The Art Fabric: Mainstream

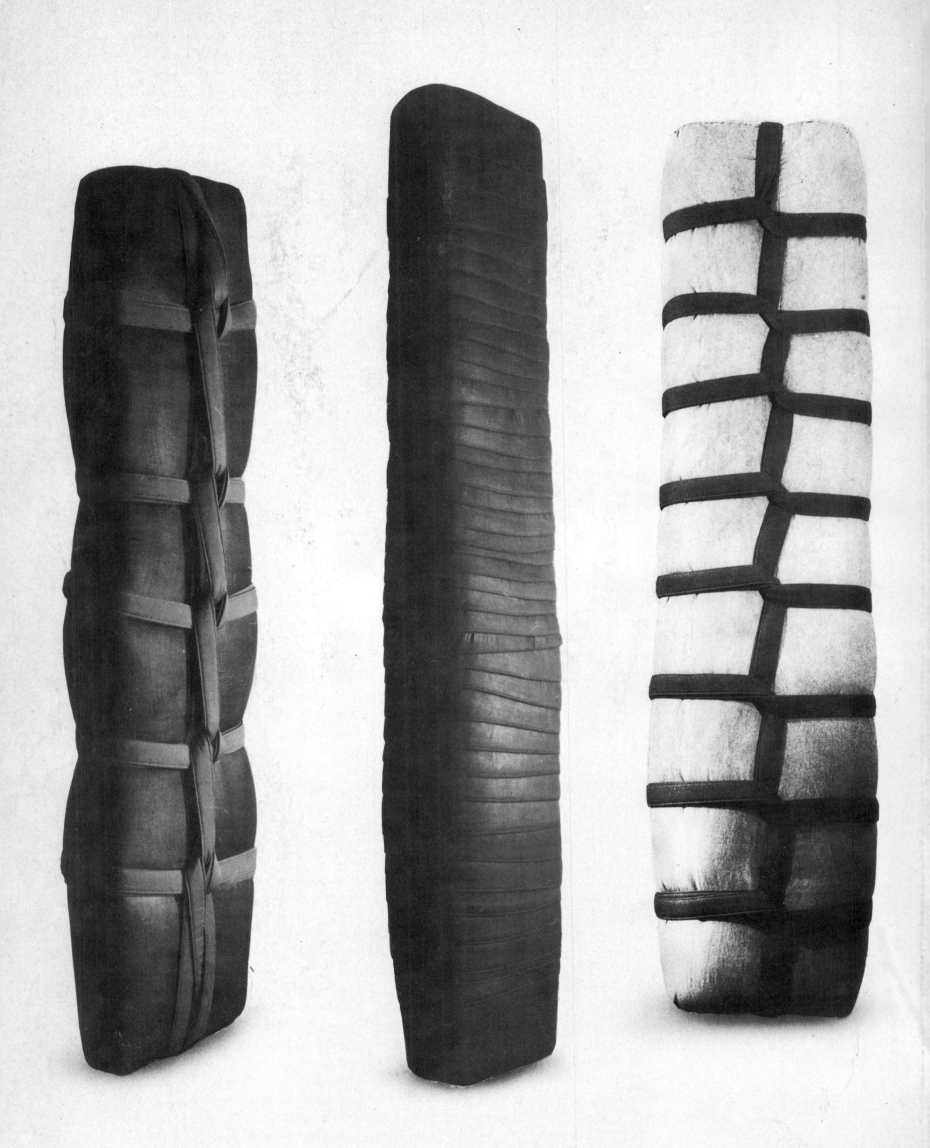

The Art Fabric: Mainstream

Mildred Constantine/Jack Lenor Larsen

 **Van Nostrand Reinhold Company**
New York Cincinnati London Toronto Melbourne

ACKNOWLEDGMENTS

The authors would like to express their deepest thanks and appreciation to all the artists who have provided us with so much inspiration and information; to the museums, galleries, and collectors for their cooperation; to Helene Margolies and Louise Irizarry for their untiring assistance in readying our manuscript for publication; to Ned Harris, the designer, and John Garrigan, Milda Vizbar, and Louis Vasquez for their wisdom and support; to our publisher and editors, Nancy Newman Green, Leslie Wenger, and especially to Irene Demchyshyn, all of whom have been more than supportive in the vicissitudes of production and provided astute and steadfast editorial guidance.

To Erika Billeter of the Kunsthaus in Zurich and to the British Crafts Centre we wish to acknowledge with thanks their cooperation and unstinting interest in our subject and in our endeavors.

The publication of this book coincides with an exhibition selected by the authors and presented under the auspices of The American Federation of Arts with the aid of a grant from the National Endowment for the Arts. We wish to express our gratitude to The American Federation of Arts for the opportunity to present this national traveling exhibition.

Library of Congress Catalog Card Number 80-25003
ISBN 0-442-21638-6

Printed in Japan
Designed by Ned Harris
Published by Van Nostrand Reinhold Company
A division of Litton Educational Publishing, Inc.
135 West 50th Street, New York, NY 10020

Van Nostrand Reinhold Limited
1410 Birchmount Road
Scarborough, Ontario M1P 2E7, Canada

Van Nostrand Reinhold Australia Pty. Ltd.
17 Queen Street
Mitcham, Victoria 3132, Australia

Van Nostrand Reinhold Company Limited
Molly Millars Lane
Wokingham, Berkshire, England

16 15 14 13 12 11 10 9 8 7 6 5 4 3 2 1

Library of Congress Cataloging in Publication Data

Constantine, Mildred.
  The art fabric: mainstream

  Bibliography: p.
  Includes index.
  1. Fiberwork. 2. Art, Modern—20th century.
I. Larsen, Jack Lenor, joint author. II. Title.
N6494.F47C66   746'.09'04   80-25003
ISBN 0-442-21638-6

DANIEL GRAFFIN France
La Longue *1976*
97" × 16" × 12"
L'Autre Longue *1976*
90" × 16" × 12"
Celle en Trois *1976*
78" × 24" × 12"
Incluses *1976*
97" × 16" × 12"
wrapping; indigo dyed cotton
(description on p. 113)

CONTENTS

MAGDALENA ABAKANOWICZ
Poland
Self Portrait *1976*
mold cast; bast fiber
life size

1 THE ART FABRIC

single fibers are like letters of an alphabet

with them one can form words and sentences then

create prose and poetry

like a single letter a fiber has characteristics

which may be sequenced towards an infinity of forms

this unlimited potential for interpretation

is basic to artists working in art fabric

There is an axiom that a work of art can stand any response we bring to it.

This book is concerned with artists who create in the Art Fabric medium. It presents our estimate of their worth, how their art has evolved from that of the first generation, and what they have to pass on to the future. Together, the illustrations and comments, the artists' concerns and philosophies, and our own criteria give recognition to the collective sweep of Art Fabric.

The works shown in *Beyond Craft,* our first book on Art Fabrics, testified to the rich fulfillment to come. In it we recorded the history of this movement through the 60's, detailed the antecedents, and documented the evolution with the work of individual artists. Our objective now is to concentrate on Art Fabrics of the 70's. We examine the distinctive aesthetic tendencies of both a new generation of artists and those in mid-career. In this way we continue to document this major art form in its explosive mainstream.

For this book we have selected those Art Fabrics that satisfy certain criteria: works that involve knowledge of and respect for the nature of chosen materials; works that illustrate an understanding of the disciplines of structure, control of technique, and the freedoms that emerge from that understanding; works that, in their nature, satisfy not the style but the aesthetic qualities of art.

In *Beyond Craft* we proposed a nomenclature to identify those works we term Art Fabric. We also cite Irene Emery, one of the world's foremost authorities on fabric classification: Deriving from the Latin *fabricare,* meaning to build, to fabricate, the word *fabric* is the generic term for all fibrous constructions. Further Emery defines *textiles* in specific reference to woven fabrics (i.e., fabrics with two or more sets of elements interlaced at right angles).

Craft is mastery of material and technique to produce an object by hand; add to these skills the intention and imagination of the maker. If the beholder is drawn into the world of the maker's values, sharing the vitality, intensity, and mystery, he may recognize the essential elements emanating from a work that goes ''beyond craft.'' Only then does he sense that *the distinction between the crafts maker and the true artist is precisely that the former knows what he can do and the latter pursues the unknown.*

Worth looking at are all those visual arts that emphasize tensions between form and content, that have a felt presence, that offer emotional impact, or that make an intellectual statement: in short, works experienced in the memory as well as in their presence. These works project authority.

Thus, a painting, a sculpture, a building, a book, a pot, or an Art Fabric—any medium used in any mode of expression inseparable from craftsmanship—may become a work of art. An indefinable process is set in motion whereby the beholder is attentive to every mark of the maker's imagination. For example, many years ago, René d'Harnoncourt, the pivotal director of the Museum of Modern Art in New York, sat with some curators viewing a group of objects destined for acquisition.[1] Among these was a hand-thrown pot by the great Japanese artist, Rosanjin. D'Harnoncourt asked if we recognized the moment at which a pot ceases to be a pot and becomes a work of art: when the artist's statement transcends utility. He recalled that in the pre-industrial past there existed a fusion of

KITQOUI ROSANJIN Japan (1883–1959)
Vase 1953
hand-thrown Bizen ware; salt glaze, red orange
9″ h.

Collection: The Museum of Modern Art, New York
Gift of Japan Society, Inc.

utility with the qualities that make an object pleasing and perhaps even beautiful; this fusion was neither noticed nor discussed but recognized as craft that makes art possible.

Among the many working in every medium and technique, there are, of course, those with only avid ambition and uncertain ability. During the last decade, for instance, many have jumped on the Art Fabric bandwagon. Some are students and amateurs working in a scale and with a pretension far beyond their experience or skill. Some blatantly exploit commercially a market won by others. Some are fine crafts makers and gifted designers but are without poetic vision.

But there is little difficulty in distinguishing the innovations of the true artist and the different impulses of the followers. Sure talents surface with such vital purpose and force as to demonstrate their very considerable creative achievement. These talents are individual and diverse. Their personal imperatives are clear and authentic. Today their expanded range of form is parallel to that of painting, sculpture, and architecture.

THE MAINSTREAM

Art Fabric functions in the mainstream of contemporary art and shares its artistic diversity. One would have hoped that—with a shared point of view that recognizes the pluralism in art today—the old questions of art versus craft would have long been resolved. But in the late 70's many were still searching for clarification. As late as 1978, so esteemed a critic as the late Harold Rosenberg made some controversial points about the makers of images and objects:[2] ''As art moves farther from its origins in the handicrafts, the possibility of objective standards of value is reduced to the vanishing point. Crafts, with their measurable skills, cannot be reconciled with the interests and practices of art in our time. The skills of the modern artist are the opposite of those of the craftsman: instead of acquiring techniques for producing classes of objects, the artist today perfects the means suited to his particular work. His technique—and, indeed, his self as an artist—tends to be his own creation.''

Among others Rosenberg had failed to recognize or appreciate the unconventional use of

Cloth Kuba, Central Zaire *19th C.*
cut and looped pile; natural and dyed raffia
23.5" × 12"

Collection: Cranbrook Academy of Art Museum
Kuba ''velvets'' served no function, but as works of art they were the ''gifts of kings to kings.''

craft media that the artists are using to produce art that goes beyond craft.

(Contemporary art criticism to the contrary, the three major art exhibitions shown in the United States in the 70's were of artifacts: ''The Treasures of Tutankamen,'' ''The Splendors of Dresden,'' ''Art of the Peoples Republic of China.'' *How old must craft be to be considered art?*)

In response to Rosenberg's comment we are treating this search for clarification in some depth and are involving the thinking and expertise of our respected peers.

CONSTANTIN BRANCUSI *Romania (lived in Paris) 1876–1957*
Table of Silence *1938*
One of a series of monuments in Tirgu Jiu, Romania, Endless Column, Gate of the Kiss, *and* Table of Silence.

"The stools encircle the table in a stately round dance. . . . You cannot sit on the stools and eat at the table. . . . It is the transformation of material, formal and symbolic properties which provides the visual experience which becomes absolute: existence as thing, even existence as symbolic is surrendered for existence in the light of perception alone."15 Brancusi welcomed this commission because it brought his work into an open, public environment. It reflects his feelings that "simplicity is not an end in art, but one arrives at simplicity in spite of oneself, in approaching the real sense of things."16 Table of Silence is a unity—a whole in which no part is seen outside the whole.

facing page

top
MAGDALENA ABAKANOWICZ *Poland*
Heads *1970's*
from "Cycle Alteration"

bottom
MAGDALENA ABAKANOWICZ *Poland*
Working in her studio in Warsaw 1974–75

Like Brancusi's tables and stools, Magda Abakanowicz's sisal and burlap bundles are intended to be seen in groups. Their repeated, seemingly identical forms have a rhythm of their own; any one implies the others in view. Whereas Brancusi has transformed function through an exaltation of form, Abakanowicz transforms through allegorical reference. Each of her outer structures is different; mostly surfaced with sewn sacking, they seem to exist as forms that grow in nature. These organic works are one aspect of this artist's reincarnation of the human figure. Dating from the early 70's this direction includes the seated figures, heads, and headless torsos, shown on pages 32 and 33.

11

In discussing the diversity in contemporary visual arts and noting an absence of a unifying mainstream, Lawrence Alloway, the esteemed and outspoken critic, has taken issue with what he sees as the restrictive tendencies of contemporary criticism.[3] ''There is a serious conflict between the profession of aesthetic freedom and the selection of some stylistic traits at the expense of others . . . . The criticism of art, spoken as well as written, is failing to cope with the multiplicity.''

In a later communication he stated: ''The exclusionary trend of American art writing has not spared the crafts. It was in the 18th century that different aspects of the arts were precisely separated. The more distinctions that we can make between things, the better of course, but systems of classification need to be tested and revised. This has not happened with any regularity in the visual arts, and painting and sculpture have remained the core subjects of 'fine art' theory. As P. O. Kristeller pointed out,[4] other subjects, such as gardening, engraving and the decorative arts, the dance and the theatre come and go according to writers' interests. The crafts, even when clearly outside a category of utility, are generally assigned a lower status than the 'fine' arts. The expansion of the definition of art, after Duchamp, easily includes postcards but not tapestries, Xerox but not weaving. This is due to a prejudice against craft as the residue of an earlier manual phase of culture. As a result, discussion of the crafts gets left to craft critics as specialists and art critics rarely feel called on to estimate, for example, fiberworks as sculpture. No general theory of art as a form of communication can afford to leave the area of craft out of account.''

Thus, placing art in craft media on a level less worthy than other visual expressions perpetuates an outdated hierarchy. Why does this attitude still exist in the minds of institutions devoted to contemporary art? Why has art history enforced these exclusions? Forward-looking academic trends in thinking about the arts stress that all forms of creativity must be recognized as valid statements. These statements must be considered worthy of serious comment and study. A revolution in art criticism is long overdue. The power of form making and the specific energy created by dynamic artistic gestures on every level of human experience must be acknowledged.

Cloth—wrapped, compressed, nonutilitarian, has played an early and important role in 20th century art concepts. Dadaist Man Ray wrapped an ''enigma.'' Christo some forty years later wrapped a building. In the early 60's Claes Oldenburg had introduced cloth (muslin) as a basic material for his art forms—''Wrinkled, torn and creased surfaces, rippled edges, expressing the physical sensations, visual perceptions and poetic associations that the object arouses in the viewer are assumed to be relative entirely to his own experience.'' The interest in cloth has extended to the use of compression, laundry elements for environments (see Sheila Hicks, pp. 38 and 39) and totem-like forms (see Graffin, frontispiece).

CESAR (BALDACCINI) France
Jeans 1975
compression; cotton
47 1/4" × 39 3/8" × 5 1/2"

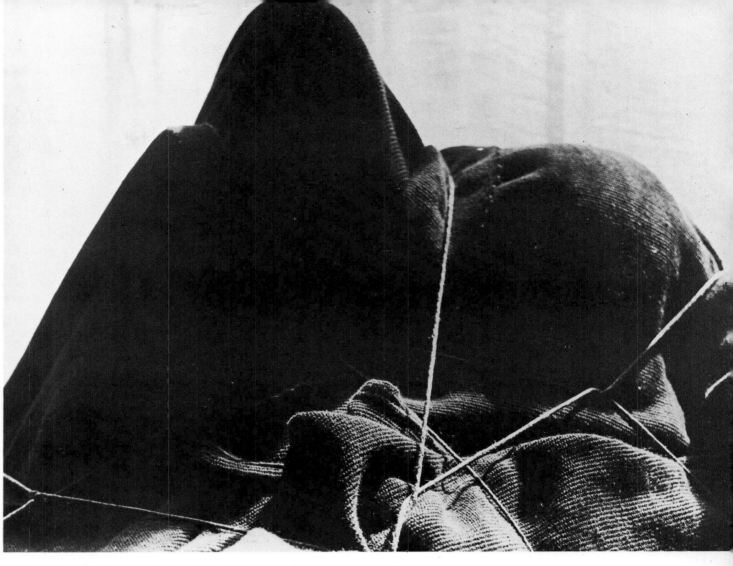

MAN RAY U.S.A. (lived in Paris) 1890–1978
Enigma of Isidore Ducasse *1920*
mixed media
17 3/4" × 22 7/8" × 9"

CHRISTO (CHRISTO JAVACHEFF) U.S.A.
The Museum of Modern Art Packaged *1968*
scale model: painted wood, cloth, twine, and polyethylene
16" (including 2" painted wood base) × 48 1/8" × 24 1/8"

Collection: The Museum of Modern Art, New York.
Gift of D. and J. de Menil

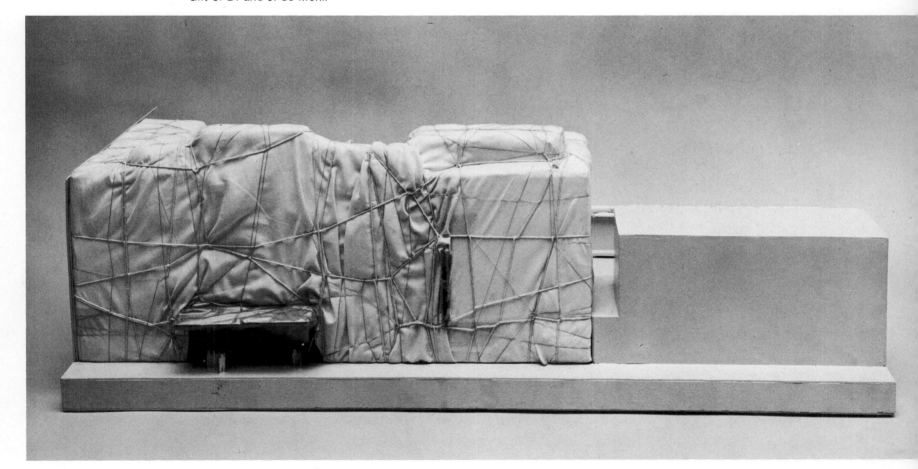

EVOLUTION OF THE ART FABRIC

All artists have ancestors. The character of their work evolves neither in isolation from the other arts nor in a linear pattern. It goes forward in leaps or connects by complex and circuitous routes. The contemporary history of Art Fabric does not begin in the 1960's. It started with the tapestries commissioned by William Morris in England in the 1870's. In this aspect, modern Art Fabric is well past its own centennial. Our interest in tracing its development is to give the legitimate facts of its evolution.

Nikolaus Pevsner offers a most succinct explanation of design history in his seminal book, *Pioneers of Modern Design.*[5] Pevsner points out that 20th century style had been set by 1914. "Morris had started the movement by reviving handicraft as an art worthy of the best men's efforts, the pioneers about 1900 had gone farther by discovering the immense, untried possibilities of machine art. The synthesis, in creation as well as in theory, is the work of Walter Gropius. . . . At the end of 1914, he began preparing his plans for the reorganization of the Weimar Art School. . . . The opening of the new school, combining an academy of art and a school of arts and crafts, took place in 1919. Its name was Staatliches Bauhaus, . . . it was at the same time a laboratory for the handicraft and for standardization; a school and a workshop. It comprised, in an admirable community spirit, architects, master craftsmen, abstract painters, all working for a new spirit in building. . . . Gropius regards himself as a follower of Ruskin and Morris, of van de Velde and of the Werkbund. . . . The history of artistic theory between 1890 and the First World War proves the assertion. . . that the phase between Morris and Gropius is an historical unit."

It is recognized today that, for the development of the Art Fabric, the Bauhaus was of major importance.[6] This in spite of a later change of emphasis from abstract tapestry to a machine aesthetic and design for production. Arthur Cohen has pointed out[7] that "the decline of the prestige of the decorative arts in modern times, the relegation of decoration to a lesser status in the pantheon of arts, arose from the fact that economic and class considerations intervened, the artisan coming to regard himself as a slave of the rich and therefore déclassé—at a time in post-revolutionary Europe when egalitarianism and disintegration of class boundaries had accelerated and came to erode his self esteem. It was not that the artist made more money than the craftsman. It was rather that the artist was regarded as a free man—free to create and starve if he chose—whereas craftsmen were always guilded, bonded, and sustained by a feudalism of station and a feudalism of imagery."

It could also be said that the craftsman was usually bonded by the client commissioning him. Most often he worked as an artisan to the dictates, drawings, or cartoons of architect or decorator. To a lesser extent painters commissioned for portraiture, decoration, or the recording of events were confined as well. And so, when in the late 19th century photography became popular, art for art's sake triumphed.

In the aftermath of World War I, economic collapse was followed by an artistic boom in the 20's. Working in Paris, the artist Sonia Delaunay was one of those who disregarded all conventional limitations and obstacles. In 1922 she was designing interiors and in 1923, sold her first "Simultaneous" fabrics to a silk manufacturer in Lyon. Her atelier for printing these fabrics and the manufacture of coats made of wool tapestry was begun in 1924. In her paintings she also began to alternate colored surfaces with painted paper and fabric. Her book *Tapis et Tissus,* written in 1929, can still be read today as one of the most valuable espousals of the Art Fabric.

In Paris the "Exposition Internationale des Arts Decoratifs et Industriels" finally came to fruition in 1925. Planned as early as 1916, it was repeatedly postponed by the war and its aftermath. In 1930 the group L'Union des Artistes Modernes (formed in 1928, with the slogan "the beautiful in the useful") produced their first exhibition.

The impact of this French contribution to post-World War II design did not truly manifest itself until the exhibition "Les Années '25'," which was shown at the Musée des Arts Decoratifs in Paris in 1966. Drawn from that museum's collections, it united Espirit Noveau, Stijl, Bauhaus and Art Deco. It emphasized the coexistence of these "styles" during the years around 1925. Common to each of these movements was the extraordinary diversity: plastic arts—painting, sculpture, graphic arts including advertising—architectural drawing, arts for the theatre, furniture, lighting, tapestry, weaving, printed fabrics, ceramics, and glass were shown. Manufactured objects were dominant, from the porcelains of Royal Copenhagen to jewelry, silver, and costume accessories.

A particularly important revelation came with rooms designed by the great French *artistes decorateurs* such as Jacques-Emile Ruhlmanni. Allied to theatre, embodying some of the characteristics later identified with *Art Decoratif,* both the interiors and individual pieces spoke of fantasy, elegance, rich materials, pattern, and Parisian chic. Old crafts such as marquetry and lacquer were revived. Murals and reliefs were important. Textiles emphasized exaggerated texture in new materials. Prior to this 1966 exhibition, these aspects of modern design had been summarily excluded in documents and exhibitions of the postwar period. Their presence was at aesthetically satisfying and historically (particularly for the present) of utmost interest.

The influence of the machine itself, to which all other influences became subordinate, was the strongest concept to emerge from all the work produced during the 20's and 30's. Did this produce a decline in values in which the craftsman's touch disappeared? Did craft lose its place in society? During the worldwide depression the withering of national economies and private fortunes certainly robbed craft of its main support for unique works. And thus the movement away from craft as an element of environment was inevitable. Those people working in craft who found employment were making prototypes for production. All this caused the crafts world to thin its ranks, and some craftsmakers were obliged to become more flexible in their direction. Yet there were survivors, among them Wharton Esherick, Loja Saarinen, and Maja Grotel (who was head of the ceramic studios at Cranbrook), energetically producing the single unique object.

Revisiting the great houses of Frank Lloyd Wright[8] and the Finnish and Cranbrook homes of Eliel Saarinen is both instructive and rewarding. They contain so much detail and craftsmanship, love of materials and distillations of the past. With their concern for pleasing our senses and spirit, these houses *are* art, as are many of the craft objects within them; so perhaps are the prints and the few small paintings. (And so it ever was in Japan and other countries of East Asia: gifted craftsmen were as highly prized as sculptors and private art was as apt to be in lacquer or ceramic as in painting.)

We noted in *Beyond Craft* that, well before World War II, the United States was the fortunate host for master weavers who became the seminal force for diverse achievements in several parts of the country. The West Coast, the Great Lakes areas (Cranbrook Academy of Art in Michigan and in Chicago), and Black Mountain College in North Carolina produced "schools" of artists working within individual concepts. What were the concerns and contributions of these masters? In the 40's leading weavers were designing prototypes for production, a legacy from the Bauhaus and Wiener Werkstätt programs. As masters of the loom they concentrated on the visual and structural aspects of weaving. They also produced rugs and Art Fabrics that illustrated concepts and thinking of their time. Thanks to European teachers—as Loja Saarinen, Anni Albers, Trude Guermonprez, Marianne Strengel, and Marta Taipale, —such brilliant artists as Ed Rossbach and Lenore Tawney were nurtured.

The French tapestry exhibition at the Metropolitan Museum of Art in 1947 illustrated the contributions of the modern painter. In these "portable murals" it was evident that the weaver's skill remained completely subordinated to the iconography of the tableau. (Even in 1974, on the occasion of the historical exhibition, "Masterpieces of Tapestry," held at the Metropolitan Museum of Art, the critics went into verbal ecstasies in describing the iconography, with hardly a mention of yarns, structure, or of the weavers' contributions. Compounding the ambiguity between the painter and fiber, a 70's travesty of this esteemed art is the colossal "Miro" tapestry in the East Wing of the National Gallery of Art in Washington, D.C. Designed by the artist, freely adapted by the weaver Royo, it is the epitome of contradiction of concept and materials.)

The Fifties

As evidenced in the "Milan Triennales" held during that decade, the 50's revealed winds of change. For the first time Art Fabric joined other aspects of architecture and design. The Eastern European participants were exhibiting Art Fabrics that were deserving of special attention: a work by Jagoda Buic was awarded the silver medal in 1957. Poland's sole entry was a presentation of Art Fabrics such as had never been seen in the Western world. The immediacy of their impact owed much to the richness of handspun wools and vegetable dyed colors. In this expression of the weaver's art, image was subordinate to texture and structure.

In order to understand fully the emergence of the artist-craftsmen as exponents of the freest range of expression, it is necessary to point out that they were heirs to America's Abstract Expressionist movement of the 50's. Painting became an adventure, often chaotic, but free from all restraints. The painters revelled in their freedom and found it imperative to express form with content—implied or barely stated. When invited, a broad audience responded with profound involvement.

In keeping with this revolutionary mood, artists changed the definitions of painting and sculpture. They neither catered to the art establishment nor were they deterred by political oppression. By abandoning the conventions of easel, canvas, oil, and brush they expanded the very limits of painting, both in concept and pure physical size. Works measuring 10 feet high by 120 feet wide electrified a growing audience for modern art. As the modern style became the dominant vocabulary for building, these large works were often selected for the public spaces within and corporate clients joined private collectors as patrons.

As old antagonisms toward abstraction began to break down, the human figure all but disappeared in sculpture. In the 50's new sculptors assembled rather than modeled or carved. Diversified materials, found objects, and iron components were welded to produce works that were visually compelling. Modern techniques of blending and brazing metals enhanced the surfaces.

As America became the center of art, artists were heroes and their creativity was acknowledged. This burgeoning cause of modernity was, for a time, so powerful as to unite art and architecture, design, film and dance, poetry and music. This far-reaching crusade against established forms of expression enlisted a powerful minority of artists, intellectuals, teachers and students, and craftsmakers.

Because those who work in craft media are among the least celebrated, it is essential to understand how profound a change from tradition was their route. In the early 50's, when one used the word *designer* it was generally understood to include the designers who worked in hand production and/or for industry. Those specializing in design for industry—except for those working in fabrics—came to be known more specifically as *industrial designers*. The others asserted their alliance with the Modern movement under the banner of *designer craftsmen*. They knew they were professionals; they were in the vanguard of the revolution. This was as true for those working with fiber as it was for potters. That they were open and responsive to all of the arts in the 50's helped to account for the diversity of the 60's.

In North America the Studio Craft Movement became important to the first generation of postwar students (especially to the potters). They conceived of their medium as more expressive than utilitarian and—parallel to painters and sculptors—their lifestyle centered in the studio rather than in the workshop or factory. Here the creator and artisan were one and the same, and production was small. Mostly recent graduates of art schools, employed as university instructors, identified with Studio Craft, with incomes and studios that suggested expressive rather than production work, their nomenclature evolved. By the end of the 50's, the term *artist craftsman* was established to distinguish those craftsmen not working for production. This, in turn, was succeeded in the 70's by the term *artist,* or the unfortunate *fiber artist, glass artist,* etc.

Although studio craftsmen worked much like painters and sculptors, they had no galleries to market their work and hardly any museums to exhibit, collect, and espouse their cause. An underground without economic base, they were sustained by a camaraderie of mutual encouragement and participation in the larger cause of modern art and, more specifically, modern design. Support was derived from teaching posts in universities and from the rare collector or architect who was knowledgeable and appreciative of their work.

New York's Museum of Modern Art, then spearhead of the international Modern Art movement, sponsored Edgar Kaufmann's "Good Design" exhibitions (1950-1955)[9] and "Textiles U.S.A." (1956)[10] both of which included handweaves. These works were originally woven as production prototypes; as the connection with industry seldom came to fruition, the pieces became virtuoso orchestrations of color and texture neither functional nor "suitable for framing." Just when custom handweaving was on the wane, weavers needed a more expressive medium than fabrics for architecture could provide. They aimed to encapsulate, in small hangings, a poetic essence that would satisfy themselves and the individual collector.

In 1979 Rose Slivka, former editor of "Craft Horizons," summed up the 50's:[11] "U.S. crafts have been hailed over and over again during the past year as a 'renaissance'—a well-meant but uninformed interpretation . . . . While the publicity certainly has succeeded in spurring public interest, it has, at the same time, perpetuated a serious fallacy and revealed the depth of misunderstanding about what actually is taking place. This is not merely a revival of crafts. This is not a nostalgic return to the handmade object. . . . We are, as we must be, irrevocably an industrial society . . . . The crafts and craftsmen have always been with us to a greater or lesser degree, but today they are filling a *new* need, meeting a new condition and a *new* demand. . . . We are creating new values in an entirely new situation—a handicraft culture growing within a powerful industrial society.''

The Sixties

The explorations by Anni Albers, Trude Guermonprez, Ed Rossbach, and Lenore Tawney founded a movement away from the format of "exhibition lengths." The "Fabrics International" exhibition (1960) forecast dimensional work in a variety of new interpretations of long neglected techniques.

In Lausanne, Switzerland, the "Biennale Internationale de la Tapisserie" was inaugerated in 1962. Although paintings by modern artists reproduced in tapestry by

ROBERT RAUSCHENBERG U.S.A.
Bed 1955
mixed media
75 1/4" × 31 1/2" × 6 1/2"

Collection: Mr. & Mrs. Leo Castelli, New York

A composition that includes such pedestrian household furnishings as a pillow, sheet, and patchwork quilt bespattered with paint. This is a highly charged emotional object in which the elements no longer have a usefulness but are preserved. Rauschenberg's loving irreverence for fabric, fabric objects, and fabric painting called attention to fabric as a medium and the potentials within it.

artisans dominated, the work of the Poles Magda Abakanowicz, Jolanta Owidzka and Wojciech Sadley represented a new and promising departure.

"Woven Forms" (1963), held at the Museum of Contemporary Crafts in New York, presented important American innovations by Lenore Tawney, Sheila Hicks, Alice Adams, Dorian Zachai, and Claire Zeisler. Erika Billeter, whose untiring efforts on behalf of new forms of expression brought the exhibition to the Kunstgewerbe Museum in Zurich, created the title "Woven Forms"[12] because no accurate definition was yet available for these new and unusual textile objects: "However they were displayed, they were strange objects and opened completely novel possibilities for the art of textiles that, until then, had been known in Europe only in the form of gobelin tapestry. The woven objects had their individual shapes and their own personal expressions, and they realized themselves solely through the various techniques that were arranged in free combinations."

The second Biennale opened in Lausanne in 1965, with the Dutch and the Polish contingents showing works that were experimental and influential. In 1966 the Saõ Paolo Bienal awarded its gold medal to Abakanowicz. In the 1967 Lausanne Biennale, the East Europeans from Poland, Yugoslavia, and Czechoslovakia surfaced in full force. Their definitive break from the classical concept of tapestry contributed largely to the ferment of the present Art Fabric Movement.

Joshua Taylor, in his brilliant book *America as Art*,[13] describes the 60's as a moment in time when the artists sought "identity through uniformity. Many different names have been used to describe the various pursuits of artists with like motivations—at one point, beginning in the late 1950's, titles of art movements were multiplying so rapidly for the benefit of the New York art market that criticism was almost reduced to being a glossary of terms—but it might be more useful to remember that all of the tendencies were, to some degree at least, a response to a

given situation. And in this case the situation with which they dealt was most acutely felt in the United States.''

Op and Pop imagery was uniform, while techniques from the painterly to the graphic were not. Accompanying this uniformity was the purity and precision of minimalism, particularly in primary sculpture.

On the other hand, this kind of cohesion hardly existed in the work of Art Fabric in the 60's (this decade saw violent social upheaval in which the linkage of history and style was so evident). Basic expression had to do with freedom, revolution, and primitive vigor. Often aggressive, the message was orgiastic and territorial. The 60's may one day be designated the period of discovery likened to the Fauves and to Abstract Expressionism in painting; it also relates to Brutalism, which appeared in 60's architecture. As defined by the critic, Ada Louise Huxtable, Brutalism denotes heavy, aggressively articulated, rough surfaced, hovering masses—words that can indeed be ascribed to Art Fabric of the 60's.

First in the United States in Lenore Tawney's shaped weavings, then in Europe in Magdalena Abakanowicz's mid-60's breakthrough, we saw the departure from the traditional rectangular format. Free silhouettes, high relief, and fully three-dimensional works followed. Many were free of the wall altogether; often they did not hang but were self-supporting structures on floors and pedestals.

Working with large elements—finger and wrist thick—permitted the making of very large pieces in small amounts of production time. Often the works resembled blown-up sections of primitive or historical pieces. Some are very much like the microphotographic enlargements of bits of nature, and—if not the perfection—they have the same fascination. In other words, they are like small sections of a cloth, mat, or basket stripped of function and old reference, and then magnified to the 100th power (p. 167).

URSZULA PLEWKA-SCHMIDT Warsaw, Poland

Plewka-Schmidt combs pre-dyed sisal and twists it into loose roving that she knits or knots into dimensional forms. Here she is shown sitting in the midst of her Warsaw exhibition.

The monumental scale in Art Fabrics was no doubt influenced by the very apparent success of oversized canvases so visible from Jackson Pollack onwards in the 50's. As likely the cause was the architects' acceptance of very large works in all media. The new buildings—short on detail, austere if not plain— demanded visual focus. Larger works related best to "important" spaces and could be most easily protected. In addition there was the sheer impact of the first great Art Fabrics. They demanded attention, as was the need at the time. Finally, the Lausanne Biennale required a minimum of ten square meters, befitting of the great galleries of the host museum and of Lurçat's[14] (founder of the Biennale) stipulation for "large wall pieces. Tapestry, it is the mural marching hand in hand with architecture." Other exhibitions tended to follow suit until, in 1977, Lausanne reduced the minimum to five square meters and in 1978, there was no size limitation.

above
RITZI AND PETER JACOBI Germany
in their studio in Hamburg 1977

left
AURELIA MUNOZ Spain
at work on Xerxes Vegetals in Barcelona 1973

facing page

NAOMI AND MASAKAZU KOBAYASHI Japan

Their house, in a mountain valley two hours north of Kyoto, is as structured and ordered as their work. In a common room used for working, sitting and dining, stands Masakazu's large Kawasaki loom; beside it is a typical woven piece. On the sleeping mezzanine the wooden structure of the hip roof dominates all. The only objects are a shelf of books, a fouton covered with a Masakazu's printed cotton and Naomi's long black and white pyramidal forms.

Typical materials of the 60's were sisal in ropes and cords or as a loose fiber, and loosely spun raw wools. These materials readily provide visual and tactile interest. They *read* as fiber, contrasting admirably with bland interior surfaces or holding their own with brutal ones. More than this, the stiff "body" of these coarse elements contributes to the stability of intuitively conceived fabric structures. Finer, softer yarns would, in such open meshes, too readily succumb to the pull of gravity and the ravages of time, transport, and soil. Color tended toward monotones. Black and natural white were almost equally popular. Whereas techniques still included the tapestry joining (gobelin), single element structures such as knotting, knitting, twining, and sprang became more and more evident. "Own technique" frequently appeared on European captions, while "off-loom technique" was coined in the United States, where for some years Cranbrook Academy's fine collection of looms went into storage.

The Seventies

To the extent that any strong action breeds reaction, one might have expected the liberations of the 60's to foster an opposite trend. It did. However, the main attributes of colossal size, organic dynamism, raw expression, and intuitive searching did not die in the ensuing decade. Nor did the romantic aspects of Personalism and revolution. Probes into the past continued seriously and unabated.

Many of the leaders of the 60's have matured in their styles. Their improved craftsmanship and control, nuances of refinement, superior construction, and continuing technical virtuosity are to be commended.

Why does fabric now have more visibility in all the arts? Why are we now ready to enjoy the sensuality of fabrics in all of its myriad forms? Are we seeking relief from the austerity of standardized interiors or from the hard-surfaced, unrelieved facades of our topless buildings? Have hard-edge geometric surfaces surfeited both the artist and the spectator?

Has public taste caught up with and absorbed what once was new?

Working directly with cloth and other "non-art" materials, some artists have broken the barriers and changed the definition of what constitutes art. This can be seen in the work of Eva Hesse, Sam Gilliam, Man Ray, Robert Rauschenberg (p. 17), Colette (p. 241) and Christo (p. 234) among others.

By the mid-70's it was evident that some radical changes were afoot in the choice of materials. Interest in dye and needle techniques stimulated the increased use of silk and, especially, cotton. Fabric—usually fine counts of mill woven cotton—became a prime material. As described in chapter 3, such cloths were dyed, machine embroidered, darned, fabricated, stuffed, or woven as strips. Fabric became—in other words—a major raw material.

Rope became even more important as a material and, with it, some new techniques as well. At the other extreme, non-woven Art Fabrics appeared in felted wool and in cellulostic fibers formed into paper. (We should make it clear that the material here is the fiber itself, not felt or paper.) If the potential of these "new" old techniques is still not exploited, important breakthroughs should result: enthusiasms for both felting and paper making are high.

A major aspect of the 70's was a renewed interest in fabrics that are not only loom woven but loom controlled. Unlike tapestry, these pattern weaves must be planned out and "built in" even before the warp making is started. There was an emphasis on formalist, structuralist methods and analytic investigation. The rules of the game were pattern repeats or lack of them and, usually, choices of simpler yarns than the lush complexities of the 50's.

In chapter 5, *The New Classicism,* we describe how this new sense of order and moderation, modest size and unusual calm emphasized an inner power. This power can be likened to Josef Albers' long series of squares within squares. If not as visually exciting as the contemporary work of Abstract Expressionists, it probably did not occur to Albers: he was among those whose passionate involvement was in ideas, not in action.

The artists of the 70's worked on wall pieces, on floor pieces, and on pedestal pieces. There was both classic order and expressionist disorder. The artists went through stages of abstract vision, the making of objects, and depicting the human figure. They worked for architecture, for theatre, and in the landscape. They created work to be in. They expressed ecological and social concerns.

However uniform our world may be, the high visibility of these artists and their continuing thrusts into exploring frontiers make us recognize Art Fabric as a phenomenon germane to our times and compatible with art in its present-day potential. That it is of broad international concern, that it has received widespread recognition is evident in the following pages.

JAGODA BUIC Yugoslavia

Of the Sun
Of the Stone
Of the Dream *1973*
At the Musée d'Art Moderne de la Ville de Paris, 1975

2 EXHIBITIONS OF THE SEVENTIES

While artists are eager for commissions to bring their work before a wide public, it is the museum and/or art gallery exhibition that provides recognition, alerts the attention of collectors, and constitutes a document of development.

Each epoch finds its expression in the emergence of a particular art form. Yet in the 60's, when Art Fabric reached an ascendancy and importance in the expression of contemporary art, it is astonishing to account for only four major exhibitions in the entire United States.[1] This in spite of that decade's proliferation of museums and exhibition halls.

In Europe, however, major exhibitions had been shown yearly, if not more often. In 1962, the Centre International de la Tapisserie Ancienne et Moderne (CITAM) in Lausanne began its spectacular and seminal "Biennale Internationale de la Tapisserie." The exhibition attracted major works and introduced new artists and new movements that helped to shape the response of critics, historians, and public alike. In a single exhibition (1969), as many as 26 countries were represented by over 80 individual works, and in Lausanne the exhibition had been seen by over 20,000 visitors. In recent years these Biennales have traveled to Japan, Portugal, and Denmark. Since the mid-60's the São Paolo and Venice Biennales have also been exhibiting Art Fabrics.

In the two examples of work shown in this chapter—Francoise Grossen's presentation shown in the 1977 Biennale (p. 26) and Daniel Graffin's shown in the 1979 Biennale (p. 40)—one can see the radical change from tapestry-woven hangings. Three-dimensional fiber forms and mixed media have dominated the Biennales since 1967. It is quite natural for die-hards to be concerned about the direction of this world-famous Biennale. However, they must recognize that the changing character of Art Fabric reflects and parallels an art world in state of flux.

The pluralism of the arts in the 70's, together with the growing awareness of Art Fabric, have generated a new international interest and response. Considerable force and diversity in Art Fabric have worn away the ambivalence and insulation of museum and art galleries. We can now point to major exhibitions that have provided support and recognition for what is sometimes considered outside the realm of formal and academic "art."

"Deliberate Entanglements" (1971) in Los Angeles was the first major exhibition of the decade in the United States. Organized by Bernard Kester for the UCLA Art Galleries, the exhibition was also shown in Portland, Salt Lake City, San Francisco, and Vancouver. The Galleries' then Director, Frederick S. Wight, stated that[2] "expression is open-ended. The work is inherently linear and pliable, the end result massive and formal. Does this not say that one of the oldest of arts has become the newest?"

There were a large number of group and one person exhibitions in the United States, among them "Fiber Structures" (1976), held in Pittsburgh in conjunction with the Convergence Conference sponsored by the Handweavers Guild of America.

An outstanding international exhibition, "Fiberworks," was presented in 1977 at The Cleveland Museum of Art. William E. Ward so successfully installed this exhibition in the 36-foot-high spaces of Marcel Breuer's new wing that it seemed to be designed for the Art Fabrics shown. Ward had a sympathetic awareness of the diversity and respect for the individuality of each of the seventy-seven pieces. His extraordinary use of theatre lighting dramatized the work which, for the most part, was extraordinarily fine. Hicks' laundry elements appeared for the first time. Tawney's large tapestry glowed as if it were precious metal. Penalba's black cascading sculpture received the space it demanded and Horiuchi's work seemed to be perfect[3] (see pages 42 and 43).

Sherman E. Lee, the Director of The Cleveland Museum of Art, noted:[4] "The twentieth century has been a period of numerous experiments in the arts based on new concepts, materials, and techniques which have proliferated as never before in history. Some of these new developments, however, have been only fashionable and have been inappropriate exploitations of materials or techniques for very vague and general ideas.

"Among the exceptions to these trends, en-

below
LAUSANNE BIENNALE 1977
(foreground): Francoise Grossen Switzerland (lives in New York)
Ahnen Galerie
(right wall): Sherri Smith U.S.A.
Pavilion
(left): Marisa Bandiera Cerantola Italy
partial view of Chromatic Structure (see p. 196)

facing page
THE DYER'S ART
Installation at the Cranbrook Academy of Art, Michigan 1978

joying wide-spread and lasting success, has been the use of fibrous materials to create aesthetic equivalent of sculptures and paintings. New tools, techniques, and synthetic fibers have fired artists' imaginations. The variety of effects possible range from the predominantly decorative to the highly expressive. And unlike some other recent developments in the arts, contemporary fiber works rest firmly on long and substantial traditions from all major cultures. Although many new and significant forms have already appeared, the future seems to offer even further possibilities for the growth of this art.''

''The Dyer's Art,'' both book and exhibition (1976–79) brought the art and technique of simultaneously coloring and ornamenting cloth before a large U.S. audience. Both historical and contemporary manifestations of the processes and craft focused our attention on the achievements of the modern dyer. The exhibition was shown first at the Museum of Contemporary Crafts in New York; it then traveled to ten cities in North America. Above we see its excellent installation at the Cranbrook Academy of Art, Michigan.

Chicago's Art Institute has a superb collection of the textile arts of many cultures and periods. It has been supportive of the research and explorations of several artists working in the fiber medium and particularly of Claire Zeisler, whose work was presented in a major retrospective (1979) covering a period of about sixteen years. In this exhibition Zeisler clearly demonstrated her brilliance in broadening the boundaries that limit fiber techniques. She is a daring and true innovator, as can be seen in *Coil Series #IV*, in which a two-sided composition hangs over its own freestanding wall. Natural hemp, red wool, and blue polyester are wrapped over steel coils to produce a truly stunning work (p. 41).

Other major one-person exhibitions included those of Magdalena Abakanowicz (pp. 46, 47) and Sheila Hicks (pp. 44, 45); these are discussed in the section on *Environment* since both artists have been concerned with breaking away from orthodox museum installations and have created their own environments for their work, albeit each in her own way.

LOUISE ALLRICH GALLERY, San Francisco 1979
work by Lia Cook, Daniel Graffin, Moik Schiele, Masakazu
Kobayashi, Kris Dey

HERMAN SCHOLTEN Holland
Exhibition, Stedelijk Museum, Amsterdam 1974–75

JAGODA BUIC Yugoslavia
Svart Rumsbild *1975*
at Konsthantverket, Kulturhuset, Stockholm 1979

facing page
MAGDALENA ABAKANOWICZ *Poland*
Black-Brown Composition in Space *1972*
Exhibition, Huddinge, Sweden

MAGDALENA ABAKANOWICZ
Cycle of 40 Heads *1976–78*
Exhibition, Modern Art Festival, Warsaw 1978
Exhibition, Sonia Henie-Niels Onstad Foundation, Oslo
Human Structure Images from Cycle "Alterations" 1974–75

Perhaps the most energetic and influential historian and critic working within a university program is Bernard Kester of the UCLA Art Department, mentioned earlier in reference to "Deliberate Entanglements." He continues to encourage investigation, innovation and diversity in his students. "Transformation: UCLA Alumni in Fiber" (1979), the exhibition of work by his former students (among them James Bassler, Karen Chapnick, Neda Al-Hilali, Kris Dey, Francoise Grossen, Gerhardt Knodel), illustrates a level of achievement that has been recognized by their inclusion in major national and international exhibitions.

In chapter 5, *The New Classicism,* we mention the almost simultaneous 1976 exhibitions held in Amsterdam at the Stedeljk Museum and in New York at The Museum of Modern Art. Both institutions had, in the past, recognized and exhibited the outstanding artists of the 60's working in fiber, and

each had independently focused on the challenges of "classic wall-hung" work emphasizing the exploration of techniques and materials. Directed by Wil Bertheux and Liesbeth Crommelin, "Structuur in Textiel"[5] showed ten artists working systemically in some depth. Supporting the clean intellect expressed in the work, the installation achieved a serenity in the isolation of each piece and of one artist from another. The exhibition also gave Richard Landis and Ed Rossbach their first exposure on the European continent.

Jack Larsen selected pieces for a smaller exhibition entitled "Wall Hangings: The New Classicism" at New York's Museum of Modern Art. It pointed up the return to loom-woven work, rectangular formats, and more disciplined attitudes. Both exhibitions aided the understanding of the 70's changes in climate.

No one has done more for Art Fabric and the artists who have pioneered in this field than Erika Billeter, now Director of Exhibitions at the Kunsthaus in Zurich. In 1964 she brought "Woven Forms" to the Kunstgewerbe Museum. While she served as Director of the Museum Bellerive in Zurich she tirelessly and courageously presented major exhibitions by American and European artists. The Museum Bellerive continues to be a strong influence under Dr. Sigrid Barten. It is slowly building a small but important collection of Art Fabrics. Fine examples from this collection are usually installed on the grand stairway.

In 1979 Dr. Billeter assembled the very large and important "Weich Und Plastich Soft Art,"[6] which traced the development of soft sculpture from the prehistoric past through the 70's. One gallery covered historic and ethnic examples from around the world. Although modern examples shown were strong in the Dada period of the 20's and Art Fabric, which began to reappear in the late 50's, work of the 60's and 70's dominated the exhibition. To see Art Fabrics juxtaposed with works in fiber by major painters and sculptors aided in assessing the interaction of the two and the relative importance of each.

Although artists from Japan did not participate in the Art Fabric movement until the early 70's, it did not take too long for the National Museum of Modern Art in Kyoto and Tokyo to respond to the burgeoning innovations in the field. In 1976, "Fiber Works: Europe and Japan" was presented, followed by "Fiber Works: America and Japan" in 1977. In the latter exhibition, pieces by Horiuchi and Shawcroft serve to illustrate the differing trends. Toshiko Horiuchi showed *Air Contained in a Floating Cube* (p. 48), for which she knit hundreds of gold and silver lengths, stretched them into concave panels, and composed them as a cube. Then, with powerful knee-high floodlights, she transformed the whole into a haloed radiance.

Barbara Shawcroft's *Blue Circles to See Through* (p. 224), an original work of great power, was made for the same exhibition. When hung in the monumental double stairwell at the Kyoto museum, it successfully dominated the space and, because of its stepped progression, provided a mounting sense of expectation. The electric blue color vibrated through the otherwise lackluster space.

Reacting to the emphasis on large scale works shown in international exhibitions, the British Crafts Centre in London organized the "1st International Exhibition of Miniature Textiles, 1974." Acting on the premise that quality can be contained in works of small dimension, this first exhibition included over one hundred works of mixed technique and mixed media. The traditional meaning of a miniature was bravely stretched by the artists themselves and this tendency was repeated in the 1976 and 1978 presentations (p. 159).

Encouraged by the success of this program, the "1st United States Miniature Exhibition" was launched in 1979 in Santa Fe, New Mexico. Certainly these showcases provided a stimulus for small Art Fabrics in their many manifestations. However, the sheer number of entries submitted for jury selection indicated the desire of many eager amateurs to jump on the miniature bandwagon. Too often the work submitted revealed neither comprehension of the nature of materials, nor convincing intent on the part of the makers. (In the titles of both the Lausanne Biennales and the London Miniature Textile presentations we face a problem of nomenclature. The use of the word *tapisserie* in the former and *textile* in the latter would seem to indicate a conservative and traditional meaning and attitude in the field. However, in the development of Art Fabric in the 60's and 70's, this approach is sadly out of date and not applicable to today's Art Fabric character.

Perhaps least recognized for their pioneering efforts are the art galleries which, whatever art form they sponsor, serve a function without which the artist could not survive, nor the art market flourish. Some of the galleries have shifted the boundaries of their normal concerns to include exhibitions of Art Fabric; others have concentrated with growing success on craft media, especially Art Fabric.

In the United States the galleries on the West Coast were the first to show Art Fabrics. Margery Annenberg's Gallery in San Francisco long bridged contemporary and ethnic expressions. Later, Fiberworks and Kasuri Dye Works in Berkeley, and Straw Into Gold in Oakland fanned the spread of new expressions. Continuing this tradition the Louise Allrich Gallery in San Francisco has supported, through exhibitions, artists from the West Coast, Europe, and Japan. Allrich has extended her concerns to seek commissions and to obtain teaching assignments for visiting artists. She expounds her views in roundtable discussions and in print.

Interestingly enough, the oldest gallery in the United States is the Contemporary Crafts Association in Portland, Oregon, which regularly brings the work of contemporary artists to that area. In the New York area, notable are the Hadler-Rodriguez Gallery (with a branch in Houston), the Elements, and the gallery of Florence Duhl. Each gallery presents exhibitions of not only U.S. artists but of Europeans, Japanese, and South Americans as well. In Chicago, the Jacques Baruch Gallery, established in 1971, has shown work by U.S. as well as East European artists.

Regional exhibitions, competitions, festivals, and workshops abound throughout the United States, Europe, and Canada. Artists air their concerns and attitudes through symposia and roundtables. Little by little the battle for the Art Fabric has been won.

SHEILA HICKS U.S.A. (lives in Paris)
Newspaper and Thread composition, Lund, Sweden 1978
Street environment in Montreuil, France; a part of the exhibition
''Fil,'' 1978 and the ''Fête du Fil'' in which Hicks, Daniel Graffin
and John Melin participated (following pages).

Poster designed by John Melin for ''Tons & Masses,'' Lund,
Sweden 1978

DANIEL GRAFFIN France
Mallarmé's Meteorites 1979
fabricated; Carrara marble and cotton bands
22' × 17' × 16'

In the 1979 Lausanne Biennale, Graffin showed this major work.
He is once again provocative in combining cotton tapes with
polished marble, neither material subservient to the other. The
work follows a direction of media mix in all the arts.

facing page
CLAIRE ZEISLER U.S.A.
Coil Series #4 1978
wrapping; natural hemp, wool, polyester
9'8" × 6' × 5'

In Claire Zeisler—a retrospective
The Art Institute of Chicago, 1979

facing page

top left
ALICIA PENALBA
Chuchicamata
MASAKAZU KOBAYASHI
W³–W to the Third Power

top right
DEBBE MOSS
Fiber Tile Wall
RENATA BONFANTI
Algeria 5
LENORE TAWNEY
Waters Above the Firmament

center
WARREN SEELIG
Triple Planar Fold 2
GERHARDT G. KNODEL
Act 8

bottom left
MARIYO YAGI
Gen Ou-6
JEAN STAMSTA
Tarzan's Rope
JAGODA BUIC
Variabil Noir

bottom right
SHERRI SMITH
Overhang
OLGA DE AMARAL
Equilibrio en Rojo y Azul

below

left
SHEILA HICKS
Reprisage Repertoire

right
HILDE SCHREIER
Triangle 2

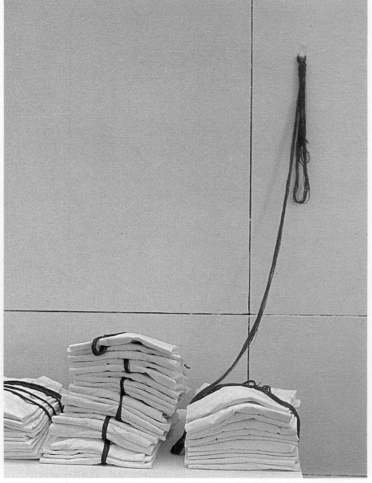

SHEILA HICKS   U.S.A.

Tons and Masses, *Konsthall, Lund, Sweden*   *1978*

facing page

left
Bands
top right
Flying Birth Bands *(one of four poles)*
bottom right
Marche Noir

below
Blouses

MAGDA ABAKANOWICZ   Poland

left
Three Black Garments   1973-74

below left
Alterations: The Seance   1976

below right
Brown Abakan and Heads
Exhibition, National Gallery of Victoria, Melbourne   1976

facing page
Exhibition, Art Gallery, New South Wales, Sydney   1976

46

TOSHIKO HORIUCHI   Japan

Air Contained in a Floating Cube   1977
knitting; linen, gold and silver Mylar

In Fiber Works Americas and Japan
The National Museum of Modern Art, Kyoto & Tokyo   1977

STRUCTUUR IN TEXTIEL *1977*
Stedelijk Museum, Amsterdam
A partial view of the exhibition with the work of Madelein Bosscher
on the left and Peter Collingwood's two pieces center and right.

WALLHANGINGS: THE NEW CLASSICISM *1977*
The Museum of Modern Art, New York
A partial view of the exhibition with the work of Kris Dey on the left
and center and Madelein Bosscher's on the right.

3 EXPANSION OF MATERIALS AND TECHNIQUES

The interrelationship of materials and techniques was never as irrevocably meshed as in contemporary Art Fabrics. Either material or technique may be the starting point, and—especially with larger elements—material and interlacing are interdependent. But in spite of this interdependence, focusing first on one then the other seems essential to our analysis. Paper, for example, is first described in relation to new materials; later, paper making is discussed under techniques in current focus.

Throughout the 70's the very definitions of Art Fabric were expanded by the broadening of materials and techniques employed. Of course this trend was a continuation from the 60's: it now seems extraordinary that as recently as at the 1962 Lausanne Biennale, the use of wool yarn was so ubiquitous as not to be identified; the only variations in technique were high warp (vertical) or low warp (horizontal) tapestry joining. In every aspect of Art Fabric the expansion continues.

Although the 70's was in some ways a less volatile decade, the headlong growth in productivity accelerated the expansion of both materials and techniques. Ancient fiber structures were often combined with ultramodern materials. A case in point is Arturo Sandoval's compositions with film strips interlaced in simple 1/1 plaiting (p. 105), a technique some 20,000 years old. Other interpretations of techniques invented millenia before woven cloth provoked increasing interest from artists of the 70's. These included such prehistoric materials as leather and felt treated in new ways. Often, but not always, these primal methods require more skill than paraphernalia, and—most importantly—they permit freedom. Broad ranges of material and scale are possible; so is dimension and the option to select materials with sufficient body for substantial forms.

More and more often, media explorations in Art Fabric parallel those in "fine arts" areas. For example, we see painters applying dilute transparent stains on untreated canvases to retain the expression of primary surface and an integration of surface and image; often the result is richly "textile." With more frequency painters have been using adhesive tapes and other resists. Both painters and artists in fiber have been attracted to the clear graded colors possible with air brush techniques. Both have succumbed to the sheer pleasure afforded by cloths freely draped, fluttering, and—often—translucent.

Moreover, the multiplicity of fibrous materials is not unique to the artists presented here. In an only casual perusal of the major art magazines published here and abroad, we are presented with work that utilizes the broadest range of materials, i.e., muslin, nylon, sisal, string, rope, thread, jute, cotton, and twine. As artists have consciously stretched their choices to move away from traditional "fine arts" media, fiber has become all pervasive.

MATERIALS

The two most spectacular materials to emerge in the 70's are opposite to each other: The first, cloth, in one form or another, has undergone at least one more process than yarn; the second, unspun fibers, used in felting and paper making, one less. Equally polar are ropes and the fine smooth yarns of the new weaves described on page 70.

To these add the shaggy sisals and the broad ranges of wools and linens which are a continuation from the 60's and the materials inventory is almost complete. Only occasionally is silk used as yarn. Only slightly more often, lustrous man-made filaments are selected for their weight and precision, light refraction, or potential flashes of clear, saturate color.

facing page
ARTURO SANDOVAL U.S.A. 1977
Cityscape #3 (detail)
plaiting; paper, microfilm, Mylar
7' × 7'

Patterned film is machine stitched to cardboard strips before plaiting. Strips of unsupported film and stitched mirror Mylar are diagonally interlaced through the plaited ground.

The last inclusion of materials must be those used in basketry. Just as basket forms and surfaces have transcended myriad traditions, so have their materials. While indigenous basket cultures are almost always keyed to a single material, contemporaries like Gary Trentham and John McQueen have been open to a wide variety of materials. Utility having been abandoned at the outset, their accommodation of form to new materials strongly testifies to the immense chasm between tradition and the Art Fabric today.

Fabric—A New Raw Material

In the 70's several common fabrics became major materials, and, for the first time, fabric rivaled yarn as the dominant stuff. Of all fabrics, woven cloths were the most common, especially mill cotton, canvas, and plain silks. Patterned cloths also counted in patchworks and appliqué. Leather, paper, and plastic films were other popular fabric types.

Fabric used as a surface to embellish with stitches or dye stuffs is an ancient concept. Its newness is in the number of men and women who felt that the medium was worth their best effort (see *Fabric Embellishment,* p. 96).

Usually unembellished although sometimes dyed, fabric manipulated as a pliable plane became, in the 70's, a major concentration. The planes are sometimes draped on a grandiose scale. They may also festoon, swag, swaddle, beribbon, bunt—dusty nomenclature for front runners of our avant garde! We shall see how fabric may also surround packages and bundles, buildings, and headlands. Fabric may also be furled, i.e., folded or compacted into a linear element for any number of fabric structures. Often it is cut or torn into strips to serve as the linear elements of fabric structure. Increasingly these ''strips'' are not torn but woven, braided, or knit in the form of narrow goods.

So, in the late 70's, cloth emerged as a material parallel in importance to yarn and cord. Why? Or, rather, why so long in coming? A wide range of cloth widths, weights, surfaces, and densities is universally available. The potential for planes of translucent color is irresistible. Then consider these planes as pliable and drapable. Pleating and tucking are possible; so are appliqué, patchwork, and quilting. Motion is available, as are inherent references to tents, kites, glides, and flags.

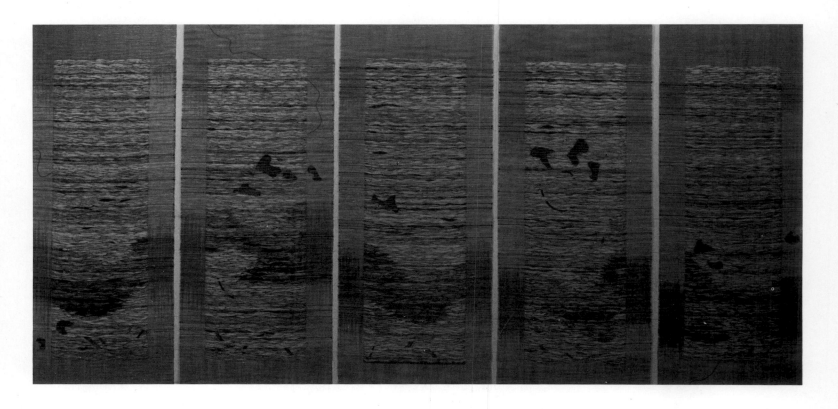

above
CYNTHIA SCHIRA U.S.A.
Seascape I *1975*
weft brocade; cotton, wool
17 1/2" × 17"

*The brocading elements are cotton tapes pre-dyed in a range of
half-tone shades. Some of the tapes eccentrically weave in and
out of the others—a technique that extends the weaver's range of
expression. It also serves to tie down the very long weft floats.*

facing page
Beyond The Mountain *1975*
brocade, warp ikat, local dyeing; cotton tapes
7'6" × 15'6"

*For the five panels of her large hanging, also shown in color on
page 102, the artist ikat patterned the warp, then superimposed
the brocade as above.*

Gerhardt Knodel, weave master at Cranbrook Academy of Art, was certainly one of the first to fully exploit the potentials of cloth. His early experiments were glades of suspended, free-hanging panels dyed in pastel color ranges. In these layered translucencies he saw the potentials for reflected and transmitted light. Their partial enclosures related to the tent forms that had long enthralled him. He was quick to realize the flexibility of modular panels which could be composed and recomposed in any number of ways; multiplying the size would be easy. Large commissions would be possible without prohibitive cost, and transport and cleaning were simplified. From this began Knodel's fascination with a system that could—like a great, complex Venetian blind—pivot and traverse "before our very eyes," and even at our will. Two of these compositions, accepted for the 1975 and 1977 Lausanne Biennales, did not, in that vast, light-drenched, competitive space, "come off." On the other hand, *Act 8,* first shown in "Fiberworks" at the Cleveland Museum in 1977, came off magnificently. The photograph on page 42 illustrates, if not its kinetic magic and sense of place, the sureness of his suspension system. Commissions came quickly. For *Free Fall* at the Detroit Plaza Hotel lobby (p. 219) he specified very special hand-woven yardages with banded repeats to punctuate the fall of the cascading structure. For others, like *Gulf Stream* at Houston (p. 218) cloth specification was subordinate to the tension and compression of his space frame.

It follows that the closest to Knodel is his former student, Pat Campbell. She came to study with him after teaching at Kansas City Art Institute. Shown on pages 56–57, her work speaks of stresses between the taut discipline of the rigging and the fragile stretch of the cloth membranes. Her movement is frozen and without motion. She wrote:[1] "In this recent body of work, I have addressed myself to what I feel are some of the drawbacks of contemporary architecture. In considering possible solutions, I turned to Japanese architecture, already an important resource for contemporary design, and discovered particular aspects worth reconsideration as answers to our problems in urban interiors. The quality of soft light filtration through the *shoji* screen, the openness yet in-timacy of special division, the use of natural materials, the evidence of handcraftsmanship throughout interiors, whereby simple construction techniques such as bindings are used in window spaces are all important resources in my recent work. . . . The space frame may be compared to the grid of woven structures; the bindings and ties of primitive African architecture may be compared to baskets or the use of off-loom techniques by the fiber-artist.''

All of the above is in reference to unembellished cloth. Multiply these cloth types by the application of printing, including the myriad resists, embroidery in all its aspects, embossing and perforation—the possibilities extend limitlessly. (Needle techniques, page 115; surface design, pages 96, 97–101; works fabricated of cloth, pages 120–121.)

Narrow Fabrics

Narrow fabrics and narrow goods are trade terms for categories of fabrics woven, knit, or braided in widths of eight inches or less. Formerly, selvaged ribbons, military braids, and straps were principal end uses; today braided shoelaces are still common, as are tubular woven firehoses and numerous narrow fabrics for industrial use. Their economy and strength speak of integrity. They are especially admired and used in Art Fabric by a group of Americans exploring the potentials of large-scale plaited structures. Among them are Sherri Smith, Susan Jamart, Mark Pollack, and Arturo Sandoval.

Narrow fabrics need not be industrial. Olga de Amaral has designed and woven the long selvaged bands with which she plaits pieces like those on page 81. Mariette Rousseau-Vermette and Ann Sutton (p. 161) have machine-knit tubes for this purpose. Candace Crockett and Lillian Elliot have made narrow tapes in the Egyptian card weaving technique and then joined them to form wide pieces.

facing page

bottom
WARREN SEELIG U.S.A.
Fabric Tiles *1979*
folding; cotton
31" × 31"

Throughout the 70's Seelig wove striped cloths then folded them into a variety of forms. Here he used common striped ticking, folded it in the manner of a complex origami. He repeated it thirty-six times to create a rich interplay of graphic pattern versus shadowed relief.

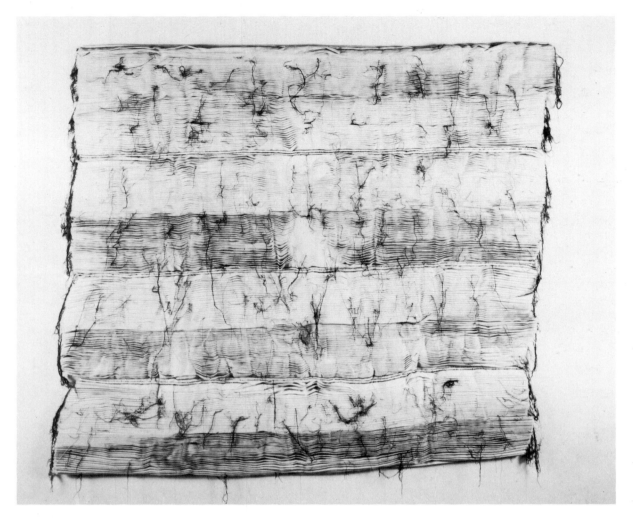

MALKA KUTNICK U.S.A.
Untitled 1978
pleating, sewing; cotton duck, thread
61" × 71"

Full widths of cotton cloth are accordion pleated lengthwise, then
stitched through with black threads. The surface variety derives
from the interplay of folded fabric and mats of black thread ends.

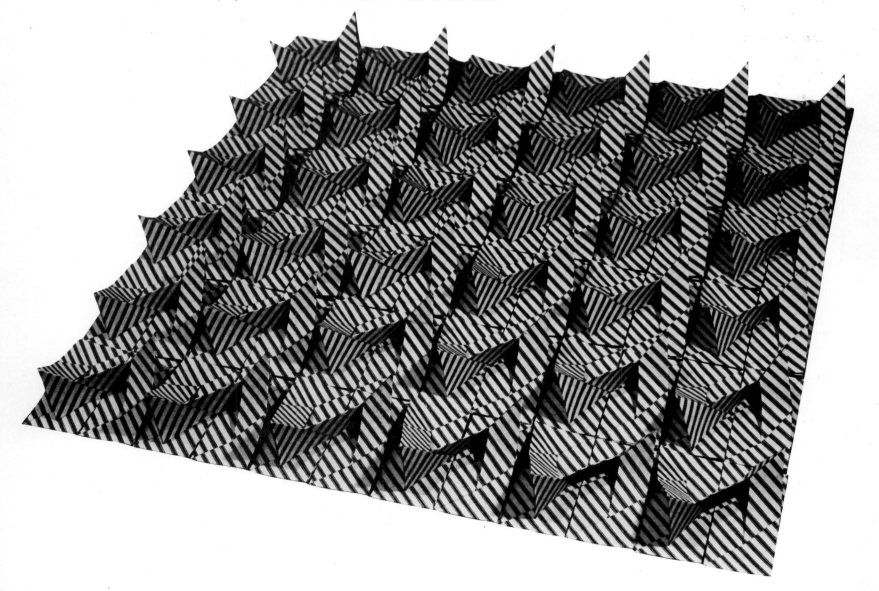

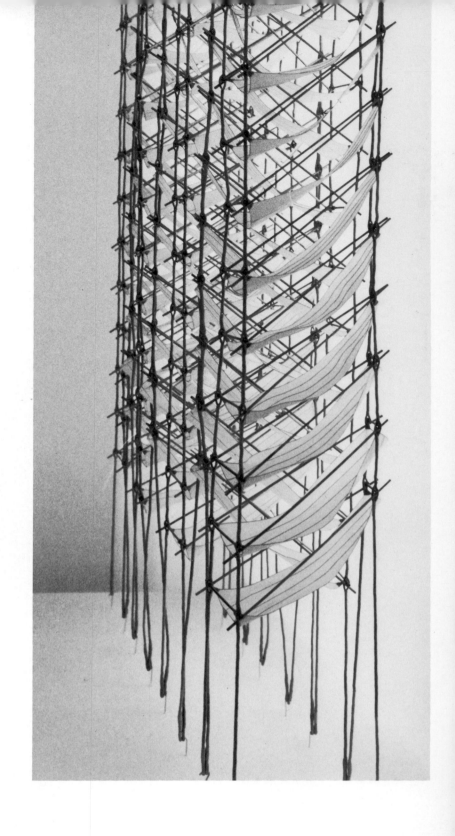

PATRICIA CAMPBELL U.S.A.
Constructed Light Wall I 1978
fabrication; shellacked fabric, paper cord, wood
8' × 8' × 15"
side view (above)
detail of front view (right)

facing page
Constructed Light Wall II 1978–79
fabrication; shellacked fabric, paper cord
8' × 6 1/2' × 18"
side view (left)
detail of front view (right)

Campbell's Light Walls *succeed because of their extraordinary
play of translucencies and their rhythm of repeated forms. Except
for faint references to such wind devices as sails and gliders, they
are unprecedented in technique. The shellac gives the cloth body
and protection, and the color of golden honey.*

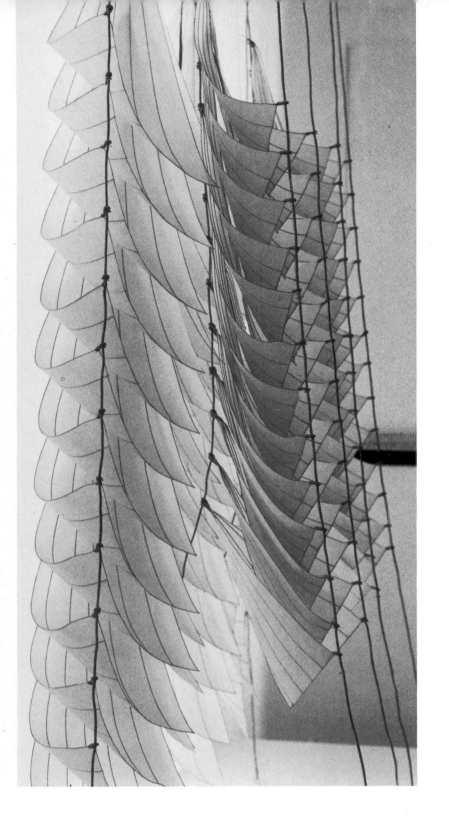

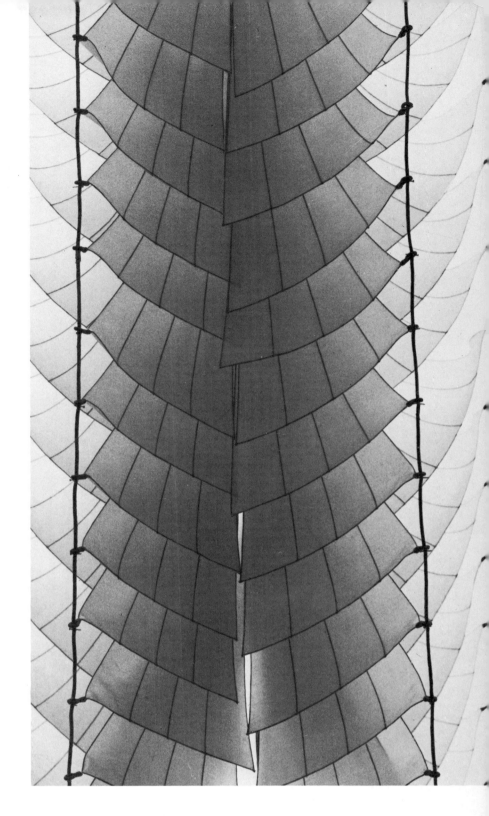

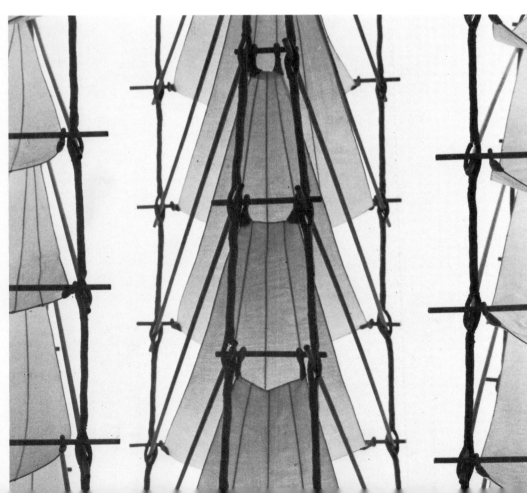

The patinated battery cable is a flat braid; it is plaited with the same order and angle of interlacing to form a contemporary example of plaited plaiting.

facing page

An extremely successful work because the variations within the star are consistent with it. The bleaching also emphasizes the weave structure within the tapes. The optical box pattern is subordinated to an implied relief, and the serrate edge is a convincing finish. Similar in its coloration and dye patterning, her Anthracite, (p. 104) is more ambitious in scale and format. The large piece ripples slightly as it hangs, exaggerating the flickering lights within it. The 1978 Textile Triennale at Lodz awarded it a special silver medal. Using colors in a full or partial spectrum, Smith has experimented broadly, softly fusing one into another. These polychromes seem less successful, perhaps because the dull cotton tapes, when dyed, do not have brilliance.

Three overhand plaited forms are linked together during the weaving process to form a single piece. The color relates to the structure of each component as well as to the whole.

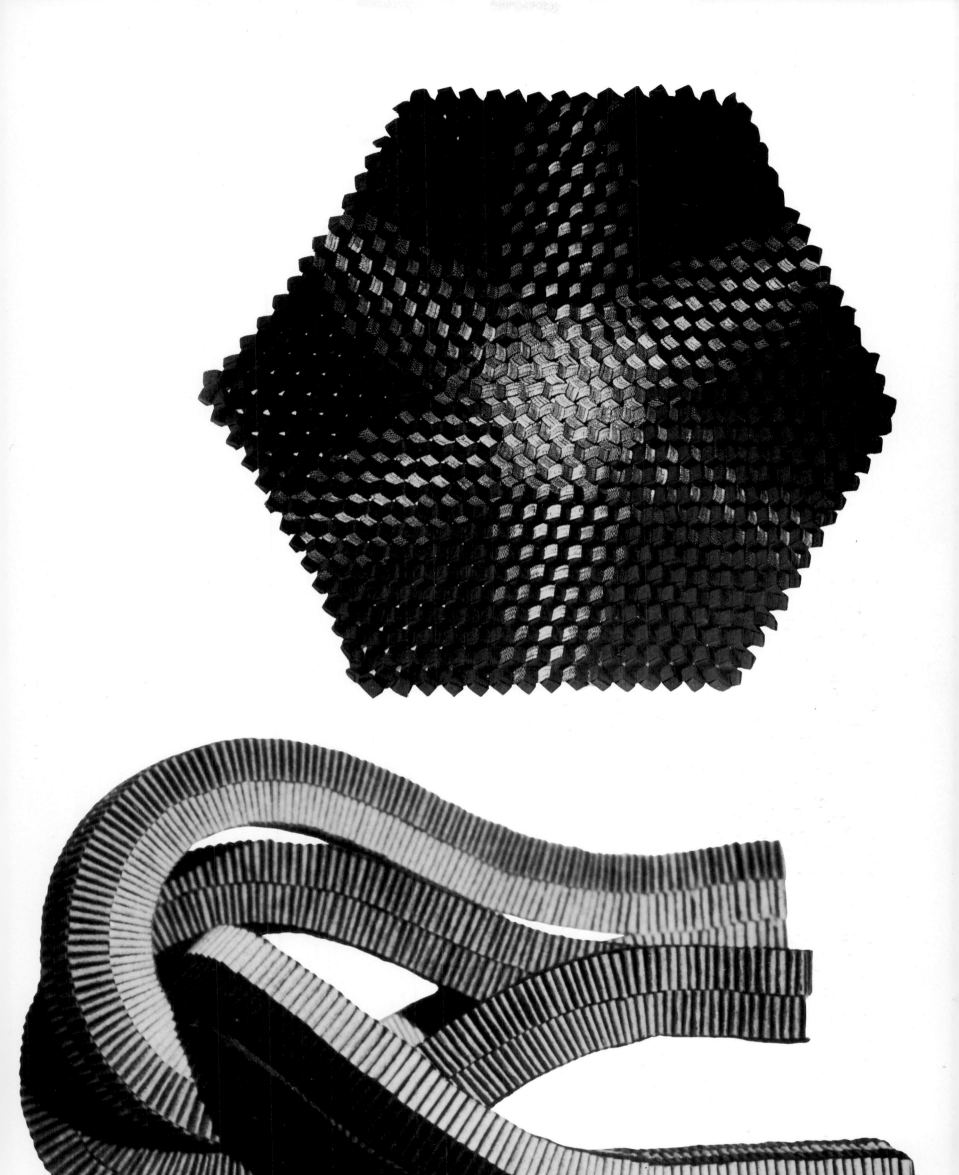

Paper is another fabric which has only recently begun to be used for Art Fabric. Again, Rossbach was first and he continues to work in recycled paper. By the 70's Dominic Di Mare was making paper for the elements of his "letters" and "manuscripts" shown on pages 152 and 153.[2] His theme is paper's connotation as message and autobiographical record—private and undecoded. With twisted paper tapes he achieves the strength of cord, then at each end unfurls a small tab. Most often his paper elements are combined with found objects, bone, honed hard wood, raffia bindings and—in the woven manuscripts—yarn. Massed, these pristine fetishes recall sensations of forgotten rituals.

Harry Boom of Amsterdam folded paper for small works like the one shown on page 137. He then "coated" them with powdered graphite to achieve a new surface of quiet beauty. No one has used paper as knowingly and consistently as Neda Al-Hilali. For the lightweight bulk of her *Tongues* (p. 238), she twisted brown craft paper into linear elements, then plaited these into sizable dimensions. Like a *raku* teabowl, which can in a single evening be formed, fired, used, and broken, this ephemeral aspect of paper is appropriate to the exuberance of a rite. But, as shown on the jacket and on pages 106 and 107, most of her plaited paper works are both serious and durable. The cohesion of the dyed and patterned surfaces is leather-like and resistant to soil and abuse.

As shown on page 108, the Jacobis have combined wrapped elements and tapestry joining with charcoal drawing on great sheets of "rice" paper. It is as if—for the first time—the tapestry cartoon had not been obliterated by a dense cloth and then separated from it. The successful media mix derives from denominators common to paper, drawing, and yarn—especially the airy freedom of the drawn images that recall the fiber character. The consistent color, or rather the lack of it, is a unifying factor: the palette is the black, white and gray of drawing.

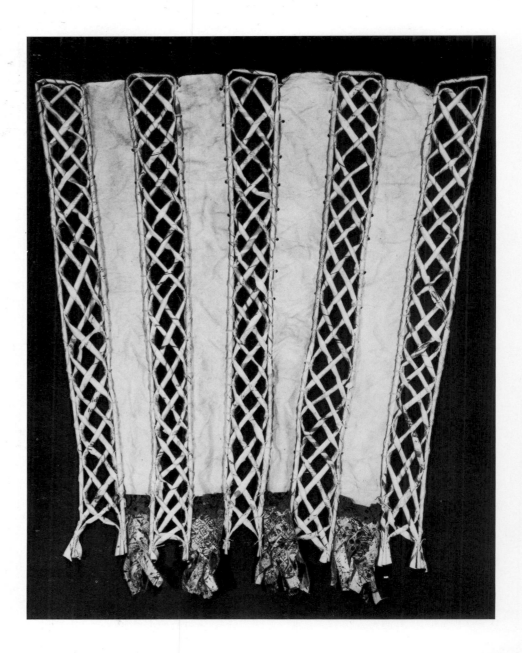

above
RITZI AND PETER JACOBI Romania (live in Germany)
Transylvania I *1972*
tapestry, drawing; goat hair, horse hair, paper
18′ × 20′ × 5′

Throughout the 70's the Jacobis have combined woven work with drawing on paper. The combination is unified by the palette and image—especially the fiber-like drawing and drawing-like fringes.

facing page
ED ROSSBACH U.S.A.
Peruvian Tunic *1976*
plaiting; paper, cotton
56″ × 48″

Canvas bands fringed with narrow strips of printed cloth are combined with paper. The rolled and plaited newspaper suggests the strap work of Irish manuscripts.

Leather

Leather, a pliable plane of protein fiber, is indeed a fabric. In the 70's it appeared for the first time in Art Fabric—not as leather craft but for elements of weaving and plaiting. Jolanta Owidzka found beauty in the stiff, patinated leather of discarded industrial beltings. For his major commission at Basking Ridge, N.J., Daniel Graffin plaited thick straps of top grain leather over a square rigging. The other elements of his long, dimensional friezes are triangular, with massive suede leather wefts so crammed into the spaced warp as to become the surface.

Claire Zeisler's gigantic cascades of suede are achieved with a variation of the paper-cutting technique, which makes a long, jagged streamer out of rectangles. Masses of these undyed or crimson suede streamers plunge downward like a dry Niagara, absorbing light and sound, and creating deep shadows in their recesses.

Although Zeisler has also illuminated suede with mythic embroidery, the neat folios of her *Pages* and *Chapters* are better known. For these, squares of natural chamois are bound in crimson, stacked, and folded diagonally (p. 151).

facing page

top
JOLANTA OWIDZKA Poland
Leather Exercise 1976
weaving; leather, hemp, silk, linen
31 1/2″ × 39 3/8″

Old industrial beltings of waxed leather recycled for a small hanging. To exploit tonal subtleties within the leather surface, she wove the beltings through a spaced warp of hard, polished linen.

bottom
DANIEL GRAFFIN France
The Passage of Ramses *(detail) 1976*
plaiting, indigo dyeing; leather, cotton

Commissioned by Vincent Kling for the American Telephone & Telegraph Co., Basking Ridge, N.J.

The taut, sail-like forms were plaited of cowhide and, in the center, of suede so tightly crammed as to form a repp.

below
CLAIRE ZEISLER U.S.A.
Red Forest 3 *(detail)*
cutting; leather
10′ × 10′ × 6′

Like a great Niagara, Zeisler's scissor-cut suede strips cascade to the floor. The power is enhanced by the play of pale natural against deep crimson.

right
CARLA MUNSTERS Holland
3 Elements 1976
sewing; PVC, grass seeds
98 5/8" × 70 7/8"

Two sheets of transparent plastic sheeting are sewn together to entrap the seedheads of various grasses in pockets. The contours of the pockets reflect the organic rhythms of contents revealed in the clear plastic. Compared with glass and frame, her flexible fabric solution is lightweight and unbreakable.

below
ARTURO SANDOVAL U.S.A.
Blue Sky Grid (detail) 1975–76
plaiting; photo silk-screened vinyl, Mylar, veiling, thread
4' × 4'

Sandoval's whole series of plaited films depend on the reflectivity of the strips he interlaces. Vinyl, Mylar, and veiling are layered and machine stitched. Transparent paints are sometimes applied.

Film

If we substitute the more comprehensive term "fabric" for cloth, plastic film becomes a factor. At the Bauhaus weave shop, Cellophane in folded strips was prized both as an extreme in the range of textures and as a hallmark of the new era. One of the first Americans to recognize the potentials of plastic film, Ed Rossbach folded it for plaited baskets and combined its "punk" colors in braided nets. Struck with the statement implicit in throw-away materials, he wrapped polyethelene film around folded newspaper, then bound it with string to achieve continuous elements for weaving and plaiting. Plaited and coiled baskets such as the one on page 125 are more recent. To date he may be the only artist to have exploited the thermoplastic potentials for molding or bonding plastic sheeting; with only the heat and pressure of an electric iron, he has fused small patchworks of opaque polychrome film.

For his large plaited pieces Arturo Sandoval cut iridescent polyester films into strips and stitched to them materials such as photographic films, veilings, and mirror Mylar to achieve surface patterns and often, a reptilian luster. His *Pond with Scum,* shown on page 105, is painted as well. He writes:[3] "My approach to my most recent work concerns the selection of visual elements to form an abstract environmental vocabulary of sky, landscape, and city. I am intrigued with the evanescence and permutations of these primary sources. I use contemporary industrial materials, such as video tape, Mylar, Lurex, webbing, microfilm, battery cable, roofing tin, movie film, computer tape and printout as my major materials because they are products of our time created by a technology which influences almost every segment of our modern day culture. They present many visual possibilities (color, shape, texture, reflection, scale and pattern) for abstraction by their material nature; their color and surface texture is predetermined by the technological process that manufactured them. They also are pliable and can be woven on the wall or floor; this affords a more direct involvement with the construction and processing of each woven collage. I have complete freedom to experiment and make changes because the entire surface area is visible and accessible to manipulation. The total form creates a sense of environment; whereas, the materials and structure invite intimacy."

Helena Hernmarck weaves strips of mirror Mylar film to achieve high reflectivity. The tapestries shown on page 212 achieve their reflective transparency through wefts of film strips punched with holes by a sequin manufacturer. The mirror surface provides reflectivity; the holes, transparency.

Glen Kaufman of Georgia was one of the first to find beauty in plastic sheeting. He employs film expansively to achieve the eerie magic of *Polycloak* on page 251. Carla Munster of Amsterdam sewed two sheets of transparent plastic sheeting to entrap the seedheads of various grasses in pockets for her *Project de Foin*.

With transparent plastic tubing knotted into a woven ground, Madeleine Bosscher of Holland achieved the luminous reliefs shown above and right. The precision of their sheared contours, the symmetry of the minimal forms, and the reflective transparency of the new material contrasted completely with anything contemporaneous. By the 70's she started to use woven cotton as her material. In the Stedelijk Museum exhibition, 1976, and later at The Museum of Modern Art in New York, she first showed a series woven with tens of thousands of disks cut from white mill cotton. Although these reliefs are as monolithic as the plastic tube series and the collective impact of systemically multiplying a single element *ad infinitum* is as impressive, their surfaces are totally opposite. Both the visual and tactile sense of the cotton is soft. One senses the fiber and yarn ends; the surface is densely opaque.

facing page and right top

MADELEINE BOSSCHER *Holland*
7 Banen 1973
knotted pile; polyethylene tubes
90 1/2″ × 197″

Bosscher is shown in her studio knotting plastic tubes onto a vertical warp. Finished, her seven-part hanging is an extraordinary example of Minimal Art. All is subordinated to the richness of a deep, translucent texture.

right bottom
Small Squares 1976
weaving; cotton

Tens of thousands of mill cotton squares are woven into the white-on-white hanging. The shadow lines and the matted thread ends produce a richly opaque texture.

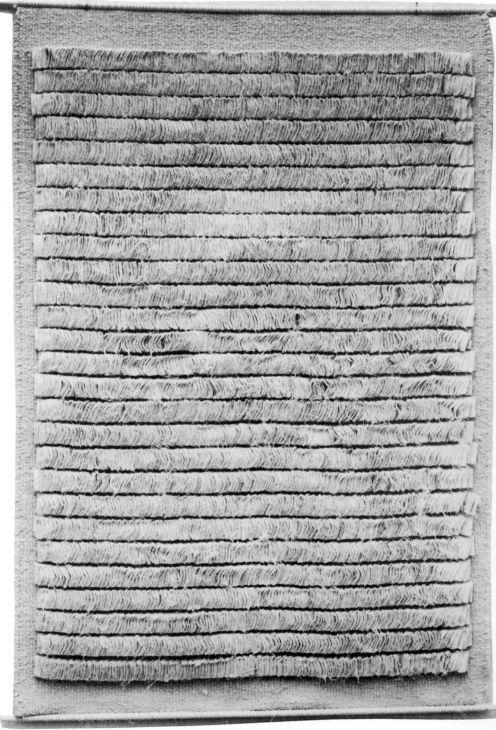

Metal

With no stretch of the imagination can one construe metal as a fabric. Still, in the vision of those concerned with fabric, metal elements may take on this character. The thin metal wires and strips are not forged or welded but are used in the manner of yarns and slats. But only rarely. In spite of the good reasons for considering metal for works destined for public areas, it is still little used. Its resistance to fire and water, soil and abuse are strong recommendations. So are its reflectivity and the pliant resistance of metal wires and cables. Especially in the bronze wire baskets of China and Japan, in medieval armor, and in Celtic strapwork, historical examples are not lacking. Some of the best instances of Art Fabrics in metal come from metal workers moving into the fabric area. Sculptor Dusan Dzamonja of Yugoslavia, for instance, has moved from hard metal forms to chain mail. His *Tapisserie en Fer S* has the characteristics of folded and draped fabric. It is sculpture; it is *fabric*—all but indestructible.

For her series of large silvery reliefs, Cynthia Schira wove 3/4" strips of thin-gauge aluminum through a spaced linen warp. After weaving, these softly resistant planes were pulled into the forms she chose. Some, like the one illustrated, are made the more monumental by an ordered symmetry; others asymmetrically relate unlike forms in a vertical composition. In addition to holding the strips in place, the linen yarn "filters" the metallic glare; the casual rhythm of the linen slubs subtly breaks the monotonous metal surfaces and heightens the contrast in reflectivity between the flat, rounded surfaces.

To achieve the weighty, luminescent pleats of her untitled work, shown on page 194, Nancy Guay used malleable copper wire for its weft. During the 70's Mario Yagi combined mirror-finished cast metal forms with her twisted bast fiber "ropes." In many instances, including the major commissions, the fiber was all but incidental. In the work shown on page 75 the fiber is equally important to the gleaming steel.

below
ARLINE FISCH U.S.A.
Reflections in a Golden Eye
tapestry; silver, gold, on aluminum sheet
2 1/2" × 5"

In extremely small scale, jeweler Arline Fisch has strung a warp on an aluminum frame, then, with eccentric tapestry, has woven fine wires of precious metal.

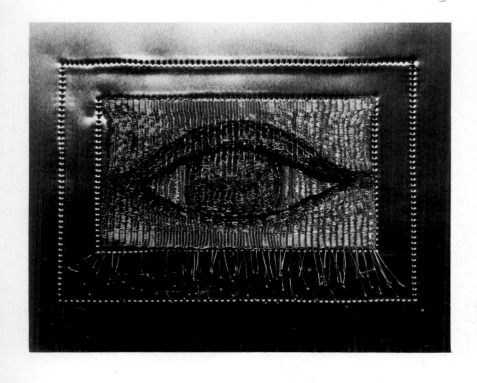

facing page

top
DUSAN DZAMONJA Yugoslavia
Tapisserie en Fer S 1979
chain mail; steel
115" × 115"

A sculptor's move toward fabric has resulted in fluid forms densely textured and resistant to time and abuse.

bottom
CYNTHIA SCHIRA U.S.A.
Four & Three 1973
weaving; aluminum, linen
12' × 10'

On a conventional handloom Schira wove flat aluminum strips through linen warps, then pulled the lower portions into cylindrical forms. The play of slubby grey linen against the polished metal is beautiful; the formality of her composition is appropriate to the dressy surface.

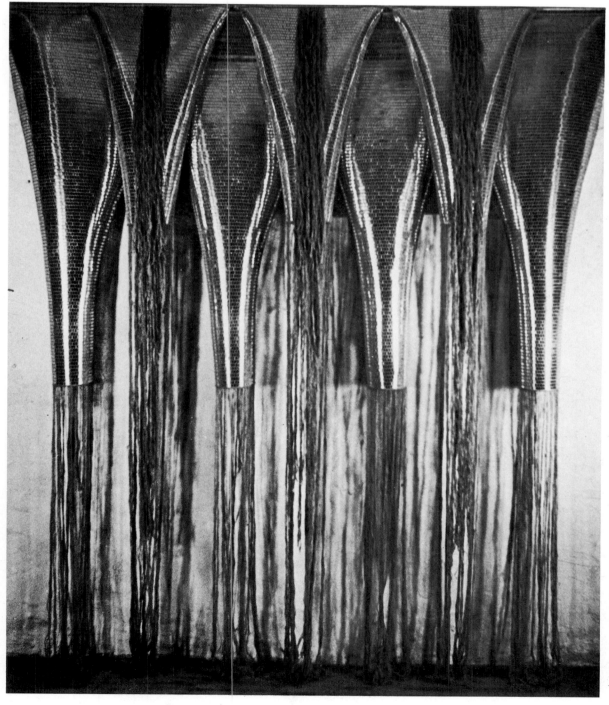

Fiber as Material

Yarn is the usual material of fabrics. Cords, ropes, slats, rovings, and slit films are among the many variants of yarn. Cloth in its many forms is a new rival to yarn in the Art Fabric. Newer still for our purposes, but historically older, is the development of fiber used directly. At least from the Bauhaus period, Germanic weavers stuffed unspun wool fiber into warps for rugs and hangings. (They also wove with sheepskin cut into strips.)

The creative, open-ended use of fiber in the ancient techniques of felting and paper making did not surface until the 70's. Although this work was still exploratory, and the dimensional potentials of both processes still unrealized, widespread enthusiasm in North America suggests the resolution and fulfillment to come. Both felting and paper making are discussed under *Techniques*.

Ropes

Since weavers' fascination with ropes predates the decade, the late 60's rope works of Abakanowicz, Fruytier, and Grossen are well documented in *Beyond Craft*. The 70's brought a wider use of this material to a larger group. Especially in heavier weights, unwieldy rope has a will of its own. Once its character is understood, it has the advantage of being in itself a major aspect of the finished work. Furthermore, rope predicates an impressive scale—often quickly achieved. And it is durable.

facing page

top
MAGDALENA ABAKANOWICZ Poland
The Rope—Its Penetration—Its Situation in Space
The Festival of Art, Bordeaux 1973

bottom
The Big Black Rope
shown at the Arnolfini Gallery, Bristol 1973

In the early 70's Abakanowicz continued to explore the potentials of very large scale environments using the enormous ropes of ships' hawsers. Often they were covered with black sacking to mask their spiral rhythms and the joining of one to another.

below
JACKIE WINSOR Canada (lives in New York)
Double Bound Circle *1971*
wrapping; rope
15 3/4" × 50 3/4"

The strength, polish, and associations of large patinated rope are appropriate to the circle as the symbol of continuity.

In the 60's Keith Sonnier, Robert Morris, and the late Eva Hesse were among those who incorporated rope in their compositions. Later, Jackie Winsor responded to the uniform surface of ropes and to the process of coiling (p. 70). Critic Robert Pincus Witten, in reporting on Winsor's first major rope works,[4] described her enjoyment of the ''slow trance-like process of exhaustive coiling or binding or winding.''

While Francoise Grossen's knotted ropes were never brutal, her mid-70's solutions took on a new finesse. The Chinese twists emphasized both the ply and the natural luster of the hard twisted, honed smooth sisal. As seen on page 110, her new pallette—deep amethyst tones—furthered this sense of polish. Similar gradations of color, when they appear, as in the detail of *Cinq Rivieres* on page 110, so totally reinforce form and finish as to become one of the most polished statements of the decade.

Many of Grossen's pieces have been bisymmetrical and biomorphic. Others are symmetric webs with a frieze-like horizontal continuation. Through the 70's she has developed the marriage of the two in a repeated horizontal symmetry. Of these, one of the most successful and imposing is *Ahnen Galerie* first shown at the 1977 Biennale. The double row of five nearly identical forms on rectangular bases creates an alley with a power and implied significance reminiscent of double rows of temple sphinxes (p. 26).

Verena Sieber-Fuchs was a classmate of Francoise Grossen at Basel. The sensual sophistication of her massive rope works bears resemblance to Francoise Grossen's Chinese twists and to the elegant bead works for which Sieber-Fuchs is best known (p. 150). Although the rope ends spill onto the floor in the manner of Zeisler and others, their flow of energy is not random but can be compared to a root system in search of nutrient.

facing page
FRANCOISE GROSSEN Switzerland (lives in New York)
Cinq Rivieres 1974
braiding; manila rope
8' 10" × 8' 2"

By the mid-70's Grossen's rope works had achieved extraordinary refinement in the "polished" surface of Chinese braid forms. The muted richness of her deep tone colors is shown in the detail on page 110.

above
VERENA SIEBER-FUCHS Switzerland
Untitled (detail) c. 1977
wrapping; rope, cord

The "braids" are made by continuously wrapping polished cord around bundles containing six to ten ropes. Like Grossen's, Sieber-Fuchs' repetition of similar forms is paramount to the composition.

Several Japanese have responded to rope as a medium. Working with Shoji Yamahawa, a rope craftsman, Mariyo Yagi started with traditional Japanese ceremonial rope. In her early pieces she used hemp and formed her pieces so that they rise vertically, as if coming out of the earth. These are in the tradition of religious usage in Japan; her horizontal pieces also have as a frame of reference the belts once used by professional wrestlers. Moving toward a more flexible form, Yagi senses herself as the medium who moves the rope from the straight line into a curve. Her inclusion of highly polished stainless steel in some pieces serves to provide many transformed mirror images.

The ropes of Sachiko Morino define her empty packages. Some are bast fiber, but many employ the plastic multifilament ropes now universally used by marine outfitters. *Roped Air,* first shown at the 1977 Biennale, is typical of her package series in its hollow volume and correct knotting. The size, however, is unusual; so is the electric blue color. Rope-like materials are used as well. Francoise Grossen has used a number of them, including the foam tubing of her famous and buoyant *Inchworm* and paper piping cord (p. 74). More often she has employed the heavy, soft, soilable welting used to line velvet theatre ropes. Naomi Kobyashi has also used welting for the horizontal reliefs (p. 133).

Then there are ropes made for specific pieces. We have already mentioned those used by Mariyo Yagi. Marian Clayden ropes fine yarns after space dyeing them. Hicks and de Amaral were the first to spiral wrap rope-like elements in the manner of oversized gimp. de Amaral's *Cal y Canto* (p. 108) uses gimps smaller than her usual size.

Curiously, almost no one to our knowledge has explored the *craft* of rope—the splicings and knots peculiar to rope and the sea. The large Turk's cap shown next to Jagoda Buic's installation on page 24 is a singular if off-hand example.

right
FRANCOISE GROSSEN Switzerland (lives in New York)
From the Mermaid Series #3 (detail)
wrapping; paper piping cord
28″ × 8′ × 8′

More than anyone else Grossen has explored potentials of rope-like materials. Her huge Inchworm *of foam rubber hosing floated successfully on a pond in Oregon. Here she twists and wraps cord of monofilament plaited over a black paper core.*

MARIYO YAGI Japan
The One 1975 (above)
Splicing, wrapping; Korean hemp
15″ × 74″ × 7″

Of the many artists working with rope, Yagi alone has considered
the crafts of rope making and rope splicing. Her splice of red and
natural ropes symbolizes the fusion of yin and yang.

Flexible Work–1 1977 (below)
wrapping, splicing; hemp, aluminum

This artist often combines hemp ropes with polished aluminum
forms. The light color and silky surface of Korean hemp helps to
unify the two. Note the Turk's cap splice.

TECHNIQUES

During the 70's, a decade of renewed interest in the exotic textiles of Africa, Asia, and Indonesia, deepening probes into pre-industrial traditions inspired many Art Fabrics. This preoccupation sometimes grew out of a fascination with such rare structures as the split ply twining, with the definable limitations of plaiting, or with the rich craft quality of ancient dye techniques. Above all, these ancient methods permitted freedom of expression not possible on the loom or in printing and, with it, a rich coalescence of pattern and texture.

Of the Americans who, since the 50's, have drawn inspiration from the past, none is so consistent as Ed Rossbach. With insatiable curiosity he meanders through history, scrutinizing one aspect after another of the old techniques. His playful fabric caricatures, started well before he took his University of California at Berkeley post, flourished there. His reference documents are often so obscure or humble as to go unnoticed by eyes less connected with making. Rossbach has explored the mysteries of rare weaves, laces, baskets, dye techniques—what has he not? That he seldom repeats himself, rarely works in large format, and does not work for sales or commissions, has enabled him to consider so many possibilities. He is never anachronistic but ever a harbinger of new departures and ideas. Through him the past has been inculcated into the unique area surrounding not only his former department and the University but the entire Bay Area.

The credit, of course, is shared. The lively influence of Berkeley's Anthropology Department is long standing, and—with it—a very real respect for Indian basketry and tribal technologies. Teachers such as Trude Guermonprez and Katherine Westphal opened doors for two generations of students, many of whom became important as artists and educators. Margery Annenberg's gallery in San Francisco long bridged contemporary and ethnic expressions. Later Fiberworks and Kasuri Dye Works in Berkeley, Straw Into Gold in Oakland and the Allrich Gallery in San Francisco fostered the spread of new expressions in ancient techniques.

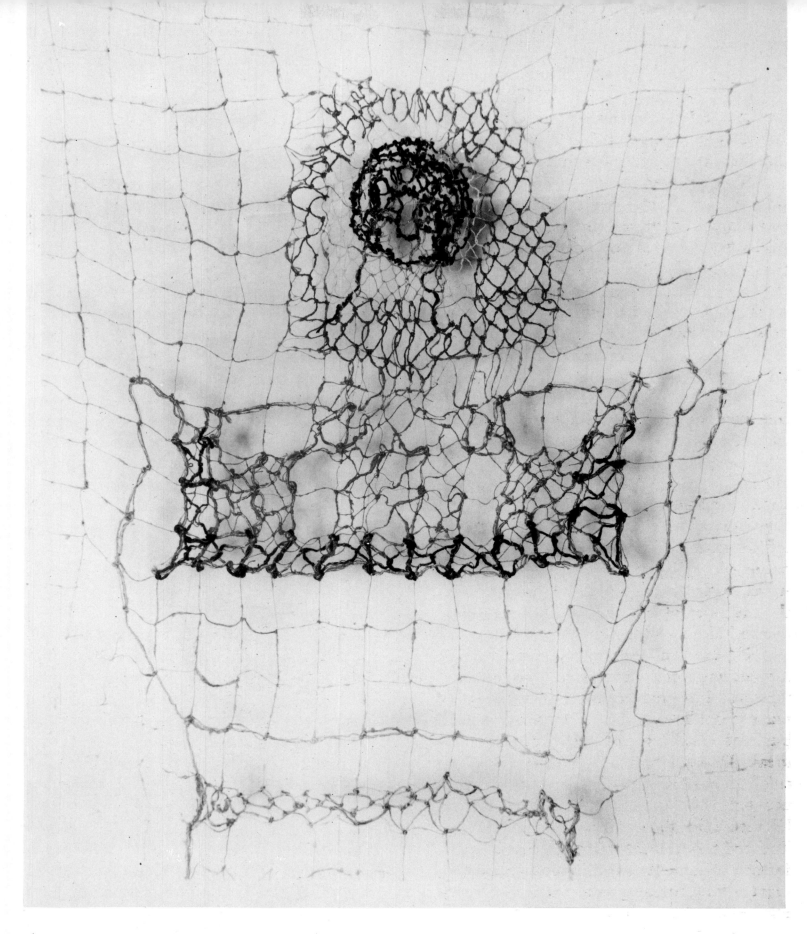

above
ED ROSSBACH U.S.A.
Coptic *(detail) 1975*
knotted netting; silk
7' × 5'

The humorous head is knotted onto an open net in colored yarns.
Although the image and color reference is Coptic, the technique
derives from Chancay ''gauzes'' of pre-Columbian Peru.

facing page
KAY SEKIMACHI, U.S.A.
Variations on a Camel's Girth #5 *1976*
split ply twining; cotton
17" × 7"

In the mid-70's Sekimachi explored the pattern possibilities of the
rare, north Indian technique of a split ply twining. As the name
suggests, the plies of one cord are split to allow the passage of
another. The locked-in construction is so dense as to make it ideal
for girth straps.

If the San Francisco Bay Area led the resurgence of ancient techniques, the whole West Coast followed suit. Through her workshops and writings, Virginia Harvey of Seattle broadened the range of exploration in such old constructions as macrame, knotting, and sprang. More recently she introduced the rare North Indian technique of split ply twining, shown on page 76. Bernard Kester encouraged an open-ended exploration of old media approaches.

Nor was this kind of historical research limited to the West Coast. Gerhardt Knodel introduced the examination of ethnic cloths to Cranbrook. While working at the Peabody Museum, Joanne Segal Brandford began her series of veil-like cloths combining knotting with local dyeing. Her examples of ikat and plangi nets were published in *The Dyer's Art;* the piece shown here on page 105 is newer, more complex in color and pattern.

All these probes into past techniques have enriched the field. Through them we have gained contemporary expressions of ikat and other resists, plaiting, roping, basketry techniques, felting, and paper making.

In the 70's we saw gobelin tapestry almost eclipsed by the advent of old and new techniques. We also witnessed the demise of those small hangings focusing on natural materials and pretending to no more than a decorative statement. The expression "off loom" describes a long period in which handweavers left their traditional tools and disciplines with some mistaken notion that weaving was retardative or obsolete. By the late 70's loom woven Art Fabrics, often small, flat, and rectilinear, were rediscovered as brilliant statements. The single element techniques of macrame, knitting, and crochet barely survived their faddish uses. Funk and junk statements in Art Fabrics disappeared. We were forced to distinguish between true artists and followers who imitated them.

Elements

A comprehension of the term *elements* is all that is required to understand the rudiments of fabric construction. An element is any linear material that can be interworked to form a fabric structure. Yarn is the most common, but strips of cloth, metal, plastic, or paper can also be elements. The first elements were grasses and reeds, wood splints and strips of bark, leather thongs and sinews—the materials available to hunters and gatherers. Sometimes bundles of fiber were plied into ropes. Twisting these fibers for additional strength led to the invention of spinning, which in turn facilitated the development of such *single element techniques* as looping, knitting, crochet, and knotting.

Sets of Elements

Braiding and sprang are examples of fabrics interlaced with *one set of elements* moving in one direction. Weaving uses at least *two sets of elements:* one—the *warp*—is stretched tautly on the loom; the *weft,* or filling yarn, interlaces horizontally across it. A supplementary warp or weft (as in brocading) is a *third set of elements,* while double cloth, with two warps and two wefts, uses *four sets of elements.* Plaiting may have one set of elements in braids, two when it resembles weaving, and three or four when the diagonals of caning are added.

Orders of Interlacing

Regular progressions of weaving and flat plaiting can be described by their orders of interlacing. The simplest, over one/under one (indicated as 1/1), is called plain weave or, in basketry, checkerwork. It is essentially a grid. Balanced twills usually progress diagonally in an over two/under two (2/2) order. Weft or warp-face twills may have a 3/1 order, etc.

Plaiting

One of the earliest and most universal of fabric structures, plaiting is at least ten times older than the loom. It takes on many forms and (consider baskets) many shapes. Because it is rarely industrialized, plaiting remains a craft and one much neglected in the West. In part the negligence derives from not recognizing plaiting in its many guises. As one of the earliest and most universal of fabric structures, plaiting is so ingrained in memory that it escapes our consciousness. As young children we learn first to plait our hair or tie our plaited shoe laces, then to plait paper mats and baskets. Later we may braid belts and lanyards, splice rope, interweave strips of metal, braid bread dough or clay or flower garlands, darn wool, or cane chairs—without ever knowing that these are all common forms of plaiting.

The term *plaiting* covers a broad area of fabric structures: flat and tubular braids, sometimes sewn spirally for rounded mats and hats; diagonal "twill" plaiting in rectangular mats; and plaiting with horizontals, verticals, and diagonals as in caning. Multiply these by the broadest ranges of materials, scale, and end use of any craft technique and one has some sense of the diversity.

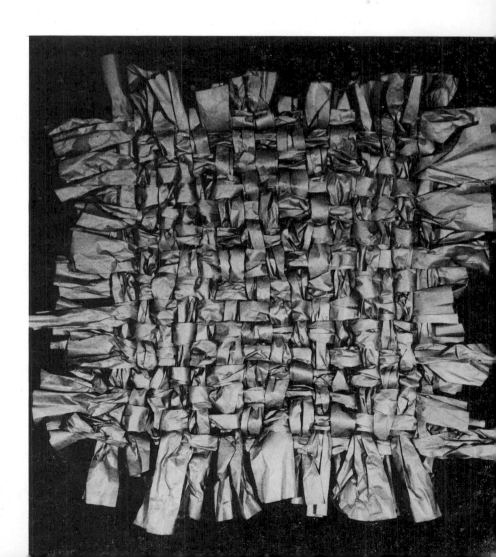

ED ROSSBACH U.S.A.
Window 1975
double plaiting; cloth, paper
c. 72″ × 45″

Outside of basketry, double plaiting is rare: as far as we know only the Byzantines used it in the manner of double cloth. With the crossing of the two layers, Rossbach achieved the vertical slashes; with two layers he had the possibility to stuff his mat into a pillowy softness. Combining cloth and paper strips is unusual. The striped paper lends a staccato rhythm. The loose ends, occasional floats, and right angle turns give variety.

It was not until the mid-20th century that Dr. Alfred Bühler first classified resist techniques as a single unit of study.[5] For plaiting, such a classification is yet to be made. To date, no dictionary or fabric classification provides satisfactory definitions. There is general agreement that plaiting with a single set (of three or more) elements is a specific form of plaiting called *braiding*. In the West these fabrics are most often simple tapes or tubes but in East Asia there are hundreds of variations, often very complex.

There is also general agreement that diagonal or oblique interlacing with two sets of elements is a form of plaiting. So are the three element interlacings shown on page 84, and three or four element canings are easily related. Controversy most often arises regarding those interlacings of horizontal and vertical elements structurally identical to weaving. In basketry these structures are indisputably termed plaiting. But *is* plaiting "weaving without a loom"? More likely, weaving on a loom is but one major aspect of the older, larger concept of plaiting. In many cultures this aspect is so diverse and preeminent as to have almost eclipsed other forms of interlacing.

In the 60's Olga de Amaral and Ed Rossbach were among the first to explore the possibilities of plaiting. Rossbach's braided plastic, plaited newspaper and baskets, and de Amaral's weighty plaited hangings have all been documented in *Beyond Craft*. Here we see his small mat of twisted paper. His large, more complex "damasks," described on page 165, are of heavy welting interlaced on a frame. Are they, then, woven or plaited—or either? Because the "warp" was wrapped first then the "weft" interlaced upon it, the term *woven* is probably the more acceptable. The distinction is subtle, ill-defined, and perhaps arbitrary.

De Amaral's work is so rich in materials and sense of craft, so strong in its expression and impact, usually combining not one but several processes, that a particular structure hardly concerns us. Director of a Bogota studio for Art Fabrics, upholstery, and carpet, she is considered a weaver and artist. Yet for ten years her major works have been primarily wrapped or plaited. Where it occurs, the weaving is primarily in broad tabs with which she forms the "shingled components" of such large pieces as the commission shown on page 217. More often she weaves heavy coarse tapes to plait such pieces as *Cal y Canto 227* (p. 108). The tapes here interlace through a "warp" of spiral-wrapped horsehair cords. More extraordinary, the horizontal tapes push out of the base plane to diagonally interlace with each other; i.e., one of the two elements splits into two elements.

Several of de Amaral's plaits are inspired by an indigenous New World technique of oblique interlacing at a steep angle, related to that form of sprang that is plaited. This technique is found among the Indians of Col-

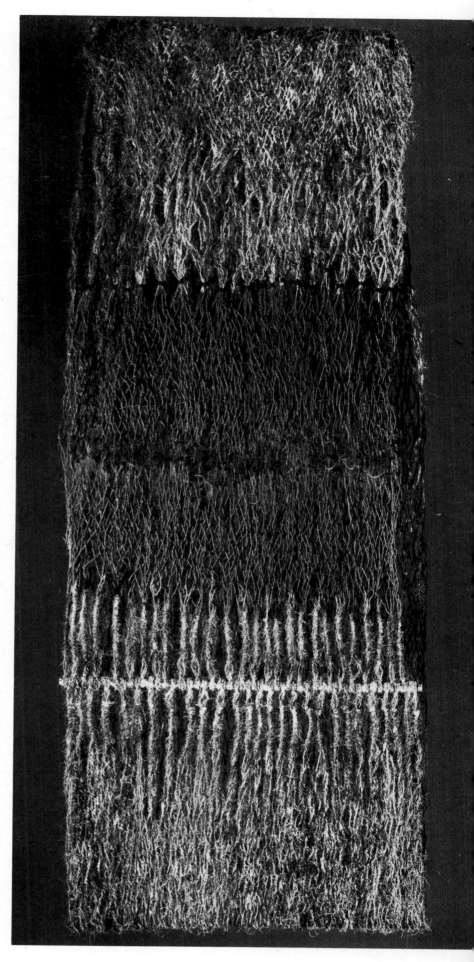

OLGA DE AMARAL *Colombia*
Cal y Canto *1977*
plaiting; horse hair, gesso
75" × 32"

De Amaral used the frame plaiting technique indigenous to the Americas. As in sprang, each crossing is mirrored at the other end of the "warp" Here the looped ends of the central red band are interlinked at either end to natural grey ones. At the horizontal dowel, yarn groups are ornamented with gesso.

ombia, who use bast or wool yarns in a
checked pattern for bags and purses. As
shown at the bottom of *Cal y Canto* (p. 108),
de Amaral mostly uses wrapped cords.

Especially in his 1/1 interlacings of plastic
film, the early plaits of Holland's Harry
Boom, shown at the 1st International Exhibition of Miniature Textiles, have this same
simplicity. Whether viewed as simplistic or
conceptual they predate Sandoval's much
larger, more complex plaited films.

The large, luminous, extremely flat works of
Arturo Sandoval are plaited with wide strips
layered with Mylar, photographic film, and/
or netted veilings. The iridescent strips of
Pond With Scum (p. 105) have a locally applied transparent stain that produces an
opalescent surface. Like a chameleon, the surface changes with the light and color reflected
on it. As shown on page 50, some of his
plaited films are superimposed with diagonal

above
JOHN MC QUEEN U.S.A.
Untitled c.1977
plaiting, embossing; raffia
14" × 12"

*The resilience of diagonal plaiting aids in the deep embossing; so
does a pattern consistent with the grain of the cloth.*

facing page

top
KAREN CHAPNICK U.S.A. (lives in Canada)
Effusions 1976
plaiting; wool
45" × 96"

*The glowing color of this large hanging derives from a dozen
jewel-toned wools grouped in order to weave as one yarn. From
the center, they shade light to dark. The frame is achieved
through a change in the order of interlacing.*

bottom
ARTURO SANDOVAL U.S.A.
Wall Weaving in Process 1976

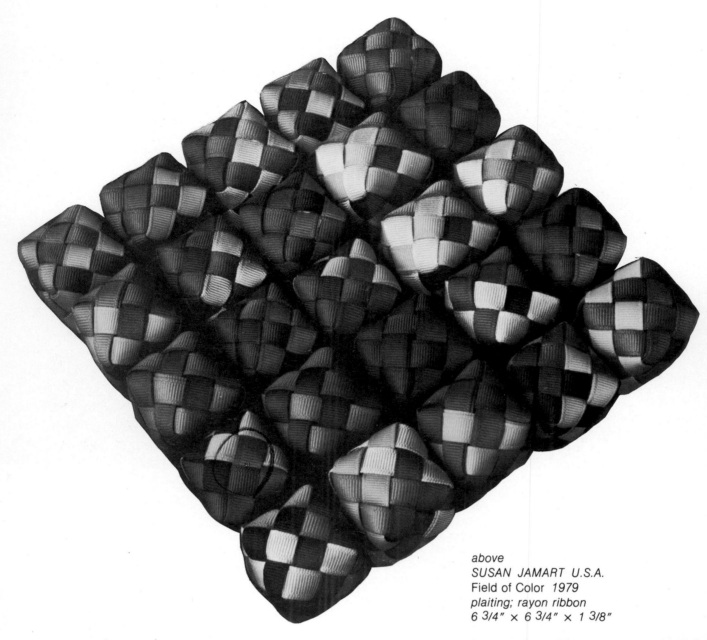

above
SUSAN JAMART U.S.A.
Field of Color 1979
plaiting; rayon ribbon
6 3/4″ × 6 3/4″ × 1 3/8″

In as many colors as Joseph's coat, twenty-five cubes were crisply plaited in grosgrain ribbon, then composed as a rhombus.

below
MARIA NEMES Hungary
String Box 1976
plaiting; hemp
7′ 7/8″ × 7/8″ × 7′ 7/8″

The visual impact of seeing through the several layers is heightened when a shadow is projected. A wet-spun hemp has sufficient body to support the frail structure.

elements. By 1979 he was deep into his *Kentucky Barn Series* in which the patinated "tin" of old barn roofs was cut into wide bands, then plaited into cohesive panels.

Similar in scale if not weight, the plaited leather bands of Daniel Graffin are discussed on page 62. Both Sherri Smith and Mark Pollack plait with broad cotton tapes. Pollack's work (p. 58) is based on 1/1 interlacing. Like Susan Jamart, whose book, *Plaiting,* aided the popularization of the construction, Sherri Smith often plaited three sets of elements in intricate color patterns. While Jamart's dimensional volumes (left) were achieved with multicolored ribbons, Smith's derived from locally dyed cotton tapes that were plaited to create predetermined patterns.

In the use of plaiting with three sets of elements and dimensional illusion both Maria Von Blaaderen's small optical box and Maria Nemes' cube are related to Smith's work described above. But in terms of scale, material, color, and density they are quite different. There is an even more essential variance: the three sets of elements in the Smith pieces prevail throughout the structure; the Von Blaaderen and Nemes works are entirely composed of areas with two sets of elements. With a single yarn, the simplest of means, both small works express structural concept as a *tour de force.*

Nemes' six-planed cube is related to several of the plaited baskets of John McQueen (p. 148) but—however geometric—McQueen's work is not minimal. Even his simplest forms are enriched with a strong sense of materials and craftsmanship. To achieve his broad range of

right
MARIA VON BLAADEREN *Holland*
Study Square *1977*
plaiting; linen
c.8″ × 6″

Using pins to support the looped selvage, the artist has interlaced vertically, horizontally, and diagonally to form one corner of an optical box.

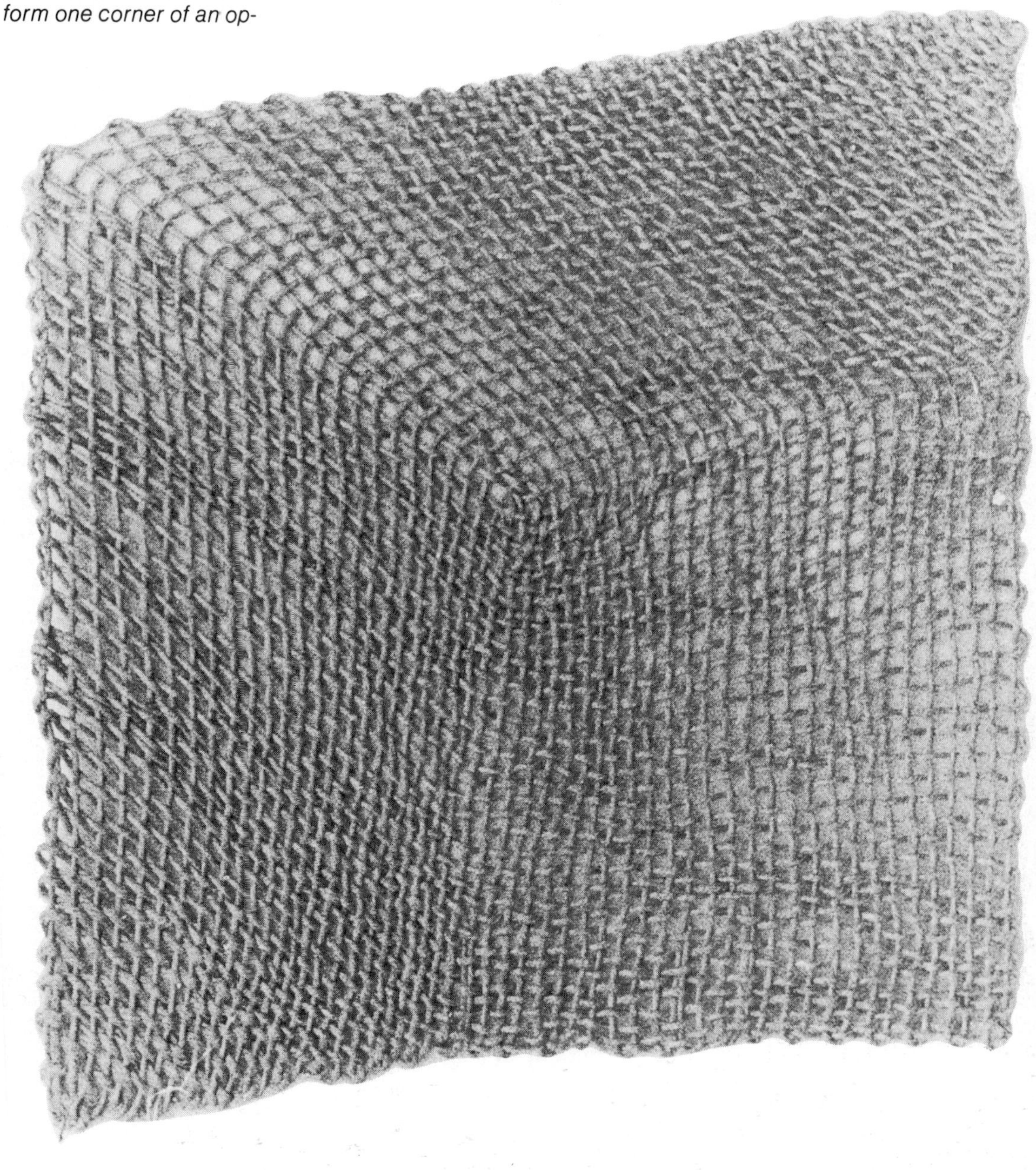

expression within related forms of similar size, McQueen uses a number of woody materials. For each he finds an appropriate interlacing. For some, as the one shown on page 147, the elements are diagonal. More often, horizontal and vertical elements interlace in the 1/1 order referred to by basket makers as checkerwork. His panel (p. 82) is from a series of small pieces diagonally plaited of raffia. The dimension created by embossing is particularly well suited to the resilience implicit in diagonal structures.

Fabric Structures

As stated above, all techniques of the 60's persisted through the 70's. But some were out of phase. By the latter half of the decade, tapestry joining and macrame knotting were only incidental to the work of Grossen, Plewka Schmidt (pp. 242–245) and Muñoz. Diane Itter used very fine, tight knotting to manipulate brilliantly colored silks into miniature mosaics (p. 159). Knitting and crochet were most often found in miniatures like those of Ann Sutton, work such as that of Marika de Ley (p. 160), and notable especially in the powerful dioramas of Eva Pachuka (pp.

228 and 230) and the large knitted work by Toshiko Horiuchi.

Lacy constructions persisted in the pictoral filagrees of the Czech master Luba Krejci, in the long series of square knotted nets by Brandford (p. 105) and rarer ones by Ed Rossbach and Lillian Elliot. With a sure knowledge of lace technique, Lizzy Funk and Lieselote Siegfried, both of Switzerland, perfected extraordinary white-on-white reliefs. These were small, painstakingly executed, virtuoso statements. One wonders how they might appear in a larger size.

Perhaps the freshest approach to technique was so freewheeling as to defy classification. Consider as a whole the cast fiber forms and stitched burlap bundles of Abakanowicz (pp. 32–33), the Lenore Tawney *Cloud Series* (p. 218), the Japanesque simplicity of Harry Boom (p. 137), and Tamiko Kawata Ferguson's mail of safety pins (p. 159). Consider the environmental works of Colette, Christo, and Hicks. All are outside established technique. Some are superbly crafted, some only concepts. All provoke our imagination, albeit differently. Some are unique *tours de force*. Others hint at a mystery, endlessly new.

left
EVELYN SVEC WARD U.S.A.
Tablero Uno *(detail) 1979*
knotting, knitting, collage, painting; sisal, cotton, ixtle on linen
14" x 12"

Several diverse techniques and materials are unified by a rich sense of structure and a propensity for enriching shadows.

facing page
LUBA KREJCI *Czechoslovakia*
Pegasus *(detail) 1976*
knotting; linen
59" x 47"

The detail gives some sense of a structure in which vertical and diagonal yarns are knotted onto passive horizontals. Although it is more than two decades since Krejci's lace panels first appeared in the West, they remain not only unrivaled but unique. They are extraordinary for an iconography constructed in air and for voids as meaningful as the solid areas.

above
ANNE WILSON U.S.A.
Swirl 1978
knotted netting; wire, gauze
4' × 4'8"

Wilson's panel speaks with the free media exploration we expect in contemporary painting. Her means is a wirey net tied with long, uncut loops to produce a varied surface on a dotted grid.

left
JOHN GARRETT U.S.A.
Wish On Wish/Winter Gate 1979
wrapping, knotting; bamboo, twigs, raffia, wire
72" × 72"

Although the first impression is structural and ethnic, the work is neither. Garrett laced the split bamboo diagonals to metal hardware cloth, then superimposed the other elements. The raffia and yarn ends are uncut and expressed.

Felting

True felt is made from wool and fur fibers. These alone have the crimp and barb-like scales that will interlock by the application of moisture, heat, and agitation. Traditionally felts have been made from knit or woven cloths (woolen blankets are usually partially felted) or directly from loose fiber. With the addition of some form of bonding agent, other fibers may achieve felt-like structures that are a type of non-woven fabric (see Jan Anderson's relief on page 112). Both a knit understructure and the loose fiber method may achieve dimensional form. Felt is potentially as malleable as clay. Felts hats and snow boots have been contoured for millenia. While traditional felt makers strive for uniformity in thickness and color, and for total homogenation of fibers, the artist has other options. Because felt tends to be durable, soil resistant, and easily cleaned, this is an excellent medium for Art Fabrics.

Joan Livingstone has, since her Cranbrook days, been working in the felt medium. Usually, as shown on page 112, she forms pieces of felt, then welds them together with a second felting process. That she has a painter's concern with color, surface, and implied image is reinforced by the "canvas" formats she often suspends from easels.

right top
LOIS LANCASTER U.S.A.
Wool Ball *1976*
winding, felting, cutting; wool
circ. 20"

right bottom
Lois Lancaster winds wool slivers into a sphere, compresses it through felting, then cuts out a wedge to reveal the "growth rings."

Another innovator, Inese Birstins, who works in British Columbia, has also put felt through a second process. First she has formed her basic ground and fused the felt to secure the color gradations she wants for her composition—from dark to light and light to dark. Then her woven strips are embedded—not stitched—into the felt, providing still another density and another texture.

In her *Kimono 2,* Michelle Heon of Quebec has used dyed and felted wool fleece as a major element. The felt garment is hung over a dyed and shredded silk cloth lining. Premeditated disintegration of both fabrics aggravates the sense of mystery. The colors of the felt—blacks, browns and greys, glossy and matte—contrast with the lighter color of the shredded silk. The effect is to perceive the garment as some primitive remains of a distant past.

Wool yarns and roving can also be felted to great effect, but seldom are. The examples shown here, both by Karen Van Derpool of Seattle, use felted roving. On the left is a small plaited basket using undyed wool felt roving as the only element. The second, right, is similar in form but is again felted; only a suggestion of the plaited structure remains.

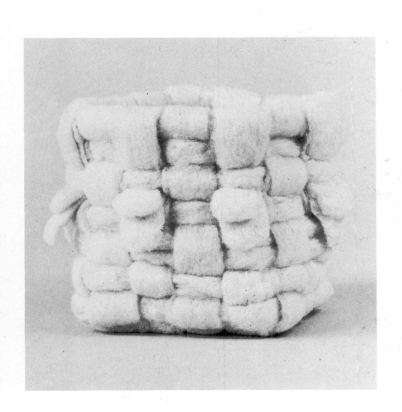

Paper Making

Like felt, paper is a wet process, non-woven fabric. The materials and process, however, are somewhat different. The fibers used are cellulosic (vegetable) fibers, principally cotton, linen, or rayon recycled from used cloth or found in wood pulps such as the mulberry fibers used for Oriental "rice" papers.

Suspended in cold water, often with the aid of a hand or mechanical agitator, these fibers form a thick syrup called a *slurry*. Traditional handmade paper is produced by raising a rectangular *deckle* or framed mesh through the slurry. As the water drains out, a damp felt-like deposit is left on the screen. It is turned out onto an absorbent cloth. For heavier papers, the mesh may be repeatedly dipped. The horizontal lines of *laid* paper result from a screen formed of small rods. A *deckle edge* is the result of fiber thinning out at the periphery of the mesh. Finishing of various kinds may be applied after the paper is dry. The point is that, once rectangular sheets of raw material are not the objective, the mesh can be blocked out like a stencil to achieve any shape. In the making, these shapes can also be pierced. More than one slurry color or fiber type can be used, and fibrous materials, such as the leaves and butterflies found in Japanese papers, can be mixed in the slurry or trapped between two layers.

Nor must the mesh be flat. Consider, for instance, a hemispherical sieve, as Dominic Di Mare did for the nested half circles of his *Moon Box* (right). Note the tenderness expressed in his natural deckle edge. On pages 152 and 153 other Di Mare papers are shown, but always as one of several materials and techniques. *Home Flight* by Judith Ingram, page 94, employs the deckle edge and some shaping plus stitching and drawn line. Its elephantine grey color was in the fiber before she turned it into paper. Here again the art is *in* the paper making not *on* or of the paper. With the mounting interest in paper making as an art form, we can expect to see more and larger dimensional work—probably in a number of directions. For example, consider the large-scale work of William Weege, whose string and paper pulp constructions are called "plaited sheets." Color is added by painting on the strings, mixing it into the pulp, or splashing it onto the finished sheets.

facing page
DOMINIC DI MARE U.S.A.
Moon Box *1974*
paper making
7" × 7" × 6 1/2"

Collection: S. Lewis, Los Angeles

Di Mare pioneered dimensionally-formed paper. The fragile
strength of his hemispheres is contained in rectilinear boxes.

right
SYLVIA SEVENTY U.S.A.
Untitled Vessel *1979*
paper making; paper, wax, leaves
d. 9 3/4"

Color, texture, and leaf inclusions are all integral. Wax is an additional binder. The fragility reminds us of paper hornets' nests.

below
ANNE FLATEN PIXLEY U.S.A.
Post and Paper Series #3 *(detail) 1978*
embossing; paper on pinewood posts
5' × 12'

Each paper piece is separately made. Each has four deckle
edges, one of which is inserted into a diagonal slot sawed into a
vertical post. The variety in color and irregularity of form augment
highlights and shadows; the whole has a surprising crispness.

above
NANCE O'BANION U.S.A.
Air: Structure *(detail) 1979*
paper making, plaiting; bamboo, enamel, pigment, linen
6' × 10'

For a large, complex composition, long paper strips with deckle
edges were made, then plaited over and under a bamboo grid. In
the light grey areas the color is intrinsic; the black was sprayed on
after the plaiting was completed.

facing page
JUDITH INGRAM U.S.A.
San Francisco High *1978*
papermaking, collage; paper, thread
23" × 31"

Three paper types were made specifically for the composition.
The center area is emphasized by the deep shadowed, deckle-
edged inclusion and tear.

Fabric Embellishment

Almost as old as mankind is the desire and need for embellishment: to decorate, to adorn surfaces—whether it be the person, body coverings, or, eventually, shelters.

From the time of World War I—and certainly World War II—ornament had been dead. A full pendulum swing away from the Victorian Era, both critics and architects found ornament and certainly applied pattern inconsistent with their industrial ethic. Like the proverbial "baby thrown out with the bathwater," the sensibilities of enriching integral pattern were as spurned as were cast embellishments applied to buildings and radio sets. Museum exhibitions and current publications followed suit, so that, when fabrics were shown at all, they tended to be pre-Columbian weaves or post-Bauhaus textures.

The first Surface Design Conference, which was held in 1976 in Lawrence, Kansas, was indeed a turning point for those working in fabric embellishment. Organizers Elsa Sreenivasam and Pat Campbell hoped for 200 delegates. From underground and out of the woodwork over 600 came. They came from all points of North America, with a sprinkling from Europe and East Asia. Out of an understanding that derived from strength-in-numbers, they founded a confederation called Surface Design, with its own publication and biannual conferences. The organization is not strong; it is primarily only North American. These are basically independent artists, designers, and craftsmen; sharing technical know-how and creating an advocacy is their common cause.

Together, they realized the strength of a new expression somewhere between weaving and painting. They affirmed that our straight-laced reaction to the overly patterned 19th century must now be over.

Dye Techniques

The fresh application of dye to cloth became a hallmark of the late 70's. From Bali to Berlin we witnessed dyed and painted fabrics in furnishings and fashion, ranging from T-shirts to ballgowns, in techniques from ancient resists to heat transfer and colored Xerox. Some were commercial, some child's play, some candidly exploratory, and some an art form. Although freedom and spontaneity prevailed, there were some attempts to achieve the *knowing* spontaneity of Matisse drawings and of Japanese calligraphy.

Especially in the resists, new masters such as Marian Clayden and Chunghi Choo devised complex compositions unprecedented in their intricate richness. Such needle techniques as quilting, appliqué, and patchwork were sometimes used in combination. Elaborate apparel came into focus. Outrageous renditions of neo-Dada and Funk came and went; it was a lively period, yet to be evaluated.

Most aspects of the 70's renaissance of dye and print techniques are covered in *The Dyer's Art: Ikat, Batik, and Plangi*. Since that book deals primarily with resists, the following is but a precis and update.

The Resists. We should explain that, until the 18th century, direct printing on cloth was not possible because vegetable dyes were only fast when immersed repeatedly, often over long periods of time. Also, until the jacquard loom was invented in the 19th century, only the top strata in the high cultures of Europe and Asia could afford figured brocades and damasks. In general and globally, richly patterned cloths had been resist dyed. In Japan, India, South East Asia, and West Africa many still are. Post-Renaissance Europeans have lost the resist traditions and, until recently, did not even appreciate them.

Indonesian terms for resists are now universal. Put simply, *batik* involves the application of fluid or semi-fluid substances that solidify on the cloth itself to form a stencil impervious to the dyebath. Hot wax, resin, and paraffin, as well as starch, rice paste, bean paste, and even half-fluid mud are used as resist materials. After dyeing, the resist is removed. *Plangi* is a general term covering a large related group of resists including tie-dye, fold dye, and stitch-dye (tritik). *Ikat* is the process of wrapping-to-pattern then dyeing segments of yarn before cloth construction begins. Modern versions with similar effects are sometimes done without resists. When directly painted on cloth, the term *local dyeing* is used, when on yarn, *space dyeing*. Warp or weft printing also produce effects similar to ikat (for an example see page 100).

facing page
top
DANIEL GRAFFIN   France
Trace Indigo #4   1978

bottom
Prise et Meprise   1978
fold dye with tritik; indigo dyed mill cotton
26" x 37" each

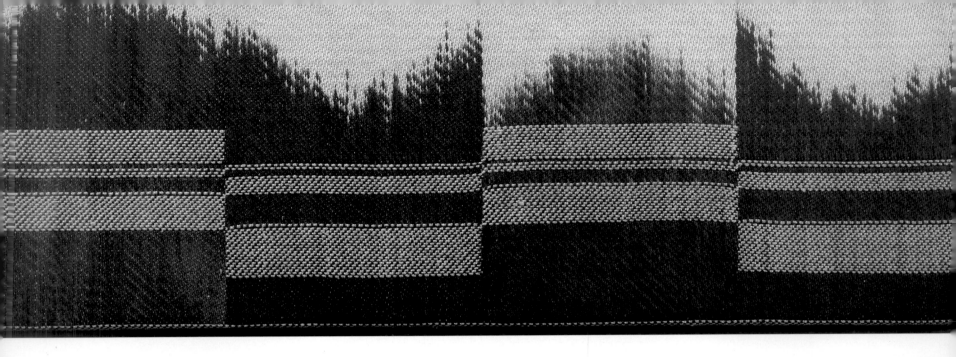

ETHEL STEIN   U.S.A.

top
Zack's Marsh   *1977*
satin damask; warp ikat; indigo dyed silk
5¾" x 15¾"

bottom
Untitled   *1977*
satin damask; compound ikat; indigo dyed silk
32" x 32"

Collection: Jack Lenor Larsen, New York

KRIS DEY   U.S.A.

Fugue   1978
local dyeing and wrapping; mill cotton strips
2' x 3'

Collection: Mr. and Mrs. E. Berliner, San Francisco

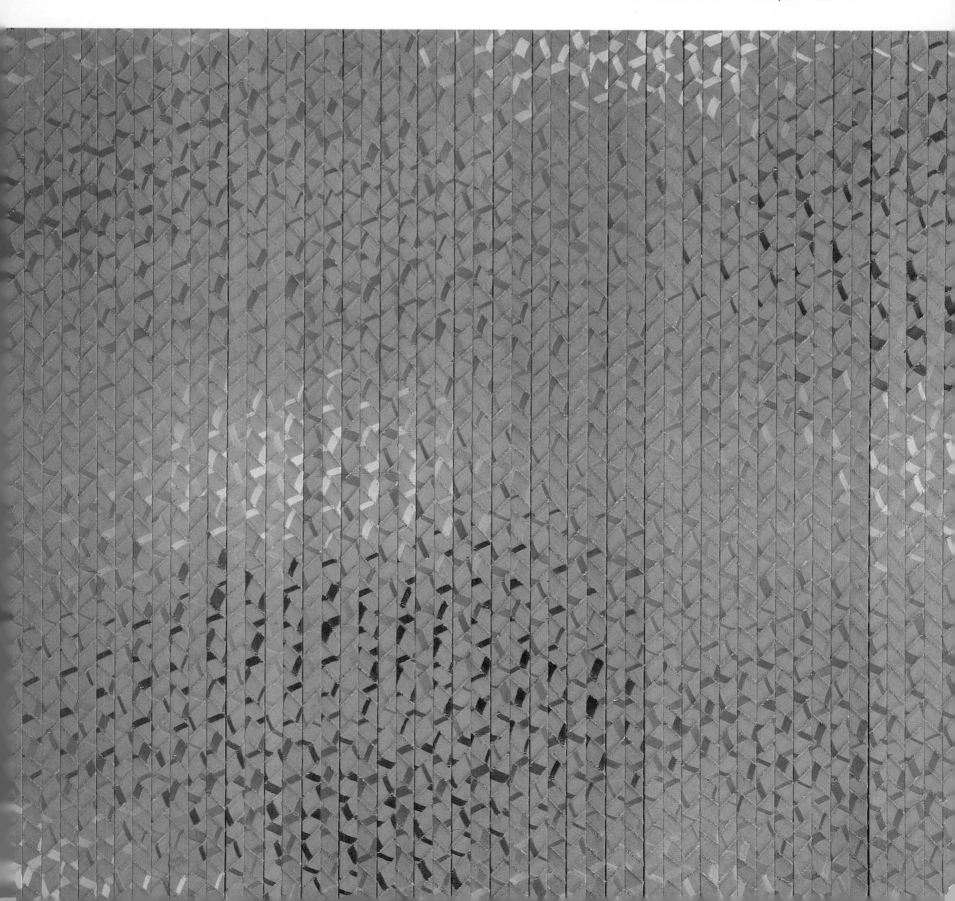

LIA COOK   U.S.A.

left
Interweave 1   1974
warp face repp; space dyed warp with photographic transfer; cotton
3' x 5'

Collection: University of Texas, Austin

right
Space Continuum III *(detail)*   1976
warp face repp, space dyed warp with shaped polyurethane weft; wool, jute, cotton
6' x 10'

Commissioned for: City Hall, Fairfield, California

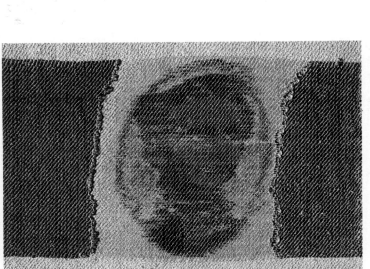

ED ROSSBACH   U.S.A.

Mad Ludwig II   1979
weft brocade; transfer printed weft; silk
4½" x 5½"

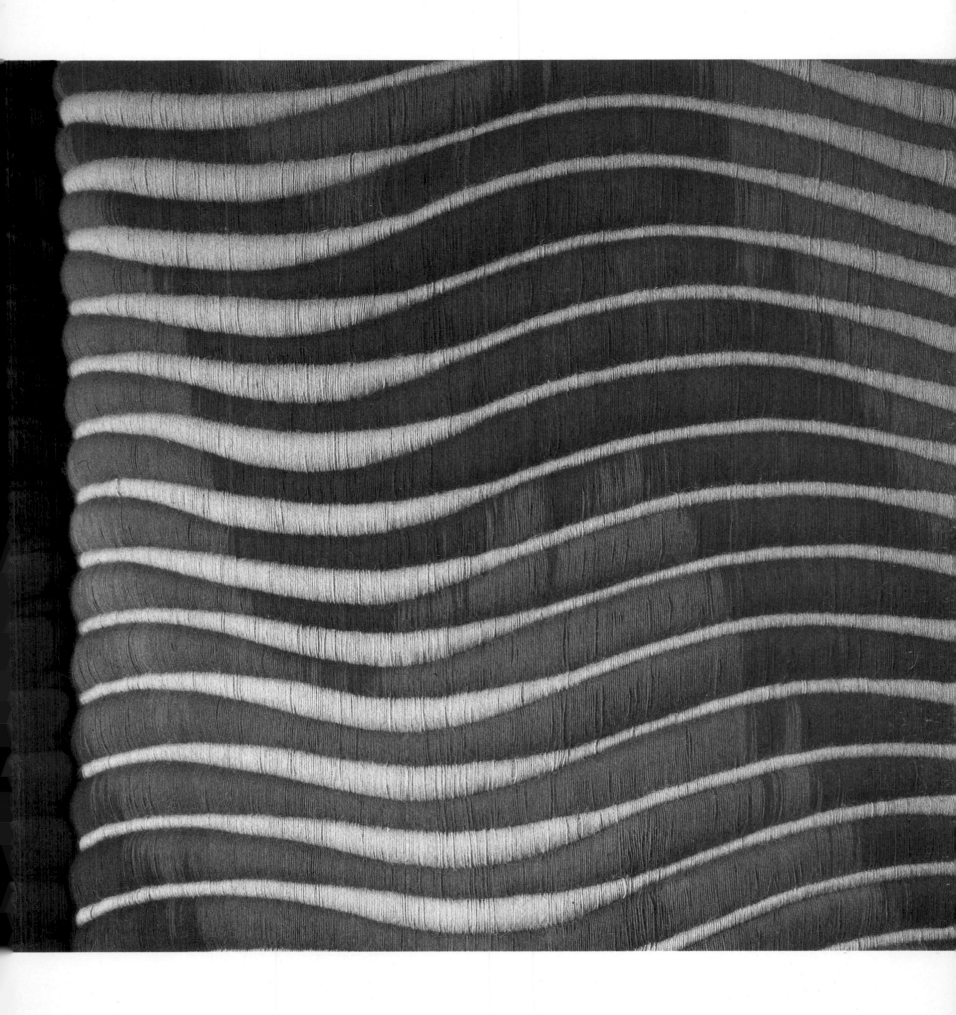

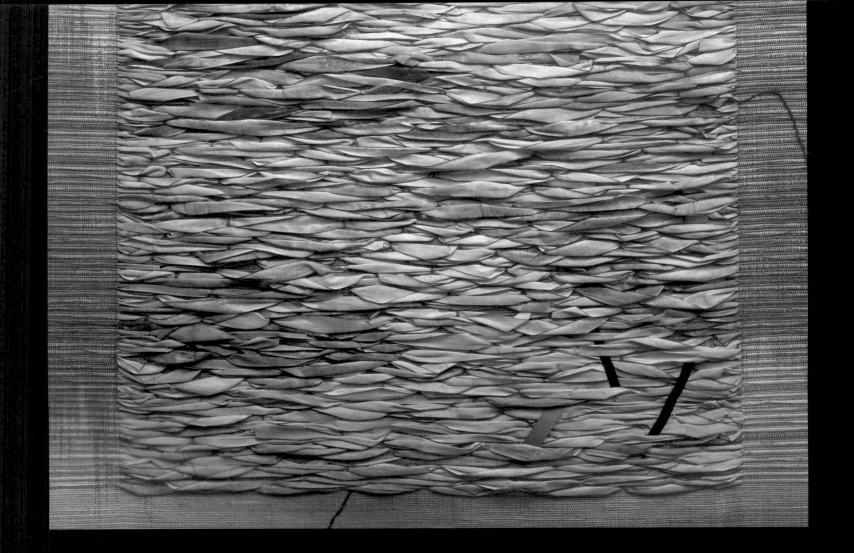

above
CYNTHIA SCHIRA   U.S.A.
Beyond the Mountain *(detail)   1975*
brocade; warp ikat, locally dyed weft tapes; cotton
7'6" x 15'6"

left
MARIAN CLAYDEN   Great Britain (lives in California)
84 Ropes   1976
roping; space dyeing and discharge; cotton roving
7' x 8'

SHERRI SMITH   U.S.A.
Anthracite   1977
plaiting; space dyed cotton webbing
8' x 11½'

Collection: Anne Bradley, Oak Park, Illinois

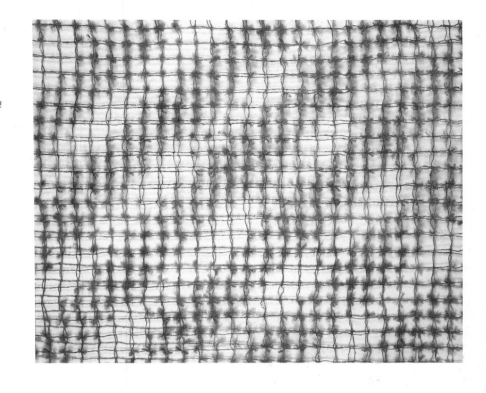

right
JOANNE SEGAL BRANDFORD   U.S.A.
Plaid Net   *1976*
netting; linen
70" x 60"

Collection: Michael and Sandra Harner, Norwalk, Connecticut

below
ARTURO SANDOVAL   U.S.A.
Pond with Scum   *1977*
plaiting with machine sewn straps; plastic, Mylar veiling,
paint, thread
9' x 9'

NEDA AL-HILALI   U.S.A.

Atlantis   1976
plaiting: dyeing and painting; paper
8' x 12½'

Collection: Muzeum Sztuki w Lodzi, Poland

top
Dark Shingle Piece   *1974*
plaiting; processed paper
82" x 70" x 6"

bottom
Coffeetable Piece *(detail)*
plaiting; dyeing and painting; paper
18" x 18"

OLGA DE AMARAL Colombia

above
Cal y Canto   1977
weaving and plaiting; linen, horsehair, gesso
53⅛″ x 39⅜″

right
Cal y Canto 227   1977
wrapping and plaiting; linen, horsehair, gesso
57″ x 43″

RITZI & PETER JACOBI   Romania (live in Germany)

above
Alina I *(detail)   1976*
slit tapestry with wrapped elements; goathair, cotton,
raw silk
2' 3½" x 10' ⅜"

right
Multicolored Exotica   1976
weaving with wrapped elements; goathair, wool
8' 3" x 3' 7"

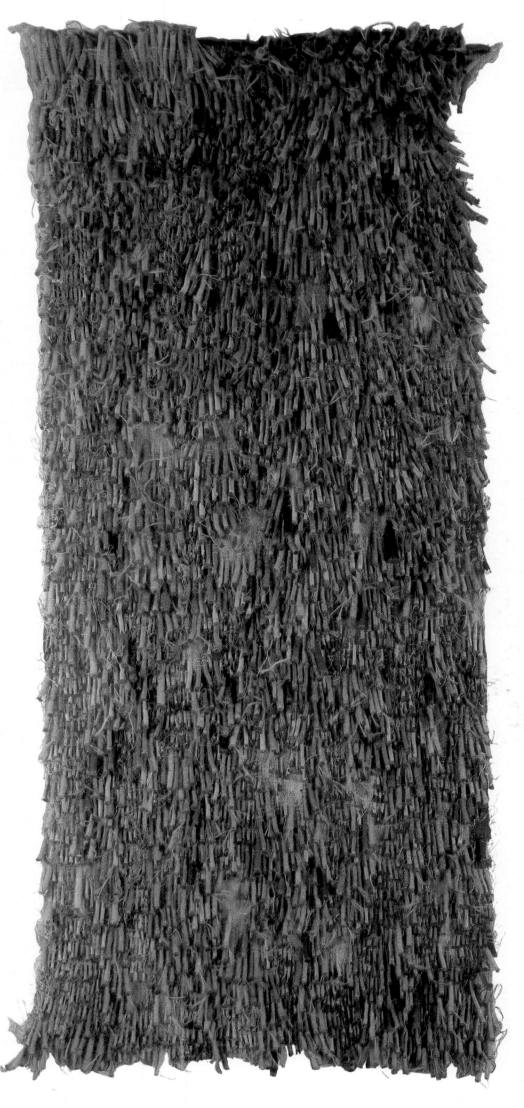

FRANCOISE GROSSEN
Switzerland (lives in New York)
Cinq Rivieres *(detail)* 1974
braiding; manila rope
8' 10" x 8' x 2'

DIANE ITTER *U.S.A.*
Change of Plans *(detail)* 1977
half-hitch knotting; linen
8" x 8"

AURELIA MUNOZ   *Spain*
Medieval Cloak   *1975*
macrame; natural jute and sisal
41⅛" x 63"

Collection: American Telephone & Telegraph Company,
Basking Ridge, New Jersey

JAN ANDERSON   U.S.A.
Stratigraphic Impressions   1977
felting and compressing; cotton, Rhoplex
4' x 6'

JOAN LIVINGSTONE   U.S.A.
Untitled   1976
felting; wool, cotton yarn
2' 1" x 2' 8"

Collection: Bill Shapiro, Kansas City

For *negative resists,* the cloth itself resists dyes, such as madder, that color only those areas pretreated with mordant. For *discharge* or bleach printing, the cloth is dyed first and then bleached with a direct or resist method. New colorants may be mixed with the bleach to replace the original.

All these techniques are particularly well suited to unique works. All convey a rich sense of craft; the image is *in* the cloth, not *on* it, and we perceive the marriage of a thirsty cloth and liquid dye.

James Bassler divides his time between California and Mexico; his work is usually woven, then over dyed with resist pattern. For resists he has used ikat, plangi and—batik. As in much of his work, the strips shown here are created with slit tapestry and joined by continuous wefts of many grouped yarns. Typical of his work, this piece has a rough hewn spontaneity. It is particularly successful in the cohesive scale of cloth structure to weave pattern of the dyed strips. The hand-drawn resist, which permits the exact fit of woven and dyed pattern, is essential.

Perhaps no one outside the United States has used dye more knowingly than Daniel Graffin of Paris. His indigo dyed totems are shown on the frontispiece. On page 97 we see his first probes into *tritik* stitch resist. The negative image is created by stitching through mill cotton and then pulling the thread so tight that it forms a resist. The cloth is then steeped in indigo, oxidized to produce the deep blue coloration, and the resists removed to produce a simple, effective dye pattern.

Ikat, the process of wrapping-to-pattern the yarns with a linear resist *before* weaving, proved especially popular with America's younger weavers. Dick Sauer became notable for having pursued a rather direct course of brilliant hangings vertically striped with warp ikat patterns. These are usually narrow in format and woven with spun silk. His weft ikat (p. 157) is extraordinary for its subtle patterning, possible only with the use of extremely fine yarns packed over one hundred picks per inch. Combining ikat with the eccentric wefting to produce the contoured ''eye'' is—as far as we know—unprecedented.

The weft of Rossbach's *Mad Ludwig* (p. 100) is also dye patterned—not through ikat but through transfer printing, a relatively new

JAMES BASSLER U.S.A.
Silk and Sisal #1 *(detail) 1979*
weaving, batik; silk, sisal
96" × 96"

Using slit tapestry technique, wide tapes were woven simultaneously on a wide loom. The batik pattern superimposed on them registers exactly with the woven form. The casual rhythms of the weaving and pattern are consistent with the draped hanging.

commercial process in which dyes are printed onto wax paper then transferred through heat and pressure onto cloth. To attempt it on yarn is typical of Rossbach's audacity: warp printing is relatively simple, weft printing, unheard of. The printed image is further enhanced with simple brocading.

In their concept and execution, Ethel Stein's damasks (p. 98) are extraordinary. The exceptionally creamy silk gives the satin surfaces a most sensuous luster. The density and balance of warp and weft are perfection. Dark/light variations within the indigo dyed areas contribute greatly. As the observer moves, the reflectivity of warp- and weft-face areas flash with kinetic vitality. The narrow *Zack's Marsh* is warp ikat. The larger, untitled piece is warp and weft (compound) ikat with a more developed damask pattern. What the authors like most about Stein's work is that, through long planning and slow execution, she has maintained a fresh spontaneity and superb craftsmanship supporting art.

As mentioned previously, ikat was invented before direct printing. Now, with the broad ranges of readily available modern dyes, many artists elect to pattern their fabric elements directly by local dyeing. On yarn we refer to this as space dyeing. In their scale and contrast the great hangings of Lia Cook (p. 100), for instance, magnify the rich variations inherent to ikat. The warp pattern, however, is achieved through space dyeing. In this case she has immersed some warp areas of a roped warp but not others. By using two warps sufficiently dense to cover the weft, the number of colors is doubled. The eccentrically undulating, thick-and-thin weft is achieved with a soft synthetic foam batting cut to shape.

Lia Cook's *Interweave I* (p. 100) employs all these techniques and devices plus a photographic image on one warp. This warp was wound, spread full width, and sensitized to receive directly the projected photo image. That the image is itself a fiber form is the visual pun creating a fourth dimension. In the late 70's Cook was working in small scale with multiple harnesses and post-weaving dye and finishing processes to achieve the shimmering low reliefs shown on page 167.

After producing what may well be the most beautiful plangi silks in this century, Marian Clayden spent a year of research in Iran (see

Dyer's Art). She returned to create her weighty *Rope* series (p. 102) in which tens of thousands of yarns were space dyed and bleached, then twisted into a frieze of arm thick elements hanging like a giant fringe. In *Tower* she has dyed and discharged cotton donkey straps. Twisting the straps as she builds up her image, they are bound and glued onto a cylinder.

Cynthia Schira has also employed narrow cloth tapes for flat hangings with the format and quietude of Japanese scrolls. The "frame" is warp faced, sometimes patterned with soft horizontal stripes or warp ikat. As often as not, three or more panels hang side by side in the manner of a triptych. Her dye process is what Dr. Alfred Bühler would call a simple resist: each tape is wound tightly into a coil; it is then immersed in dye so that the edge darkens and the flat surfaces gently shade across their narrow width. Within a single dye bath she combines strips with different fibers and constructions to increase her range of color intensities.

Only occasionally tied down by a warp yarn, long floats of cloth tape dominate the major area of each panel. Schira writes:[6] "I use the primarily interlacing structure—in plain weave. In conjunction with this structure I use supplementary wefts or horizontal elements. The supplementary wefts have no structural role and thus no physical restrictions. I can use them freely to form the visual allusions I wish to convey. I can paint with them. Yet, they are physically encased in the order of the plain weave; they are linked to the basic cloth and ordered by it but not restricted by it. I can remove these elements and still have cloth. I can add more and yet not change the basic structure. The process itself gives me a feeling of calm that I am trying to communicate visually."

Kris Dey's crisp color (p. 98) derives from locally dyeing mill cotton strips and then wrapping them around vertical rows of dowels or slats. The juxtaposition of these determines her cumulative impact. The earliest examples were large pieces composed of hefty vertical tubes wrapped with close-valved silky strips—one sensed the richness of a rare fabric swatch magnified to wall size. There followed a body of work of spring garden colors on white cotton in more complex pattern. Then, in her

1978 exhibition at the Louise Allrich Gallery, came new statements in a variety of sizes. The corrugated surfaces flattened as she moved to wrapping flat laths. Color and pattern became "less textile" with longer, freer repeats of richly soft color areas growing out of dyed neutral grounds. We were reminded of painter Cy Twombley's mature work.

The locally dyed yarns that appear in Nancy Guay's wands (p. 236) as well as the plaited works of Sherri Smith (described on page 85), and on Sandoval's plaited Mylar (p. 65) are only an indication of a pervasive movement within American Art Fabric. That explorations in dye techniques are so peculiar to America today is a riddle. Are the ongoing dye traditions of Japan "too close to home" to coexist in contemporary Art Fabric?

Needle Techniques

Of all needle techniques, embroidery, in its many forms, is the most widely practiced and there is no exception in Art Fabric. Small works are usual and miniatures like those shown on page 158 abound. Many have extraordinary charm, ranging from the primitive and naive, to Gothic fantasy, to systemic notations or color progressions. Dorothy Ruddick works in miniatures (p. 158) as well as larger "mural" size for interiors. Her embroidery is intricate and elaborately built up bare use of stitch and placement for line, mass, and volume.

Machine embroidery has a number of exponents. The best known is Emilia Bohdziewicz of Poland, who uses her dark-on-light stitched lines to expound geometric progressions. At the 1978 Lodz Biennale she showed variations of wavy horizontal lines, hung like a continuous roller towel, so that each ending was also a beginning.

The machine tucking of Holland's Corrie de Boer stands as a singular expression. Although there is a relationship in style to the work of compatriots Bosscher and Rolf and to exponents of Dutch landscape art, the de Boer reliefs are unparalleled as the most immaculate of conceptual art forms. Restrained in size, color, and material, they are so cooly nonobjective as to become purely personal statements. We show only two; a gallery full is as quietly powerful as a succession of Morris Graves' drawings.

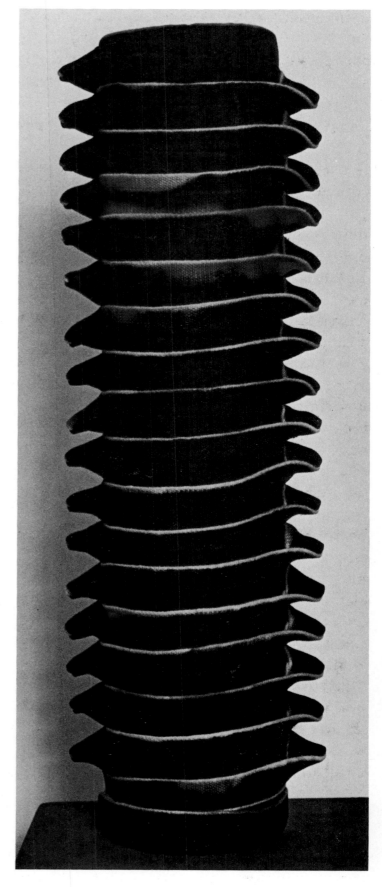

MARIAN CLAYDEN U.S.A.
Tower 1977
dyeing, discharge, wrapping; cotton tapes, cardboard
30" x 9 1/2" x 7 1/8"

Clayden's long-time involvement with dye techniques has finally resulted in a rigid three-dimensional form. Two-inch wide donkey straps were discharged to create the light edge, then wrapped around a cardboard cylinder to form the tall pagoda.

Although stitched on a similar machine, the patchworks of Lucas Samaras (p. 103) and the appliqués of Polly Hope are in every way opposite. Their heady admixtures of fabric, color and pattern, form and movement, *and* graphic implications dazzle the eye. Relatively (in contrast to Hope), the seemingly flat surface compositions of Samaras are controlled, formal, and single minded. Polly Hope creates impulsively: free of conscious mind and all inhibitions tied to form or taste—and yet, in no way primitive—her large stuffed three-dimensional forms restore childhood dreams. This is not an art one dwells on endlessly, but rather an over-sized cartoon that restores sensibility.

The enormous, widespread admiration for 18th and 19th century quilts and the popularity of architectural banners have sponsored a broadside of contemporary patchworks. For some reason, few satisfy more than a decorative function and many not even that. The pattern is *on* them. Often there is no craft and no love in them, only an all too easily comprehended facility. Pity.

LISELOTTE SIEGFRIED Switzerland
Le Bassin *1973*
needle lace embroidery; linen
8 1/4″ × 19 5/8″

Collection: The Cleveland Museum, Cleveland, Ohio

For a small white-on-white composition the disks and seed-like elements were interlaced with a needle, then stitched to the ground. The "grasses" are long loops twisted into a fringe.

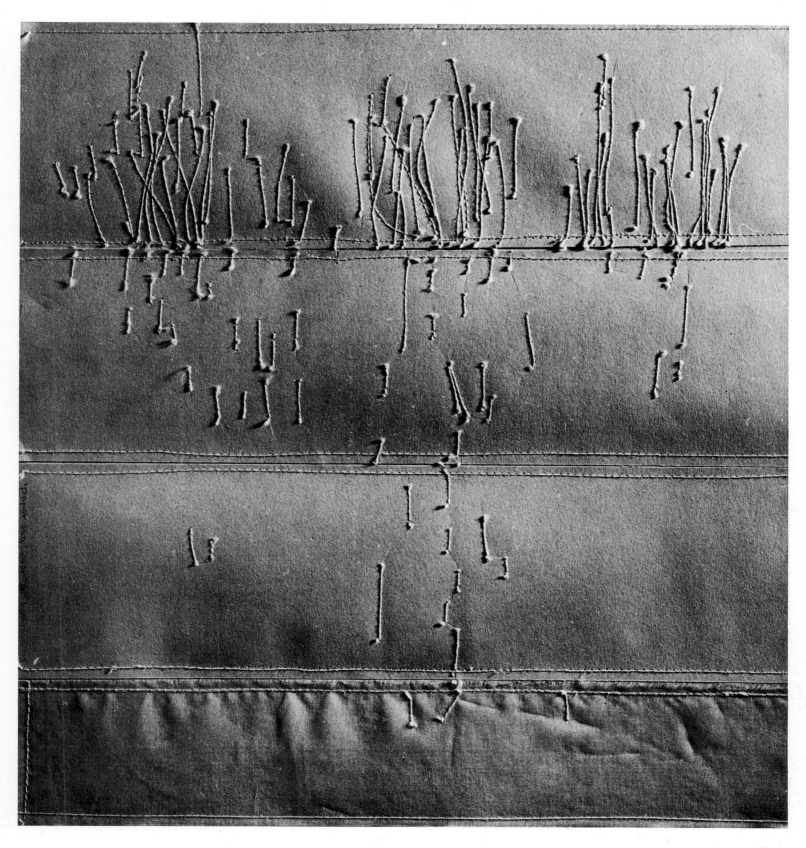

HARRY BOOM *Holland*
Paper Bag Cover III *1973*
machine stitching; paper, silk
32" × 32"

*With two kinds of machine stitching, Boom combined panels of
paper and silk. Contrasts in density emphasize the rich play of
highlight and shadow.*

above, detail below
EMILIA BOHDZIEWICZ Poland
How to Connect Some Points with Straight Lines in Different Ways
by Using Sewing Machine *1976*
machine embroidery; cotton
c. 9'6" × 9'6"

*With a zigzag machine stitch on sixteen panels of duck, the artist
enumerated the geometric possibilities of crossing evenly-spaced
lines.*

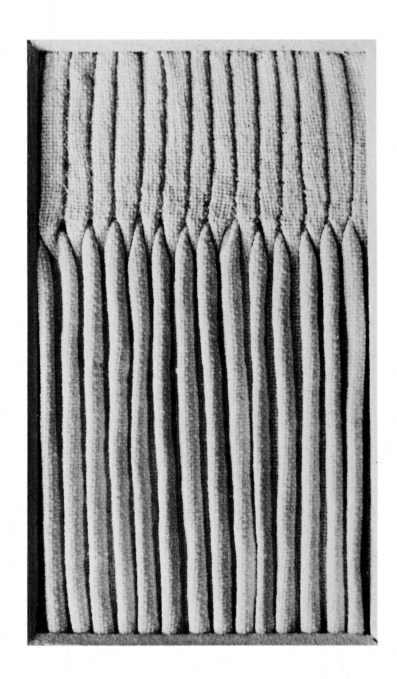

right
CORRIE DE BOER Holland
Serie A, No. 4 1972
smocking; linen
3 1/2″ × 2 1/8″

The technique here is machine smocking; the lower band is the same as the back of the upper one. The convergence of two dove-tailed bands implies symbolic fusion. Pure white cloth is crucial to the shadowed relief.

below
Serie A, No. 42 1974
tucking; linen
4 3/4″ × 3″

The regular punctuation of machine stitches supports the crisp white tucks. Meticulous craftsmanship in a small scale calls our attention to the beauty of order.

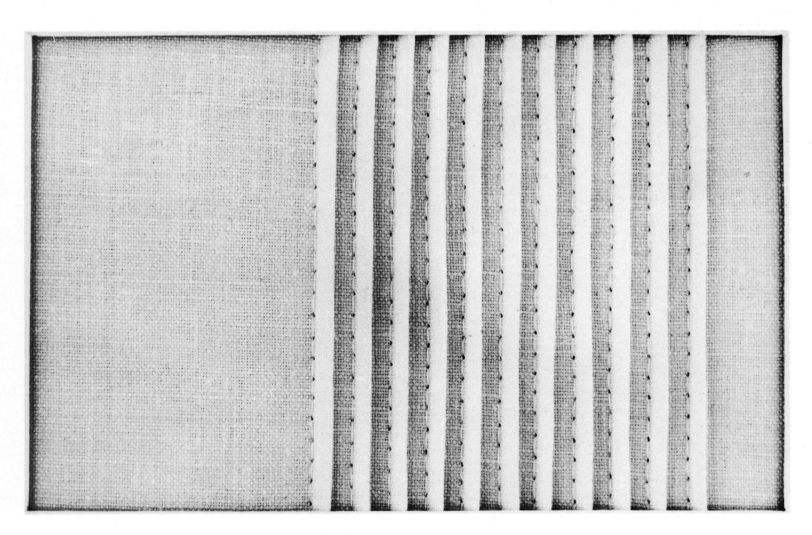

Fabricated Forms. This term is, admittedly, a first attempt to give nomenclature to a new body of work disparate in itself and mostly disconnected geographically. Machine-stitching fabric into three-dimensional works is the only denomination of pieces as diverse as Marilyn Anderson's relief (opposite) and Knodel's *Act 8* (p. 42). Pat Campbell's sail-like poetry is not stitched but bonded and then waxed to provide body and translucence (pp. 56–57).

facing page
MARILYN ANDERSON U.S.A.
Ivory Organza Structure *1974*
fabrication; silk organza
3' × 3' × 2 1/2"

Collection: Phillip and Susan Mayer, Los Angeles

Both fabric and stitches are subordinate to the play of light and translucencies. The crisp right angles and flawless execution are essential to keeping the fabric's fine scale.

below
POLLY HOPE England
Sarcophagus *1978*
appliqué, hand quilting, stuffing; cotton cloth
65" × 76 3/4"

Several cloth weights and sewing techniques combine with false perspective to achieve the considerable impact of an image associated with ancient effigies and mummy wrappings.

4 THE FLOWERING OF DIMENSIONAL FORMS

By the end of the 60's we witnessed a strong impetus toward fully dimensional Art Fabrics. Some hung in space, others spilled onto the floor. Occasionally pieces were free standing. As this trend matured in the 70's, it developed in less explored areas of baskets, objects, and dimensional miniatures. While this chapter tends to focus on small formats, dimensional forms can also be extremely large. The hand of Yoichi and the heads of Abakanowicz are enlarged far beyond life-size and some of the works shown in chapter 7 take on heroic proportions.

BASKETS

Traditional baskets are among the most successful forms. Soft or hard, they stand up to considerable abuse, accept water, resist soil, and clean readily. Baskets can be asymmetrical, or their separate parts articulated. Many shapes we now identify with sculpture may be formed with basketry techniques. While baskets are primarily symmetrical and functional, this is not a present-day limitation.

Even in the industrial nations of Scandinavia and Great Britain, traditional baskets are still made. Some areas of the United States and Canada also produce quality baskets. In Japan, both simple packing baskets and basketry as an art form coexist with post-industrial technology. The Arts and Crafts Movement at the end of the last century brought about a revival of interest in both baskets and wickerwork. Some aspects continued well into the 20th century but eventually deteriorated into pale imitations. Although design students and weavers have long appreciated the extraordinary craft found in North American Indian baskets, few have felt an urge to participate.

By the 60's Ed Rossbach was moved to attempt basketry and encouraged his students to do likewise. Although fine examples of Pomo baskets embellished with feathers and shells dominate the San Francisco Bay area, Rossbach chose man-made materials for his own work. Twining and plaiting were his favorite techniques; but his basket, shown on page 149, is coiled with newspaper wrapped in polyethylene film. The result is straightfoward and unpretentious.

Ferne Jacobs was among the first to explore basketry as an art form. She invested considerable time in research and in developing her skills before she was able to achieve such masterpieces as the one shown on page 122. On the East Coast, both Gary Trentham and John McQueen produced a long series of remarkable baskets in a broad range of techniques and materials. Trentham's coiled basket (p. 146) features jute brushed to achieve the texture of a silky fur. A similar form, shown on the same page, is imbricated with tight paper coils.

McQueen's spherical patchwork basket (1975) is exceptional for its tapestry in three dimensions (p. 147). This is a weaver's basket; his handling of form is both innovative and a *tour de force*. His 1977 cube is special for the way he coaxed resistant materials into a geometric form. This degree of skill and sensitivity is rare outside of Japan.

Using traditional materials and techniques but not relying on historical antecedents, several Japanese masters have created exceptional contemporary baskets. The Museum of Modern Art, Kyoto has a fine collection. There are also, in Japan, virtuoso baskets of bamboo worked asymmetrically to achieve the fantastic shapes required for the time honored art of flower arranging.

Innovations in basketry techniques appeared in China and the Philippines during the 70's, but this is production work for the export market. On the other hand Kae Jung Kwak of Korea explored the old technique of rush work. Many of her forms appear to be double plaited; in actuality, each layer is twined over separate ribs. The fine example on page 147 shows how this permits a nut-like outer shell lined with vertical color bands.

facing page
FERNE JACOBS U.S.A.
Coiled 1974–75
coiling; waxed linen
44" × 11" × 4"

Jacobs' sculptural forms are slow in execution, they are sure in form. In contemporary baskets, only the Japanese rival her purity and her craftsmanship.

facing page
GARY TRENTHAM U.S.A.
Black Linen Basket *1976*
coiling, knotting; linen
7 1/2″ × 29″ d.

The black inverted cone achieves its character from the deepening shadows of the inserted funnel and from the contrast of the hard coils and shaggy pile. The pile was made by knotting yarns to the surface, untwisting their cable ply, and brushing vigorously. Other Trentham baskets are shown on page 146.

MARY ASHBY U.S.A.
Cubic Expression *1973*
knotting; nylon cord
7 1/2″ × 8 1/2″ × 8 1/2″

Collection: Jack Lenor Larsen, New York

This small basket is unconventional in its structural technique; its cavity is literally filled with cut fiber ends inserted in the multiply sash cords that form its exterior. The method is similar to Trentham's, but used to a different purpose.

In Europe, Verena Sieber-Fuchs crochets basket-like forms which she covers with glass beads. The beads (as shown on the bottle on page 150) give the piece a metallic luster, while their spiral pattern assuredly ornaments its compound curves. Diane Itter uses soft yarns to achieve her basketry forms. Her miniature basket, also shown on page 150, is the foil for composing a dimensional pattern in softly brilliant polychrome.

Although the 70's have seen a real development in contemporary basketry, this is perhaps the least exploited of all Art Fabric techniques. There are, perhaps, explanations. Basketry requires special skills and extraordinary patience. Traditional materials must be gathered at a certain time of the year, then split, peeled, and dried according to time-honored traditions. There are also few connections between textiles and basketry. Weavers are accustomed to pliant yarns yielding readily to manipulation and remaining that way. Often, basket makers must work with wet materials then shrink their result to the desired shape—while trying to avoid wracking or warping.

Dimensional works employing basketry techniques and materials might have considerable appeal for use in public spaces. The stability and soil resistance is also an advantage. The potentials for poetic encapsulation of materials and structure might help to relieve the bland monotony of box-like spaces. For large spaces, there is no reason why basketry techniques cannot be worked on a very large scale: in some tribal cultures, basketry structures are worked on the scale of houses and boats (consider the famous coiled rush boats on Lake Titicaca in Bolivia). Although John McQueen has conducted workshops on room-size structures, he admits that this requires special consideration. Many traditional materials when enlarged ten-fold will not bend in the same manner as the smaller sizes. On the other hand, in twining meter-wide baskets, Rossbach found that rolled newspaper conformed to his will. So do a number of other ''new'' materials. Another means for developing large scale lies in modular units that, after completion, can be arranged as dimensional structures.

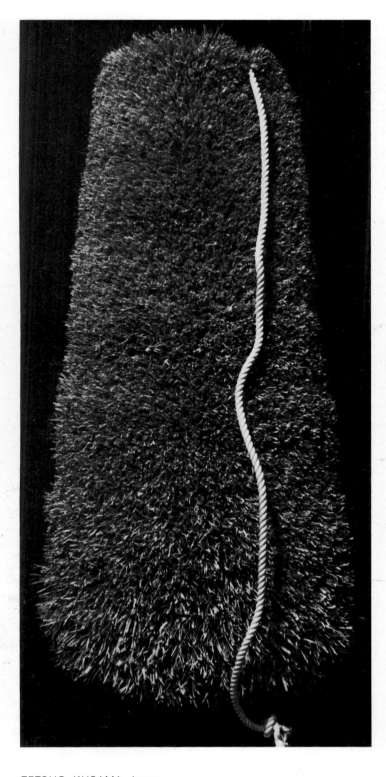

TETSUO KUSAMA *Japan*
Uneri-I *1976*
knotted pile; bast fiber, rope
52" × 26" × 10"

Typically, Kusama combines two materials, most often cord or rope with wood. Here, rope is the hard form; the soft one is the dense bristle of cut fiber ends.

OBJECTS

Today "object" is a loose term deriving from the French, *objects d'art*. By the late 19th century the term was most often applied to often useless "small extravagances" fostered by the new industrial wealth. The Paris avant-garde, especially Marcel Duchamp, chided this charade with the irreverence of his "found objects." Meret Oppenheim went further with such Dada expressions as her famous *Fur Lined Teacup*; so did Man Ray in his *Enigma of Isadore Ducasse* shown on page 13. From the 20's on, but especially after World War II, objects—that is, visual arts neither painted nor sculpted—have been part of the art community's consciousness.

John McQueen's *Cocklebur Cube* (p. 147) serves as an archetypal "object": it has form, is small, and possessed of some humor. It is a sandwich; the slices are woven squares, the binder, continuous rows of cockleburs.

Claire Zeisler has been making objects for a long time. Her assemblages of downy-soft spheres are well known and her *Pages* and *Chapters* have been widely exhibited. *Page One* (p. 151) is characteristic: natural chamois squares are overlocked with red cotton thread then stacked and folded to form a thick triangle. A series of these makes a "chapter." Zeisler has also concocted a number of intimately scaled works with materials both sensuous and secret. Her *Fragment* (p. 151) combines crochet and wool fleece.

Perhaps no one in the 70's has been as involved with objects as Dominic Di Mare. Most of his works are miniature, although, by the end of the 70's, they tended to be somewhat larger. They are built with as much care as a tribal house. His wooden materials are carefully selected, peeled, seasoned, finished, and their connections well considered. Yarns sometimes bind them into planes. The yarn ends become an integral fringe as do the tab ends of the twisted paper cords that hang by the hundreds in pieces such as *Ancient Tide* (p. 153).

Di Mare is the son of a seaman and his very name means "of the sea." In response to our talks about his *Ancient Tide* series he wrote:[1] "It gives me deep pleasure to examine and think about where the sea touches the land. The shore is a very special place and to experience it, as I do daily, is to connect with that part of me that is without end . . . like the

YAYOI KUSAMA Japan
Couch and Canvas
assemblage; cotton
c. 35″ × 83″ × 35″

Collection: Dartmouth College, New Hampshire

*Hundreds of variously shaped and sized cloth packages are first
stuffed, then stitched to a couch frame. The whole is then sprayed
white. The form is familiar, the function not.*

right
DANIEL GRAFFIN *France*
Souvenir Insaisissable *1976*
stitching, wrapping; indigo dyed linen, jute webbing

Above all, the totemic forms Graffin developed in the late 70's are packages. Often the overhand wrapping technique he employs is one traditionally used for bundles and bales. His stuffing is always sufficiently firm and resilient to achieve, in the wrapping, an undulating silhouette. The gentle compound curves produce highlights on the dyed cloth.

below
MAGDALENA ABAKANOWICZ *Poland*
Embryology *1978–79*
wrapping, stitching; jute sacking
size range from 23 5/8″ × 23 5/8″ × 47 1/8″ to 1 3/8″ × 2 3/4″ × 3 1/8″

From the Alteration cycle, about one hundred objects have thus far been produced and the number is growing.

LOIS LANCASTER U.S.A.
White Lump with Black Yarn 1976
wrapping, felting; wool sliver
10" × 7" × 7"

*Lancaster's package is familiar in form but rather unprecedented
in technique and material. Like her spheres (p. 89) the basic con-
tour is created by continuously wrapping wool sliver and then sub-
mitting it to heat and moisture, thereby achieving the stability of
felt. The black yarn is of the same wool fiber but serves as a contrast in value and scale.*

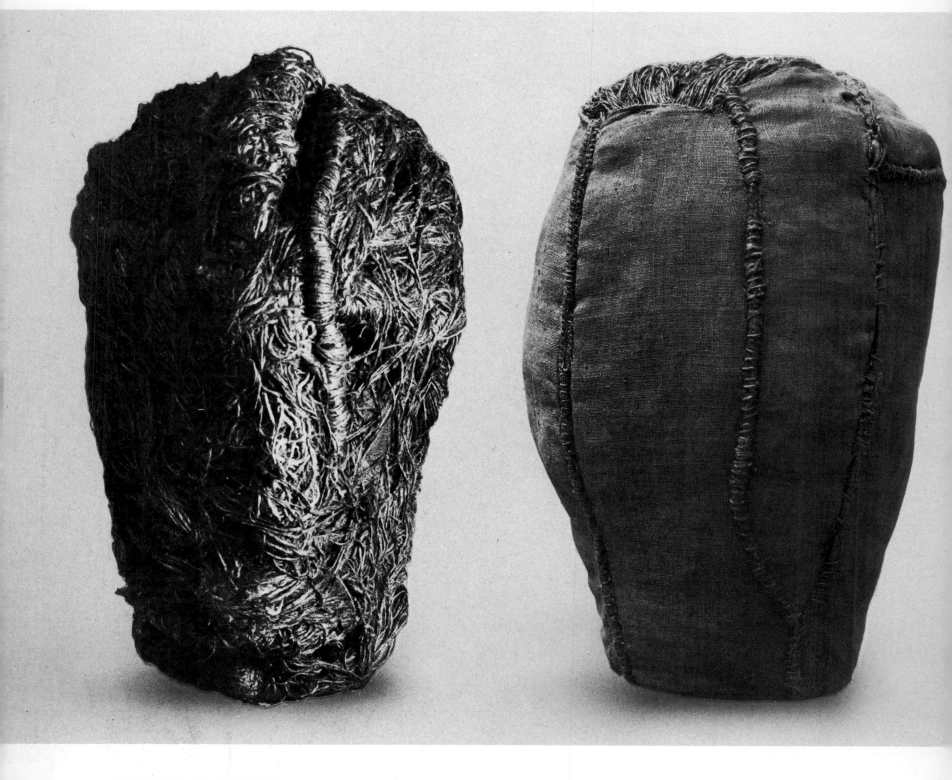

MAGDALENA ABAKANOWICZ Poland
Head 1974–75
wrapping; sisal
47" × 23" × 31"

Head
wrapping, stitching; jute sacking
47" × 23 7/8" × 31 1/2"

Head
wrapping, stitching; jute sacking
47" × 23" × 35 1/2"

Schizophrenic Head
wrapping; jute sacking
43" × 15 1/2" × 19 1/2"

The heads shown here are from Abakanowicz's long series en-
titled Alterations *(1974–75). All involved wrapped sisal; most were*
covered with pieces of jute or linen sacking. Direct, primitive
stitching is common to most, while wrapping similar to mummy
bundles happens less frequently. For her environmental exhibi-
tions, she usually composes groups of these heads to portray the
mute frustrations of modern man (pp. 32 and 33).

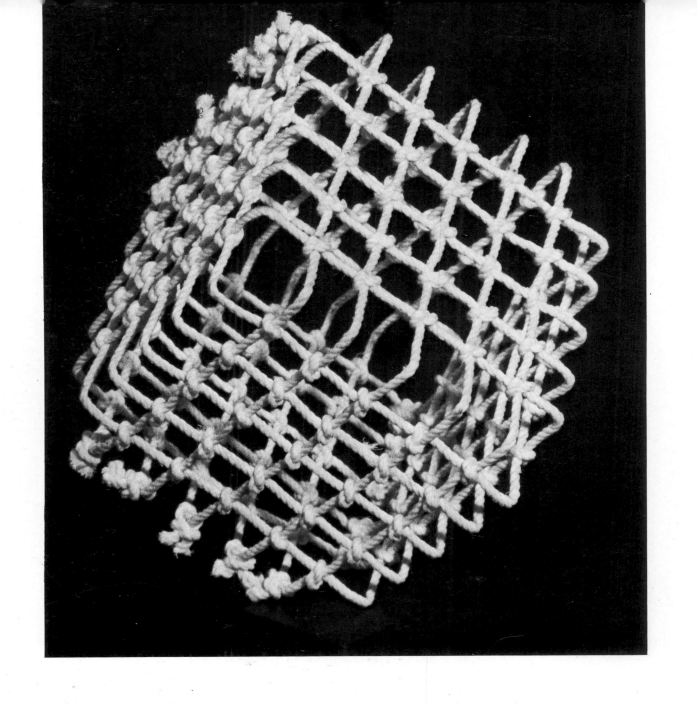

facing page

top
SACHIKO MORINO *Japan*
Silver Thraw *1976*
knotting; cotton rope
7" × 7" × 7"

No one has been as consistently involved with packages as Morino. Although she is aware of rich Japanese traditions, she does not depend on them.

bottom
WOJCIECH SADLEY *Poland*
Zadlo I *1977*
plaiting, wrapping; thread, tusk
13 3/4" × 51" × 11 3/4"
(for description see page 139)

below
NAOMI KOBAYASHI *Japan*
Pagoda-Kawa *1977*
wicking; cotton
88 1/2" × 70 1/2" × 5 7/8"

line created where the waters touch the earth. I feel very strongly at times that I am sea foam/sand/shell/light/bird song. . . . *I am that shore* . . . greeted daily by an ancient tide which leaves scattered about me materials to be examined, dealt with, and shared. The artist in me is dedicated to examining and exploring this personal shore and its contents. As I sit in my studio/ship/wave, and daily deal with this imagery of fragile sea/magic shore/tidal offerings, I would like to think we are all a part of that very special piece of land . . . *that we are all connected as is every shore in this reality* . . . and the same persistent ancient tide reappears and gently touches all of us every day.''

His handmade papers are often rolled into ''letter bundles,'' then stacked in small wooden cribs. The most complex are his ''manuscripts'' in which the paper sheets are interleaved with panels of sheer tapestry. Look closely for symbols, blind embossed to escape early detection, and for inner meaning celebrated with the most extraordinary care and craftsmanship.

Margit Sjilvitsky's folded cloth object resembles a camera bellows (p. 154). Its red center stripe pulls the eye through the aperture. On the same page we see Harumi Isobe's *Soft Stone*. The felted concentric layers are sliced to reveal their inner brilliance. Rossbach has made objects of almost every type and description, but his *John Travolta* (p. 156) is unique. His dimensional structure was created by lacing the rigid members. The portrait on cloth was heat transfer printed.

facing page
VERENA SIEBER-FUCHS Switzerland
Object 1978
crochet; metal beads
5″ × 4 1/2″ × 3″

Most of Sieber-Fuch's bead work is in the form of bracelets and
neckpieces in deep rich colorations. Her cup-like Object is abstract, without purpose or function. Its rich surface derives from
the high polish of the silver beads themselves. The artist's Bottle
(p. 150) is also a small object in the same material and technique;
the chief interest lies in an extraordinary surface at once pebbled
and lustrous.

below
GLEN KAUFMAN U.S.A.
White Maize Glove 1975
couching; glass beads
7 1/2″ × 5 1/2″

Kaufman's concentration on gloves has taken on many forms and
sizes. Some are constructed in single element techniques; other
times, dozens of common work gloves are shingled to form a large
composition. In this instance, the ordered rows of white beads are
couched onto a cotton base. The variety of contoured patterns
contributes to the whole.

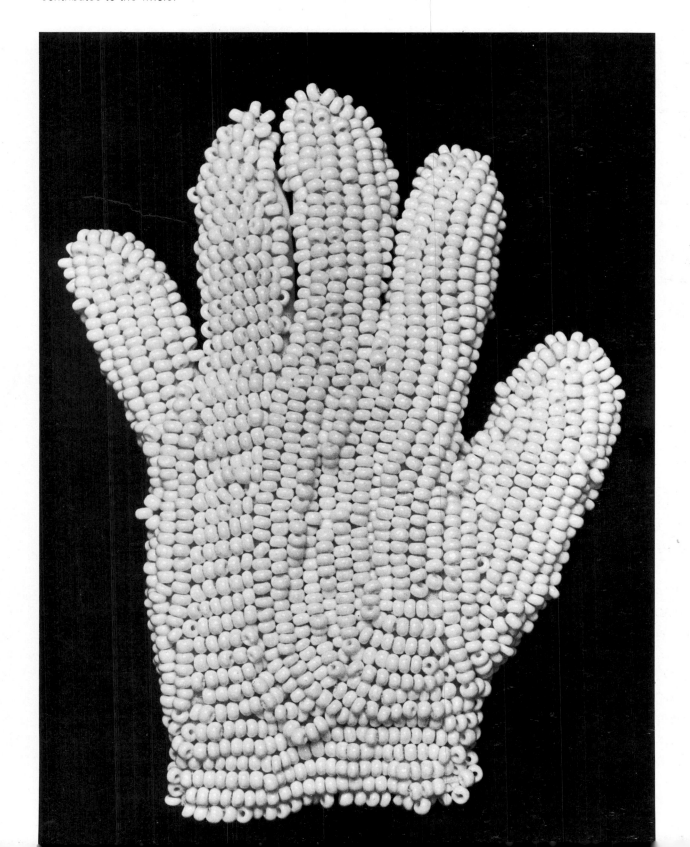

ROCHELLA COOPER U.S.A.
Page from a Miniature Score by Dvorak *1978*
screen printing; flax, glue
6″ × 8″

The miniscule scale of the printed score calls attention to the in-
tricate intermeshed fibers of natural flax.

left
LENORE TAWNEY U.S.A.
Thread Box *1968*
assemblage; box, paper, linen
7″ × 8 1/2″ × 5″

Tawney was probably first among artists working in fiber to use
the technique of assemblage. Many of these small forms were
contained in boxes; most used printed pages from old books and
brilliant blue ink. Only a few rely on yarn elements. The tiers of
linen strands shown here reflect her interest in the jacquard
mechanism.

facing page

top
HARRY BOOM Holland
"een schrijven III" *1975–76*
folding, wrapping; paper, jute cord
4″ × 3 1/2″ × 3″

Several of Boom's miniature objects are created by folding paper,
then wrapping it with cord to form a bundle. The rich black surface
of the whole derives from coating the finished piece with graphite.

bottom
SUSANNA KUO U.S.A.
Voile Ailee II *1979*
resist dyeing, wrapping; goose quills and silk
12″ × 12″ × 2 1/4″

Feathers are the subject of this miniature; they occur in the super-
structure and in the image of the stencil-resist printed silk. The
rhythms of the quills and the individual fibers relieve the rigid grid
pattern.

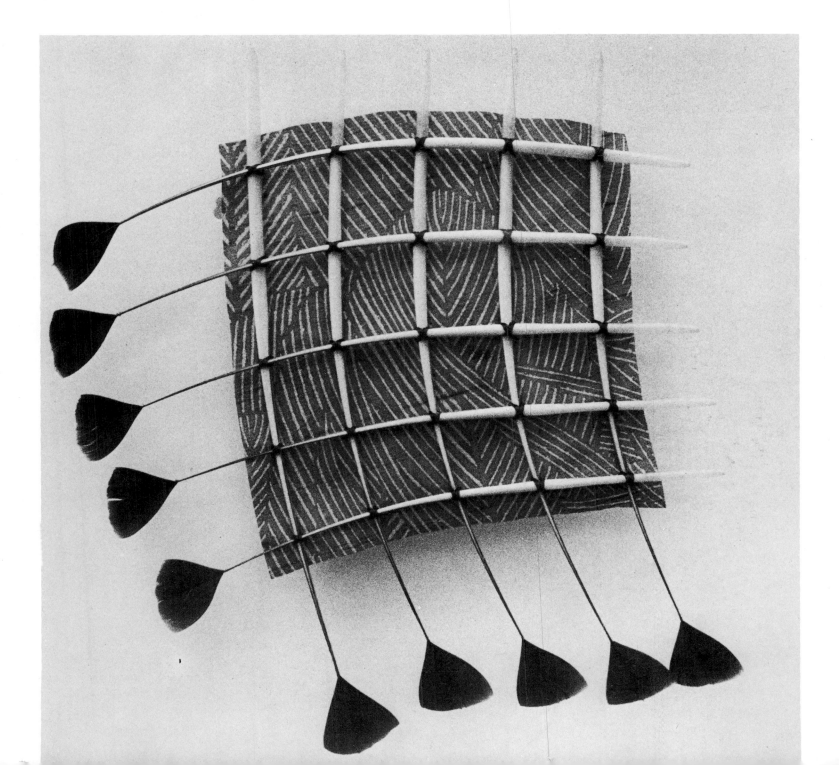

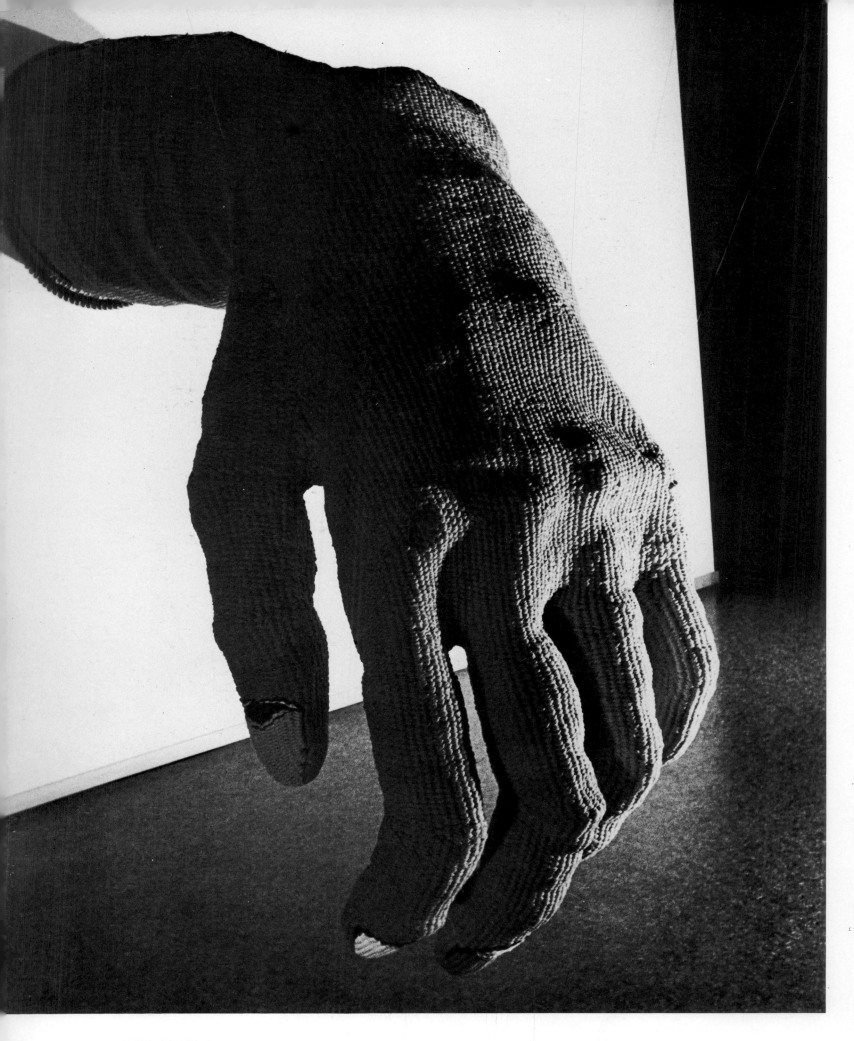

YOICHI ONAGI Japan
The Red Glove 1976
tubular woven tapestry; cotton
8 1/2' × 8' × 4'

A scale so enormous that people walking under the glove are
dwarfed, it is emphasized by the full-intensity red coloration. The
delineation of fingernails provides the only relief.

MAGDALENA ABAKANOWICZ Poland
Small Form 1975–76
wrapping; sisal
6″ × 8″ × 6″

For Abakanowicz wrapping is an unusual technique, yet with a few deft twists she has characterized the hand she knows so well. The contrast of spiral-wrapped fingers with the long floats across the back of the hand and wrist are important plastical elements.

Packages

A package is defined as a bundle in which anything is packed. It can take many forms. Fiber objects that can be classified as fabricated packages include Graffin's sewn, stuffed, and strapped forms (frontispiece); Abakanowicz's *Heads* (pp. 130–131); and Hicks' *Ephemera Bundle* (p. 155). Each gives substance to form.

Sachiko Morino packages air in her many roped works; her hallmark is the void she contains. The brilliant blue of her *An Air Sent from Switzerland* (p. 149) conveys her theme. Both it and the piece shown on page 132 are small; other works are constructed in heights up to nine feet.

The Poles, Abakanowicz and Sadley, have tightly wrapped hard fibers into small sculptural forms. Abakanowicz's hand is shown above. The tusk of Sadley's *Golden Sting* (p. 154) was wrapped so continuously with thread and metallic yarn that it suggests a bundle; it is ominous and strangely macabre.

above
SHEILA HICKS U.S.A. (lives in Paris)
Untitled 1968
plain weave, wrapping; wool
8 1/4" × 5"

Collection: Mr. & Mrs. Ralph Bettelheim, New York

This all-white, frame-woven miniature is perfect in its consistent statement. The four selvages give a sense of containment. The tab fringe is derived from ancient Peru. The horizontal progression is through grouped wefts with a triangular motif created by warp wrapping.

facing page

top
DESIREE SCHOLTEN Holland
Miniature Textile 1978
slit tapestry; wool
8" × 8"

Collection: Benno Premsela, Amsterdam

The technique utilized here is similar to that found in ancient Peruvian belts and slings: the warps become wefts where the horizontals and verticals cross (this is related to scaffold wefting). The piece is particularly effective in color; it owes much to the sparkling white squares at the crossings. A larger version was shown at the 1979 Lausanne Biennale.

bottom
ED ROSSBACH U.S.A.
Mickey Mouse 1976
double damask; linen
c. 5" × 5"

A Pop image demonstrates the contemporary implications for the damask technique. Double damask, in which each pattern area is completely covered by warp or weft, is particularly effective. The back is exactly the reverse, i.e., the ground is dark. Dora Jung's damasks, shown in Beyond Craft, *were woven with a draw loom. Rossbach's are achieved with the process discussed on page 165 (Guermonprez). See also Rossbach's damask enlargement (left).*

MINIATURES

Scale and measure exist in proportion to intention. Mark Rothko, painter of large canvases, said at the symposium,[2] "How to Combine Architecture, Painting and Sculpture (1951)" held by the Museum of Modern Art, "I realize that historically the function of painting large pictures is painting something very grandiose and pompous. The reason I paint them, however . . . is precisely because I want to be very intimate and human. To paint a small picture is to place yourself outside your experience, to look upon an experience as a stereopticon view or with a reducing glass. However you paint the larger picture, you are in it. It isn't something you command." And Henry Moore, the sculptor of monumental works, pointed out that only two scales intrigue him—the monumental and the intimate.

Scale, of course, need not refer to actual size; it can refer to the perception of the maker and the viewer. It has been said that the only possible criticism of an already existing work is in the relation of intent to result. What is the artist's intention, commitment, motivation? Can intent be judged separately from scale; does reduced form produce reduced effect? Consider the monumentality of Giacometti sculpture in relation to actual size.

In this section we are talking about work done in a scale commonly called miniature. Miniatures have a long history in almost every culture. The word itself conjures up images of ivories, porcelains, illumination, and sculpture in a jeweler's scale—all with pictorial imagery. It was the intent of the artist to focus attention onto the small, intimate image. Small works have been made in almost every media: those made of fiber can be found in Paracas needleknit figures and Chancay dolls, Pomo baskets, samplers, Venetian laces, and plaited toys. Although one can only conjecture about their purposes and the meaning of their existence, one can easily recognize their beauty and quality. Whether ritual objects, personal statements, momentos, or models, they are valid statements to be considered seriously for historic and aesthetic value.

Always a ground breaker, Sheila Hicks wove small, complete works as early as 1957. At the suggestion of Josef Albers, some pieces were exhibited in the gallery of Yale University's

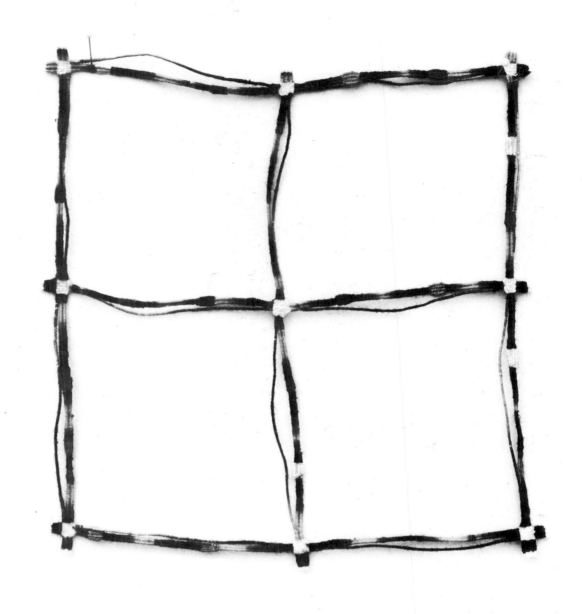

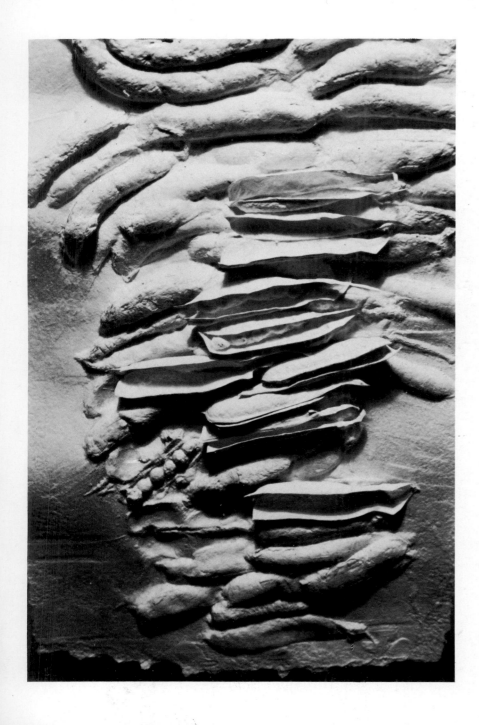

left top
BERNADETTE LAMBRECHT *Belgium*
Petits Pois *1976*
casting; cotton, pulp fiber
8″ × 8″ × 6″

*The small high relief is extraordinary for its realism versus fantasy.
The forms and scale are life-like; the stark whiteness and material
are not.*

left bottom
DON WOOD *U.S.A.*
Aspen Grove *1976*
cotton, monofilament
6″ cube

*Unlike Naomi Kobayashi's stacked wicking on page 133, the
lengths of plaited wicking in this small piece were woven through
a monofilament warp, then folded into a cube.*

facing page
DOMENIC DI MARE *U.S.A.*
Bundle/Rune *1978*
7 7/8″ × 4 1/8″ × 4 3/8″
*mixed media; spun gampi tissue, Hawthorne wood, silk; tissue
colored with pencil and ink prior to spinning.*

School of Fine Arts. Several were acquired by New York's Museum of Modern Art, and the Art Institute of Chicago. Throughout the 60's she continued to produce small works, often on a frame loom in order to have the completeness of four selvages (p. 140). But by the time the "1st International Exhibition of Miniature Textiles" was shown in London (1974), she expressed her own feelings about miniatures:[3] "They should be intimate, personal expressions—free explorations—extensions of the sketch book—which may or may not achieve art." But whether they are wiglike rag mops or mysterious thread bundles, her miniatures possess their own aesthetic.

Ed Rossbach's continuous probing of techniques is almost always expressed in small works. From 1960, both Lenore Tawney and Susan Weitzman worked in miniature. Both were shown in the first miniature fabric show, at the Museum of Contemporary Craft (now the American Craft Museum) in 1964.

International attention focused on miniatures in textile when the "1st International Exhibition of Miniature Textiles" was arranged by the British Craft Centre in 1974. In the introduction to the catalogue he edited, Revel Oddy wrote:[4] "The exhibition has been organized as a result of a growing feeling, in some cases conviction, that size may often take the place of quality in exhibitions of large-scale works. The quality of the works exhibited here should not be in question, for all the artists are of international repute. The success of their conception will be judged, correctly or incorrectly, by visitors to the exhibition—irrespective of the artists' views! The concept of the exhibition, however, is new, if not novel, and immediately raises the much debated subject of the relationship between art and size."

The small works selected for the London exhibition reflected intensely personal expressions. By the time it opened, many valid questions had been raised: What is a miniature? Are replicas of full-sized works acceptable? Is it a concept or an embryo? Should miniatures be intimate, personal expressions or dimensional sketches and exercises?

As mentioned previously, Art Fabrics in miniature appear in the broadest range of techniques and materials. Their format and function are equally broad. Some serve the artist as sketches and prototypes. Related are the models, such as Shawcroft's (p. 206) for resolving the problems of a commission and presenting the solution to the architect and client. At the other end of the scale are lilliputian replicas of larger finished works. And these too have validity as a record for the artist of a period in time.

Since that time the second and third exhibitions have been held as well as a large miniature show in Budapest, Hungary (1975) and a U.S. exhibition of miniatures (1979) organized by Mary Woodard Davis at Santa Fe, New Mexico. Although it would seem that a small scale would invite a harmonic unity, the materials the artists have chosen for these exhibitions are the most disparate of any medium. Artists often transcend their chosen media to consider unorthodox techniques and improvisations on found objects or such miniaturizations as an electrical circuit board. Small scale often suggests creative play or an expanded concept. Fantasies can be divested,

ideas itemized. As artists moved farther and farther away from drawing, these dimensional projections become the more valuable as prototypes.

Although the London exhibition specifies miniatures as 8″ maximum, some are really diminutive. A case in point is Diane Itter's tiny basket and Dick Sauer's 3″ × 4″ ikat, both shown on page 147. Both are meticulously crafted with an exquisite refinement appropriate to their scale. Although Muñoz's cloak-like form on the same page is perfectly precise, its knotted linen surface has a strength that belies its small size. Since his move to Spain, Tadek Beutlich has produced a series of miniatures; their structure, materials, and seeming spontaneity harken back to the 60's, but now his color is as varied and brilliant as a bed of zinnias. His fellow Briton, Michael Brennand-Wood, also employs full intensity color to good effect. His *Charlemagne* plays color against a rhythm of vigorous diagonals.

Some miniatures are not dimensional but appear in a flat format and, often, squares. On page 159 we see the colorful embroideries of Itter, Lundberg, and Coenen. In embroidery there is an opportunity for fine detail, a larger number of colors, and a freer expression than available in weaving. The primitive pictorial quality of the Lundberg is a surprise element. No less astounding is the flexible "mail" of Tamiko Kawata Ferguson. It is all safety pins joined together by the hundreds, then gold plated and oxidized to a rich surface.

There is no reason why any of the above are not at the same time works of art, in the way that master sketches and drawings are so considered. But some drawings and some miniatures have no other purpose; they are the beginning and the end, standing on their own merit. Consider Hick's *Ephemera Bundle* (p. 155). Those "sweepings" from her studio floor have been recycled into a visual, pulsating bundle of jewel-like colors. The starting point is what counts.

KAE JUNG KWAK   Korea
Basket   1976
double twining; rush
10" x 6" x 3"

Collection: Jack Lenor Larsen, New York

Basket   1977
coiling; brushed jute
8" x 14" diameter

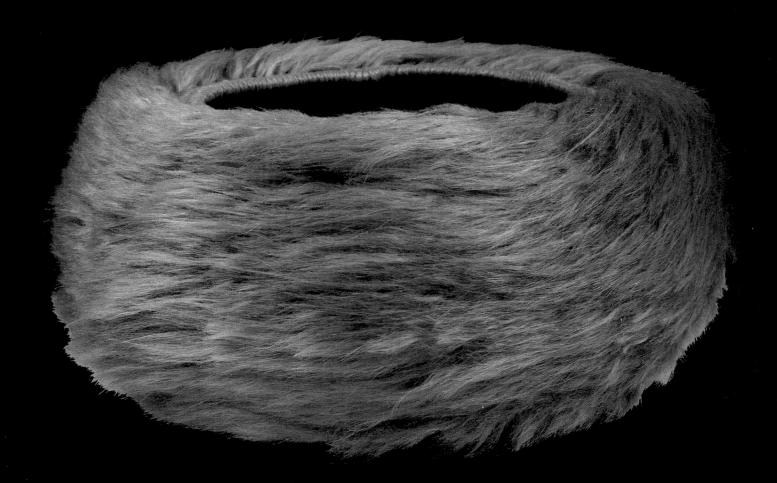

Basket   1977
coiling; paper
12" x 26" diameter

JOHN MCQUEEN U.S.A.

Cocklebur Cube   1975
weft faced repp, cock'eburs, linen, wool
9" x 9" x 9"

Patchwork Basket   1975
tapestry weave; morning glory vines,
leaves, milkweed
11" x 13" diameter

Collection: Florence Duhl, New York

147

JOHN MCQUEEN   U.S.A.
Spruce Root & Cherry Bark Basket   *1977*
plaiting
8" x 8" x 8"

Collection: Jane Hoelter, Connecticut

SACHIKO MORINO   Japan
An Air Sent from Switzerland 1977
knotting; cotton rope
14⅝" x 13¾" x 11"

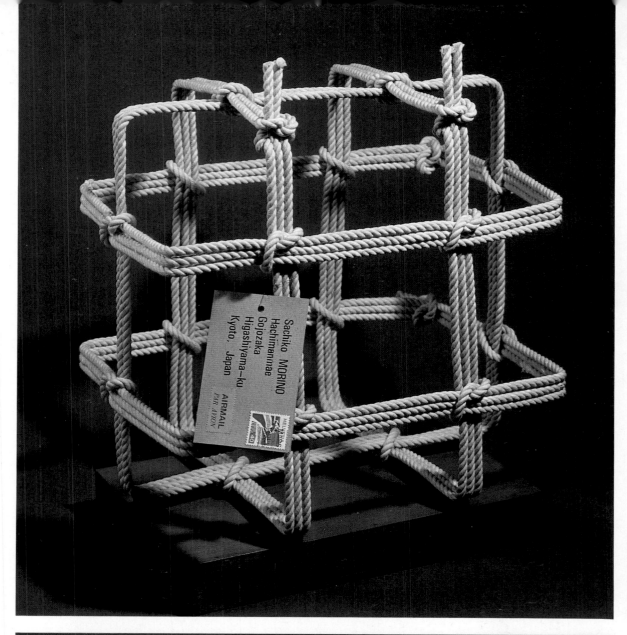

ED ROSSBACH   U.S.A.
Basket   1974
coiling; newspaper with
polyethylene film, cotton string
8" x 8" x 5"

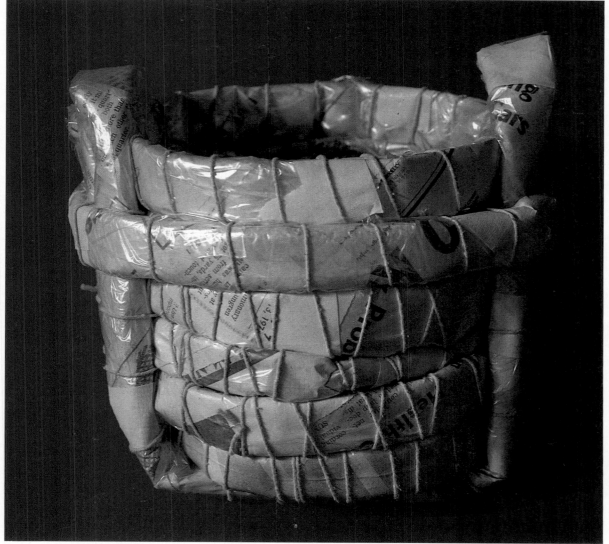

VERENA SIEBER-FUCHS　Switzerland
Bottle　1977
crochet; yarns and beads
6½" x 5"

DIANE ITTER　U.S.A.
Basket-weave　1978
knotting; linen
1½" x 3½" diameter

Collection:
Helene Margolis Rosenbloom, New York

CLAIRE ZEISLER   U.S.A.

right
Page I   1976
machine stitched; chamois, cotton
3½" x 9¾" x 4¾"

below
Fragment   1976
crochet; wool fleece, cotton
11" x 12"

Collection: Bruce N. Green, New York

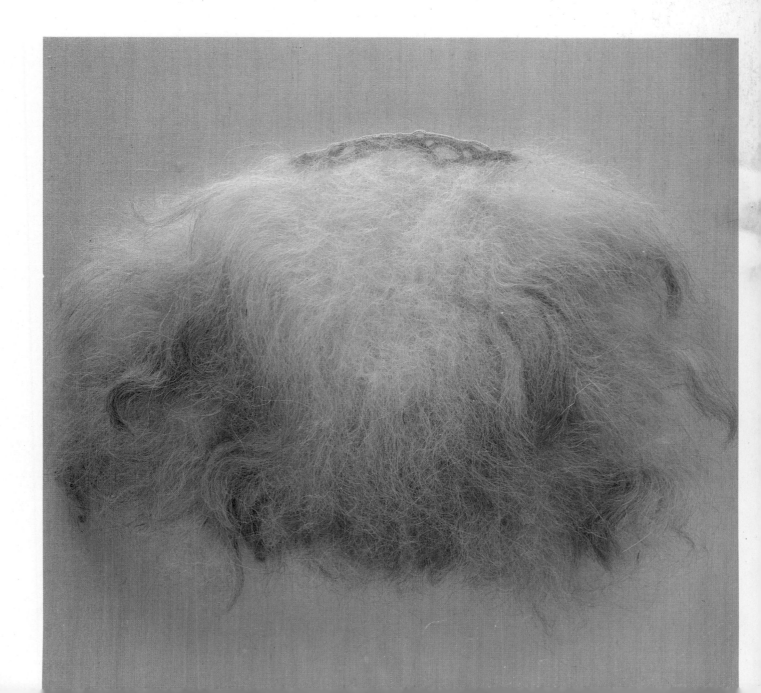

DOMINIC DI MARE   U.S.A.
*for description of plates see Expansion:
Materials and Techniques*

Pyramid #6   1976
9" x 10" x 11"

Collection: Dan Goldstine, California

Ms #12 *(detail)*   1976
21" x 12" x 4"

Collection: Mary McFadden, New York

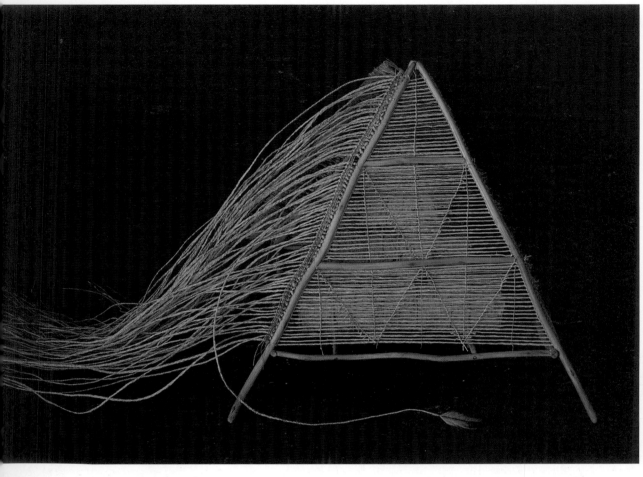

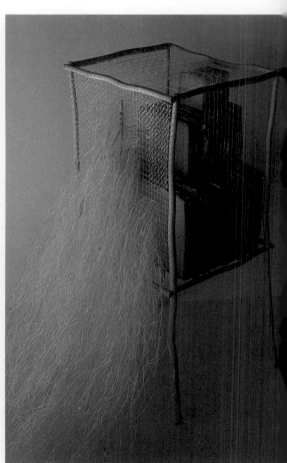

Oblation #1   1976
14" x 10" x 4"

Collection: Mary McFadden, New York

Ms #11   1976
21" x 12" x 4"

Collection: Rubenstine, New York

Shadow Oblation   1977
16" x 8" x 7"

Letter Bundle #4   1975
6½" x 8" x 4½"

Collection:
Robert Pfannebecker, Lancaster, Pennsylvania

Ancient Tide/1932   1978
11" x 9" x 10"

Collection: Dan Goldstine, California

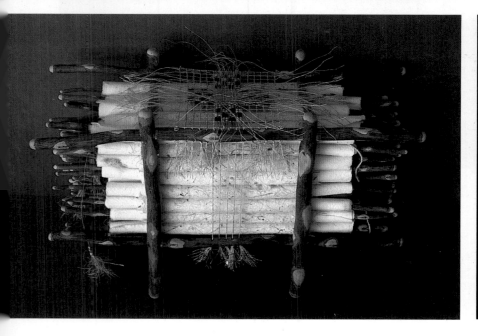

center
Blue Line Bundle   1978
4" x 7" x 2½"

bottom
Letter Bundle #3   1976
19" x 13½" x 4¼"

Curtain, Ohio, Act Six   1978
12" x 17" x 4"

Collection: D. Rudermann, Chicago

153

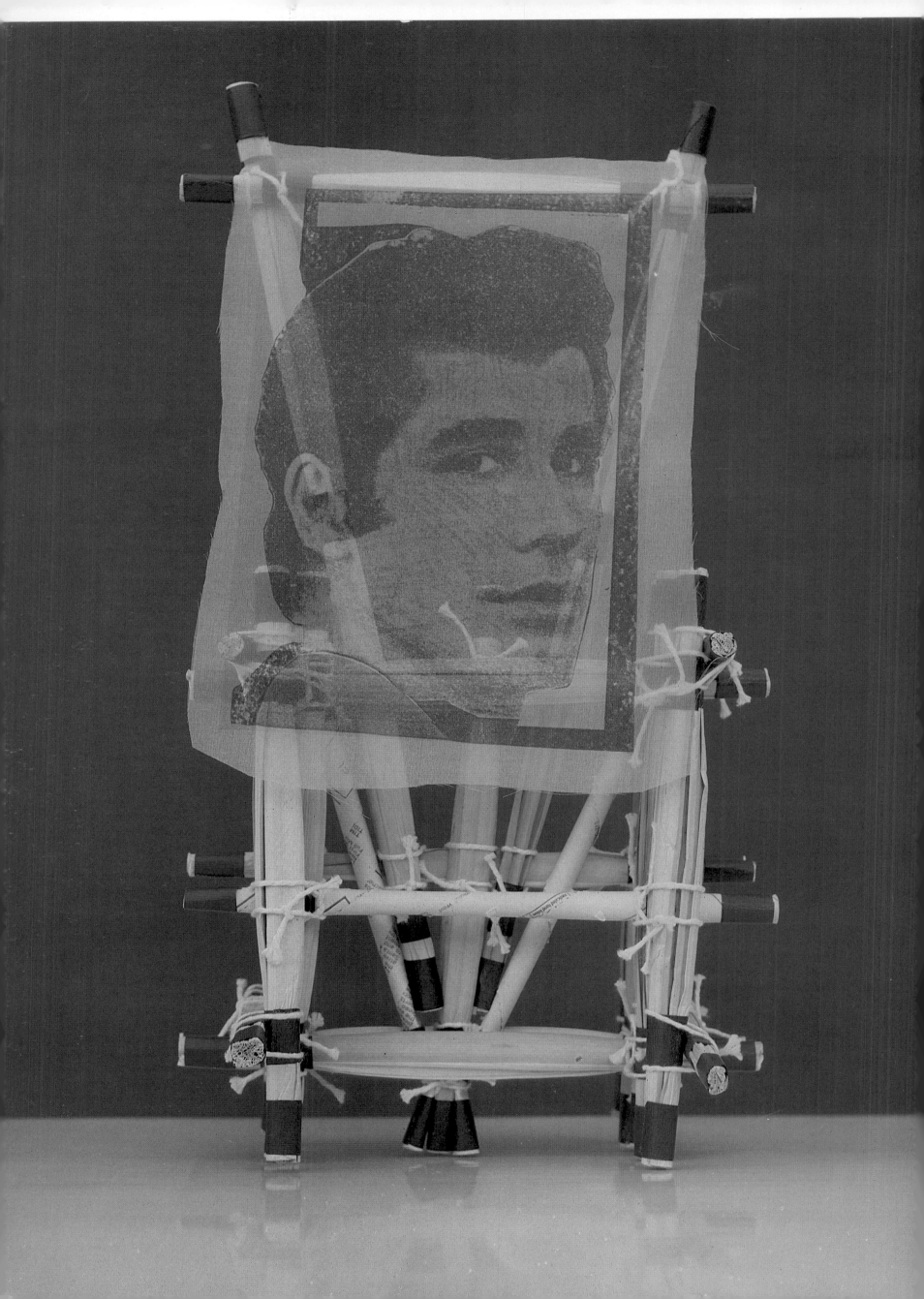

AURELIA MUNOZ   Spain
Untitled   1977
macrame, linen
7" x 5" x 1"

Collection: Jack Lenor Larsen, New York

DICK SAUER   U.S.A.
Untitled   1977
weft face plain weave with weft ikat; silk, linen (shown
turned 90°)
3" x 4"

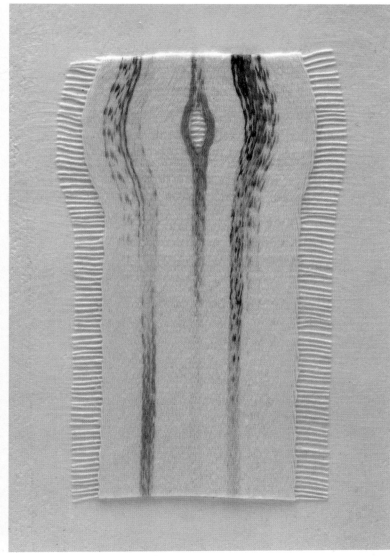

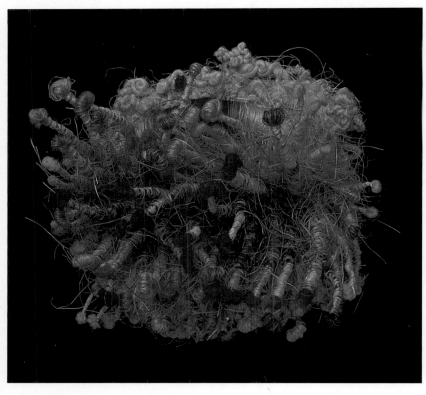

TADEK BEUTLICH   Great Britain
Vibration I   c. 1977
macrame; sisal, wool, esparto grass
7⅛" x 7⅛" x 6¼"

facing page
ED ROSSBACH   U.S.A.
John Travolta   1978
heat transfer; reeds, twine, silk organza
17" x 8½" x 6"

MICHAEL BRENNAND-WOOD   Great Britain
Charlemagne   c. 1977
embroidery and collage; wood, cloth, paint
7⅞" x 7⅞" x 1¾"

157

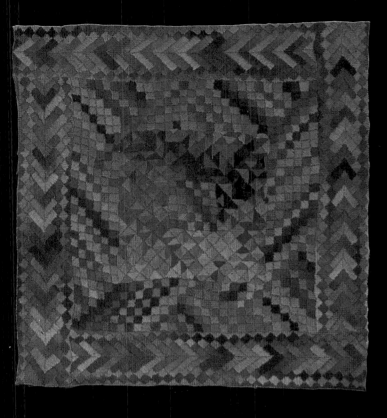

DIANE ITTER   U.S.A.
Small Insanities   c. 1977
embroidery; cotton floss on cotton lawn
3½" x 3¼"

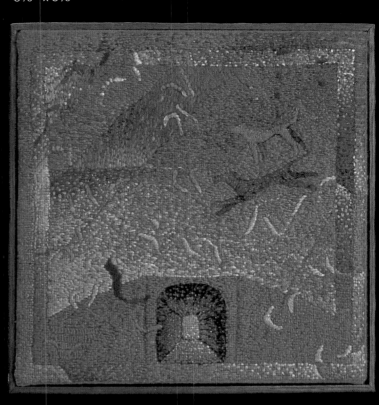

THOMAS LUNDBERG   U.S.A.
Night Dogs   c. 1977
embroidery; mercerized cotton on cotton
5⅞" x 5⅞"

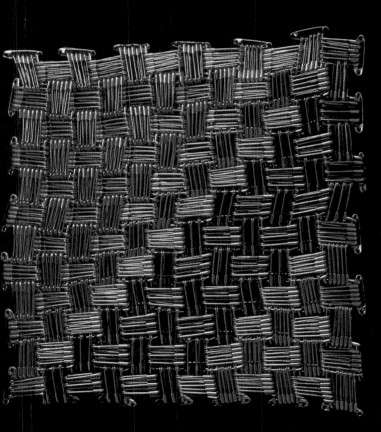

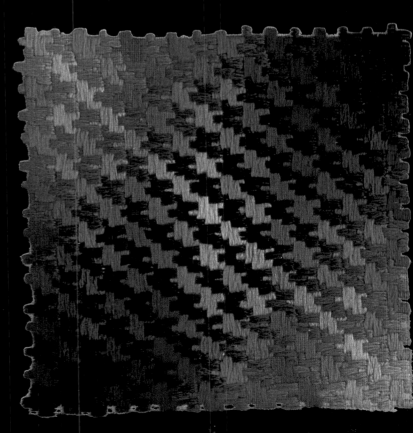

TAMIKO KAWATA FERGUSON   Japan (lives in U.S.A.)
Untitled   c. 1977
joined safety pins; brass, steel; gold plated, oxidized
6⅝" x 6⅝"

LINDA COENEN   U.S.A.
Magic Square   c. 1977
embroidery; mercerized cotton
7⅞" x 7⅞" x 2"

MARIJKE DE LEY   Holland
I am Knitting a Sweater for Myself   1979
knitting; wool

KAY SEKIMACHI U.S.A.
Basket with Brown Lines *1977*
double cloth, plaiting; linen
6" × 4 1/2" × 4 1/4"

*This extraordinary and quite perfect example of shaped weaving
in three dimensions was achieved on a conventional loom. The
wide top band was woven first; then some warps were pulled out
of the loom and the next band was woven narrower. This reduc-
tion was repeated six times. Finally the dropped warp ends were
braided to form the architectonic fringe.*

ANN SUTTON Great Britain
Endless Weave *1976*
knitting, plaiting; wool
5" × 5" × 5"

*The tubes for Sutton's brilliantly polychromed miniature are not
woven but knit. The "weaving" is in the Turk's cap plaiting. With
this technique of knitting then plaiting, Sutton also created very
large pieces.*

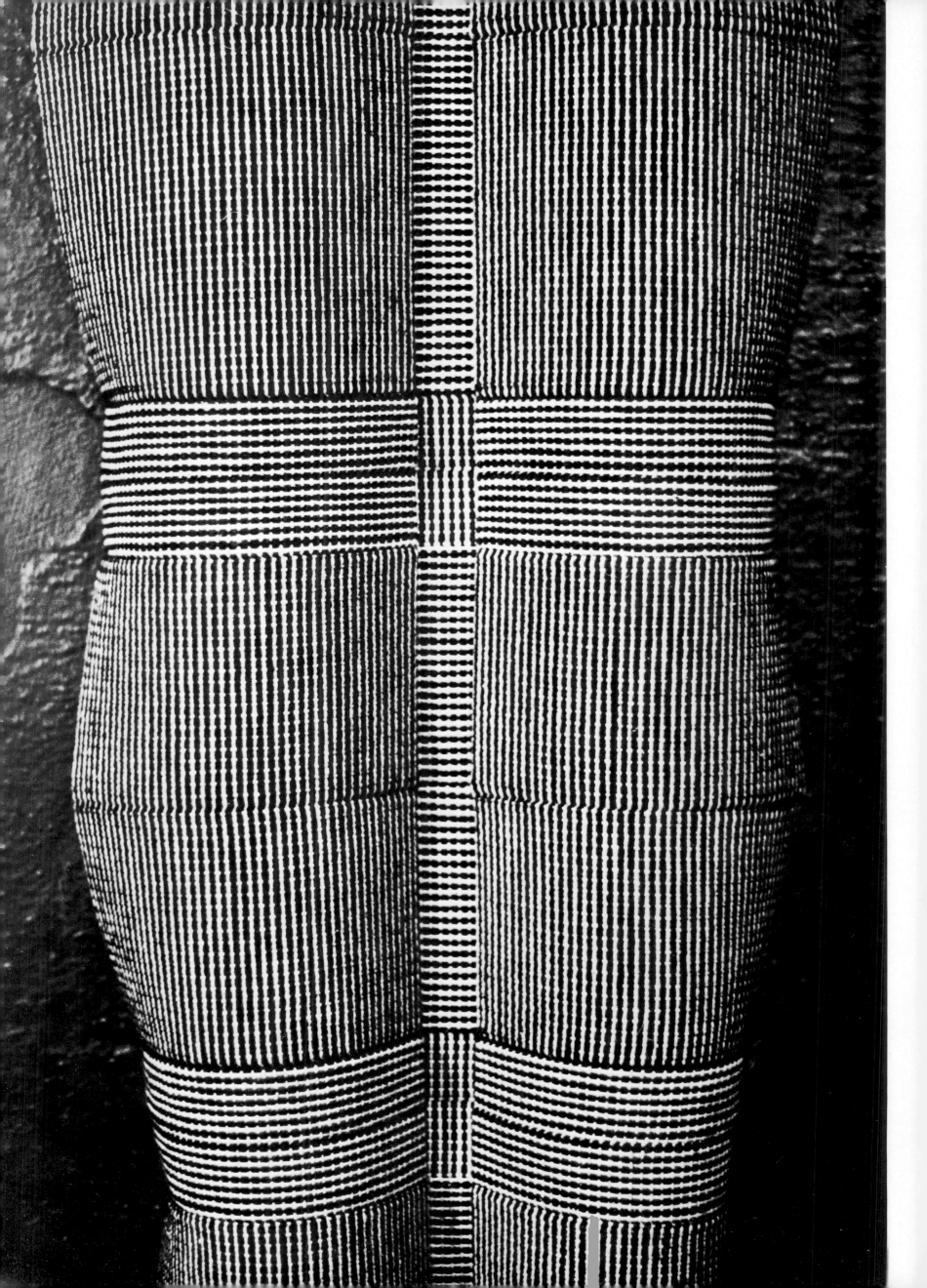

5 THE NEW CLASSICISM

Classicism is defined as "conforming to the rules and models of antiquity, especially Greek and Roman, and the opposite of Romanticism." Classicism can be said to be cerebral, simple, ordered, disciplined, and pure. It is the antithesis of Romanticism, which is emotional, heroic, and adventurous. Since a classic style is mutable from generation to generation, the artists currently involved in a classical tradition are offering works embodying new and profound ideas in a perfectly sound and "classical style."

Art Fabrics represent a transnational trend that appears, as well, in other visual arts. There are repetitive waves of Classicism in architecture and furniture design. In painting and sculpture we see revived interest in Realism, in Constructivism and Suprematism, in the Minimal and Conceptual. However, unlike the concurrent classic attitudes in architecture, apparel, and life style, Classicism in Art Fabric is not merely a revival. The work affirms rather than reiterates. It presents us with work that is mature, analytic, and programmatic. Antecedents such as pre-Columbian and Coptic weaves have been given recognition by the great art museums, which count them among their most important acquisitions.

The sensibilities at work today are often concerned with woven and plaited structures in patterns inherent to four-square, architectonic logic. In Art Fabrics of the 70's, we often witness symmetry of form or composition; a will to order and control; a trend toward meticulous craftsmanship and refinement, in moderate and even intimate size. There is also a return to wall hung work in rectilinear shapes with little or no relief. Some pieces have all these characteristics, others only one or two, and some none at all.

The pendulum has so strongly swung away from the highly charged, romantic expressionism of the 60's that it is reasonable to think in terms of a New Classicism. Not to say that the tendency is entirely new. A paradagmatic classicist, Richard Landis, was already committed to these disciplines in the late 60's. Concurrently, Moik Schiele produced ordered systems that were indeed "classic." Most contemporary antecedents, however, predate the 60's (as in the work of Anni Albers in the 1920's).

Recognition of this new will to order came in 1976 with the almost simultaneous exhibitions at The Museum of Modern Art, New York and the Stedelijk Museum, Amsterdam (p. 35). Of the latter exhibition, curator Liesbeth Crommelin wrote that the artists did not develop their approach as a reaction to the 60's. Most of them had already been engaged in working out a more analytic approach to woven structure.

TEXTILES

As stated in the first chapter, textiles are those fabrics limited to the logic of weaving. Exponents of the New Classicism emphasize exploration and glorification of techniques that are quintessentially "textile." They have to do with the magic of the interlacing in itself. On pages 17 to 22 we traced the 60's movement away from the loom toward fabric techniques permitting freedom and dimension. But almost as soon as the revolution was over, the shift toward weaving and especially toward loom-controlled techniques began, not as a rout but as a viable alternative. We are talking about the renewed interest in weaving orders so ancient as to be anonymous. In a larger sense, they are "truths" forgotten, found, and now emphasized so that we, the beholders, can newly marvel. These basic orders testify to man's ingenuity. Perhaps there is an engram in all human minds that makes woven patterns aesthetically pleasurable. In contrast to surface treatment (painting and drawing) patterns and structures are planned out and built in.

The seminal anthropologist, Junius Bird, stated at a lecture at the Museum of Primitive

facing page
WARREN SEELIG U.S.A.
Vertical Relief #5 *(lower detail) 1974*
double plain weave; cotton, wool, sheet vinyl inclusions
97" × 13"

Collection: Hadler-Rodriguez Gallery, New York
(for description see p. 179)

facing page
TRUDE GUERMONPREZ U.S.A (19?–1975)
Starlight 1970
twill weave; cotton, silk
24" × 34"

By alternating areas of different interlacings, a subtle damask patterning is created, largely dependent on directional light. The yarns are smooth, colors absent. The geometric image could be woven on a drawloom or jacquard, but it is not. Instead, the shuttle is lifted out of the shed at each pattern change, the warp yarns shifted to a different sequence, and the shuttle inserted again. The top and bottom rods, the fringe, the wavering selvages, and random striations within the pattern date the piece.

ANNI ALBERS U.S.A.
Untitled 1925
double weave; cotton
83" × 61"

Art in New York in 1963:[1] "Textiles are an ideal subject for study if one is concerned with the relationship between technology and art. The interconnections are most evident in those fabrics where the desired results—the concepts of the artist—are achieved by structural means inherent in and inseparable from the craft itself, and where careful planning is required before and during construction. All of the many and varied ways in which fabrics can be created pose distinct technical problems. Each in some degree influences, limits, or controls the end result. Each technique is a medium in itself, providing a challenge to the ingenuity, imagination, and skill of the artist. What is more, the effects on style and on expression may extend beyond textiles and influence the styles of other media where

similar controls do not exist."

This is in contrast to most contemporary weaving, in which interlacing has been the "glue" that holds together such extraordinary admixtures of materials as Jolanta Owidzka's and Désirée Scholten's in this volume or the tapestry imagery common to Aubusson and Helena Hernmarck.

In 1925, Anni Albers, the arch-classicist, made the double cloth hanging of extremely fine counts of cotton yarn shown above; this is, perhaps, the most ambitious of a series made at that time. In her important book, *On Weaving,* she says:[2] "Though I am dealing in this book with long established facts and processes, still, in exploring them, I feel on new ground. And just as it is possible to go from any place to any other, so also, start-

ing from a defined and specialized field, one can arrive at a realization of ever-extending relationships.'' Her dominant concern has always been the interaction between medium and process that results in form.

In 1970, the late Trude Guermonprez, who had worked with Anni Albers at Black Mountain College, wove *Starlight,* a damask composed of complex twills (above). Her other studies were probes into the contemporary implications of traditional interlacings. She was deeper into complex weaves than her contemporaries and, in a sense, was ''hung up'' on them. Intellectually, Guermonprez was a link pin. She had the integrity of her craft and the commitment of a leader.

Ed Rossbach and Katherine Westphal, his wife, moved to Berkeley at about the same time that Guermonprez settled in San Francisco. Although the Rossbachs' range of interest was wider than hers, a pervasive involvement with structured analysis was common to all three and to the Bay Area in the years they taught there. In the late 70's Ed Rossbach began exploring the magic of weaving with elements an inch or so in diameter. First there were plaited mats of rolled newspaper wrapped with plastic film; later, heavy, plied cotton roving interlacing on a frame, with four selvages, proved more flexible. His focus has been on the order of interlacing, not on the pattern resulting from it. Rossbach's lowly, colorless material becomes a testimonial to the idea expressed by Junius Bird and to his own sympathetic comprehension of this idea.

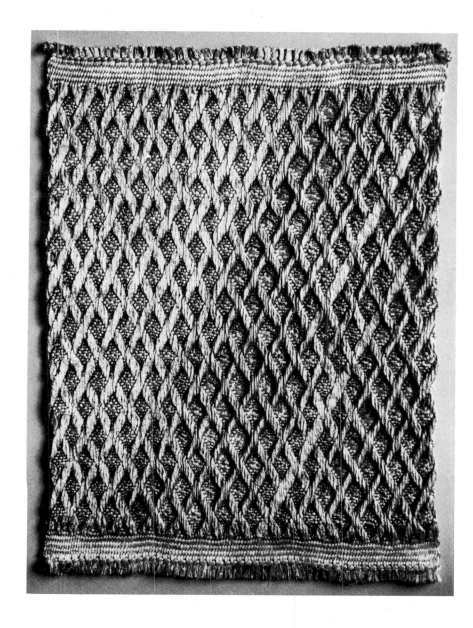

facing page
ED ROSSBACH U.S.A.
Colored Square *(detail)*
damask; cotton welting cord
25" × 25"

right above and below
LIA COOK U.S.A.
Pressed Variation *(and detail)* 1979
multiharness twill; industrial rayon,
pressed and hammered painted surface
20" × 14"

In the late 70's, Lia Cook of Berkeley paused from her monumental ribbed constructions and dye techniques (pp. 100, 101) to develop a series of small studies that she calls "pressed weaves." She explains:[3] "They derive from my interest in the interaction of surface and structure. Previously I had been working with air brush on a ribbed surface giving the subtle impression of a woven understructure. In these 'pressed weaves' I am interested in presenting textiles as an art form *without denying their textile origins.* They emphasize textile structure and at the same time provide for immediate and direct manipulation of the surface. The results have a dual reference; they are textiles and yet they refer to something non-textile (i.e. the hardness of metal or the molded surface of paper)."

She saw these studies as complete in themselves but also as a step toward something else: by increasing the scale or by increasing the overall dimension of a particular piece, the extension may be either bolts of fabric or a contained work to be shown in the art gallery/museum setting.

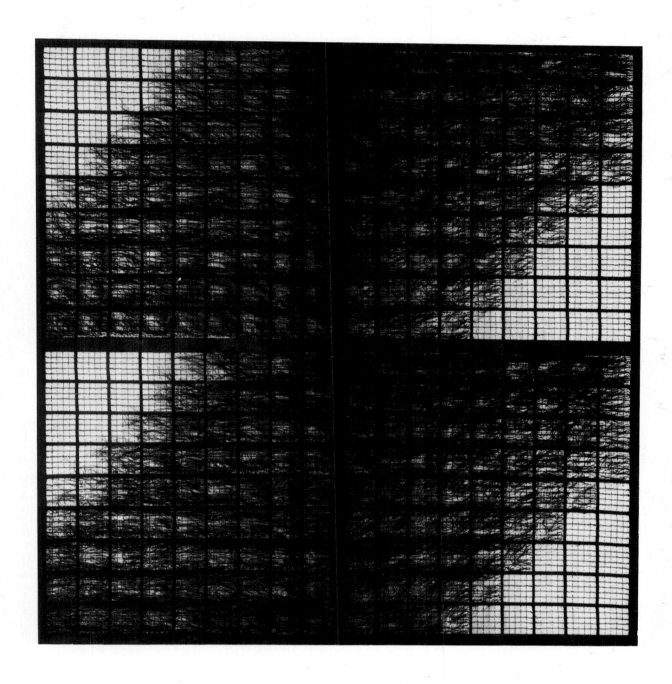

above
ANNE WILSON U.S.A.
Incline *1979*
weaving; linen, rayon
44″ × 44″ × 1″

facing page
Woven Grid *(detail) 1979*
weaving; linen, wire
4′ × 4′

In both pieces, Wilson retains the right-angle thread relationship
of loom-woven structure.

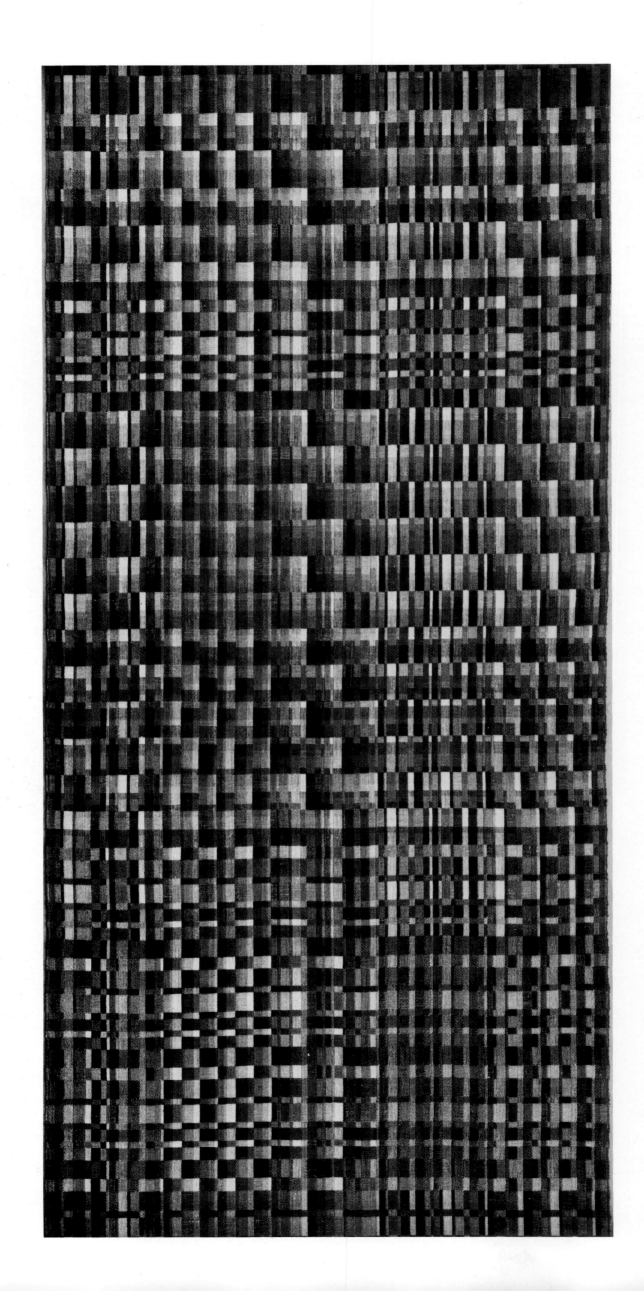

178

Double Weaves

Double weaves fall well within the center of loom controlled grid patterns. However, the appearance of double weave in Art Fabric of the 70's occurred less frequently than might be expected. Potentials for crisp delineation, systemic color-play, and positive-negative surprises within one cloth face (or from one face to the other) have been explored but not exhausted.

Richard Landis has worked consistently in double cloth since the 60's and, more recently, he has employed a new scale and material to transcend his earlier achievements. These are described in the section on *Color Systems*.

More than anyone, Warren Seelig has exploited several major aspects of double cloth constructions—first in dimensional pleated and folded forms; and then in flat hangings reminiscent of coverlets. Seelig came to Cranbrook Art Academy in Michigan with a degree in textile technology; his single-minded objectivity was quite contrary to that of his freewheeling peers—a different expression could be expected.

Confining himself to black and white cotton string and working in double cloth technique, Seelig soon discovered the potential for using the intersections of two cloth layers as an integral hinge. Working on a series of pleated fan shapes, he also found that, if the two-layered pockets between these intersections were stuffed with a stiff plastic film or a cardboard cut to size during the weaving, his pleats would be crisp and his forms rigid; this new system had such structural and aesthetic potentials that he persevered in this direction. All in white, the first fan shapes are remarkable, not only for technique but also for highlight and shadow of their folded relief. They grow from 90° fans to the 180° curves of the arches (p. 193). Framing the periphery with a band of double-woven red and black checkers was consistent with his architectonic concept.

Even more extraordinary than the pleated fans and arches are the fully three-dimensional totems that appeared later. As shown on page 193, the flat, double-woven facets—each reinforced with the pocket-size boards described above—are pulled into shape with a system of struts and guys. These pieces were so neatly engineered that they would surely have impressed designers of the early stretched-cloth airplane wings. To maximize their highlights and graduated shadows, most of the pieces are in natural white cotton.

Seelig has also produced hangings by folding striped single cloths. Some are mitered to produce a peripheral frame; others are folded into a *U* and still others are steeply angled in a repeated *W*. For all these, the arrangement of warp or weft stripes is critical to the composition.

In the late 70's, he wove the large flat double cloth shown on page 193. Part of its mastery lies in the success of its positive-negative relation of border to field and from one cloth face to the other. The incredible white-on-translucent-white areas are produced by the black and white cloth layers under the white areas of the face.

Seelig's work is varied, calculated, resolved, and unparalleled. Throughout the 70's a question remains, perhaps, about its cool intellectualism: why does it sometimes "read" so differently in photographs (where the graphic image becomes dominant) than it does in reality? Is it because he eschews enrichment so that we are confronted by his stunning technical perfection? Is this perfection too closely related to the strong line and cool neutrality of orthodox International Style architecture? It is probable that he will go beyond technical mastery to find the essence of art.

In the 60's Kay Sekimachi and Dominic Di Mare wove multiple-layered cloths that became freely dimensional hangings in space. Di Mare's work remains remarkable for his technique of not weaving the multiple layers simultaneously; instead he sequentially completes each topmost cloth, cutting its warp ends and peeling it forward onto the cloth beam.

Sekimachi's unique series of layered monofilament translucencies continues to be a hallmark of the 60's. While she has, in the 70's,

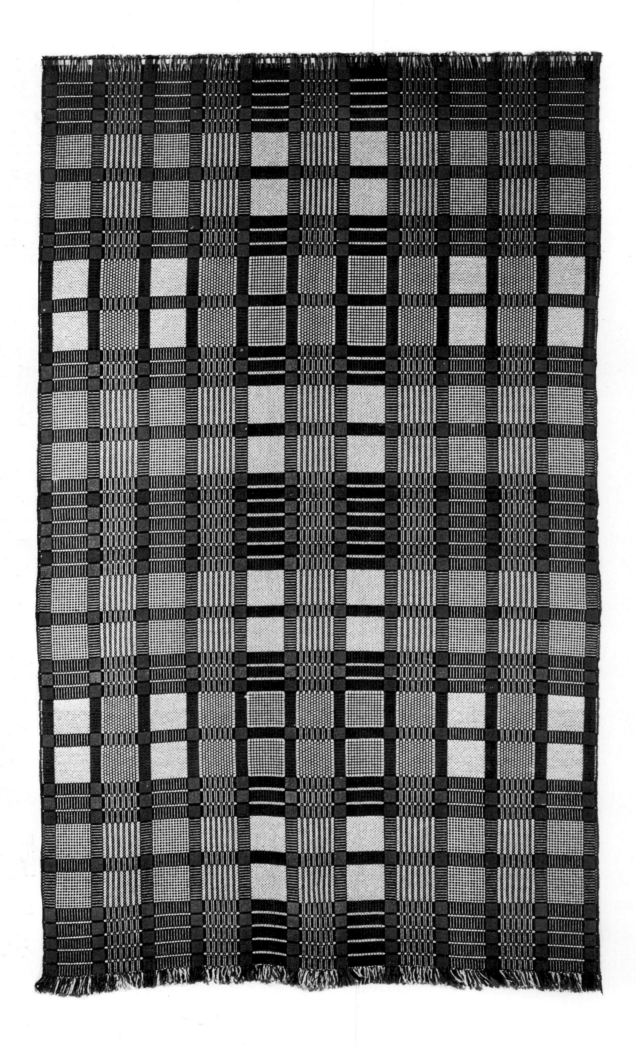

explored such off-beat techniques as split-ply twining (p. 76), her complex double cloths are more remarkable. Best known are her miniature boxes of plied linen. The one shown on page 161 is like a woven puzzle: the telescoping layers are as confounding as the Chinese filagree spheres that are carved one inside another. Other layered and folded boxes use Finn weave to achieve their strong architectronic images.

Since the time of Gunta Stadler-Stölzl and Anni Albers in the 20's, few Europeans except the Finns have employed double cloth for Art Fabric. An exception is Boleslaw Tomaszkiewicz of Poland. Trained as a painter and in gobelin tapestry technique, he developed a large series of hangings as symmetrically bordered as antique counterpanes. Still, there is about them such a satisfying quality of completeness and repose that one senses a new order or the rediscovery of an ancient one.

facing page
BOLESLAW TOMASZKIEWICZ Poland
Composition 1977
double plain weave; wool
116 5/8" × 69 3/8"

The breakup of pattern blocks with fine horizontal and vertical stripes is most unusual. So is Tomaszkiewicz's combination of double cloths with complex orders of interlacing.

right
WARREN SEELIG U.S.A.
Vertical Relief #6 1974
double plain weave; cotton, synthetic, vinyl skeleton
86" × 17"

Also shown in a detail on p. 193, Seelig alternates two blocks of vertical mini strips with two of horizontals. These are woven one-pick-black/one-pick-white but in opposite relationship to the black and white warp.

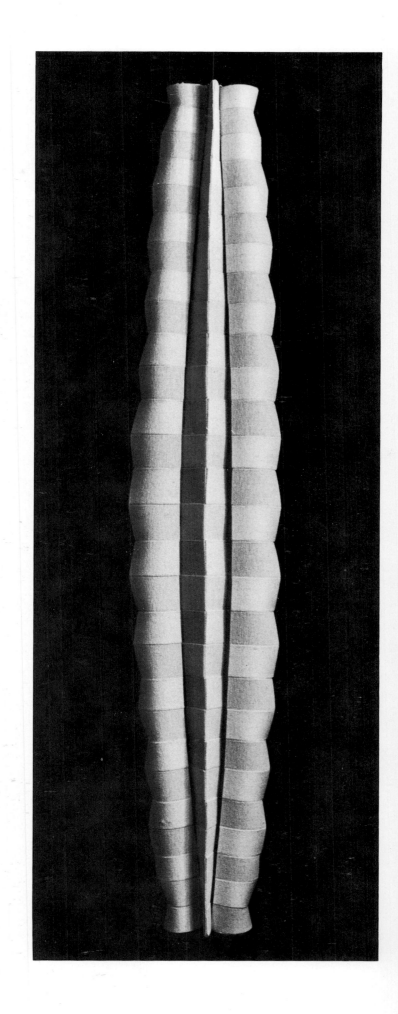

182

The weaving started at the lower left-hand corner on a vertical warp. The weft is horizontal but no side is parallel or at right angles to it. In the finished piece the appearance of oblique interlacing is brought about by successively engaging more warp ends on the left selvage and fewer on the right. The positive/negative gradation from light to dark—also diagonal—is caused, in part, by the grouped weft shading from light to dark and, in part, by very gradual transitions from warp- to weft-face areas.

In the 70's Herman Scholten of Holland wove a series of "shingled" structural systems first shown and analyzed in *Beyond Craft*. Most, but not all, are small and some are miniatures. As a group they illustrate his longtime concern with the graduated highlight and shadow of woven reliefs. In the same period he produced large works in which gradations of color are a principle element; they shade from dark to light or across the color wheel from blue to yellow. These pieces are shaped on the loom to form attenuated rainbows and lozenges.

In *Blue Shadow,* opposite, and *Ruit,* on page 200, we see a new format. Both are still quadrangles; in *Ruit,* however, the sides are not parallel and only two corners are square. According to Scholten:[5] "It seems to be cut out of a large piece of fabric with the design that might be found in a warehouse." The ombré striped warp is new to Scholten and new to gobelin technique. The shading not only persists but is extended to four directions. Equally unique is the grain of the weave, which is neither parallel nor at right angles to the sides.

The shape is based on a kite form. However, since the diagonal direction of the checks is not aligned with the form, one hardly senses the "kite," but only the appearance of mystery and the unexpected. "The 90 degree angles bind the tapestry with their horizontals and verticals: but at the same time, the diagonals, the opposition to them, provide freedom. The warp and weft are composed of groups of wool (pulling, introverted) and linen (radiating, extroverted)."

The piece is woven on a vertical warp. The "tie-up" is composed of weft ribs and crossed twills. After weaving, the corners are folded to the back to achieve the "fragment." All the rules and tenets of tradition are broken—deliberately, painstakingly, with a combination of foresight and skill. Although this piece transcends classification, it is described here because of its textile image and its concern with woven technique, with system, and with a rational order consistent with Classicism.

DESIREE SCHOLTEN Holland
Rode Stippen *(detail)* 1976
tapestry; mixed fibers
51 1/4″ × 51 1/4″

Collection: *Galerie Nouvelles Images, The Hague*

Red tapestry blocks punctuate a plane of diverse white yarns,
covering only five per cent of the total area. The main elements
are color, yarn texture, and contrapuntal spacing.

above
PETER COLLINGWOOD *Great Britain*
Black Linen Tapestry *1974*
plain weave; linen
4′ × 3′

Collection: *Florence and Daniel Duhl, New York*

facing page
LENORE TAWNEY *U.S.A.*
Wings of the Wind *1964*
drawing; pen and ink on paper
17 1/2″ × 22 1/4″

"The drawings are all based on the jacquard loom. . . . In Wings of the Wind I start with the top and bottom angled lines. These are simple arbitrary lines. You begin to draw on the far left bottom and go diagonally up to the right on top, gradually coming toward the center to the other side. Every line is made with my mind being right with the line. The part in the center—it's like a funnel. You never know exactly how that will come out. It depends on the angle of the top and bottom lines."[6]

SYSTEMIC STRUCTURES

A grid derives from a manmade sense of order; it is a network of uniformly spaced horizontal and vertical lines. It is the epitome of self-imposed limitation, premeditated order, and intellectually-conceived system.

Although a number of the woven pieces previously described or in the section on *Double Weaves* involve systemic order as a primary form, and although it can be argued that fabric structures—and the sets of yarn elements with them—are themselves systems, still other Art Fabrics are simply systems. Some of these systems are primarily structural, involving individual yarn elements, fabric planes, interlacings, or mathematical and geometric progressions. Others are principally concerned with color.

Beyond Craft traced how, in the late 50's, Lenore Tawney's brief probes into Peruvian gauze weaves and jacquard weaving had sparked her development of loom-shaped forms. Her fascination with crossed-over vertical systems of the jacquard loom-head led her to the invention of the topless reed. This, in turn, permitted her to expand or condense at will her warp widths. To better deal with the concept of image as pure form growing out of a structural system, she minimized her use of color and materials.

At about the same time and inspired by the same jacquard system, she made a series of ruled drawings on graph paper. Works such as *Wings of the Wind* (below) predate both the systemic expressions of such minimalists as Sol Lewitt and the move toward systems with Art Fabric. They predate, as well, her collage-box series, including *Threadbox* (p. 136) with its jacquard-like crossover. She has also used a systemic grid in the architectural installation discussed on page 207. Tawney has always sought the essential *order* or *system* that is the wellspring of creativity and the confluence of art and metaphysics.

Working with the same topless reed and eccentric warp concept over a fifteen-year period, Peter Collingwood developed a series of systemic structures that is remarkable for both its complexity and its adroitness of execution. Looking at such pieces as *Black Linen Tapestry* (p. 186), a layman would ponder the path of one yarn from top to bottom, but weavers are more awed by his control of tension: the yarns in each warp band—between each horizontal strut—are of a different

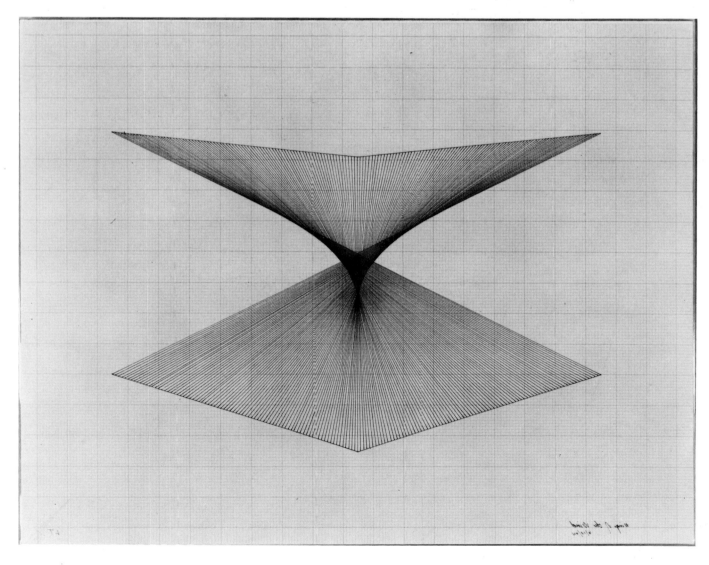

length. Accomplished with virtuoso dexterity, the systemic solution is so remarkable that it could only be Collingwood's.

In the early 70's, Marlise Staehlin of Basel developed, together with Ursula Luthy, the singularly avant-garde system of triangulated ''carpet'' elements shown on this page. The triangle was selected because it was more active, move expressive than a quadrangle. Although the flexibility of arrangement, with its hint of nomadic freedom, was thought of as an antidote to the rigid grid of modern architecture, the new module is related to it by its tight order and machine aesthetic.

Throughout the 70's Japan's Akiko Shiminuki has systemically worked in media as diverse as translucent tapestry and filaments embroidered through panels of clear acrylic (p. 192). In all of these her prismatic color is as correct as a crystal. Although the piece shown is similar to Collingwood's in its ordered layers of diagonal filagree secured by horizontal rods, both the structure and her softly iridescent close-valued color are dissimilar.

MARLISE STAEHLIN   Switzerland
(with Ursula Lüthi)
Rhombos *1977*
half-hitching; wool roving

A flexible model in which the folded Rhombos becomes a triangle.

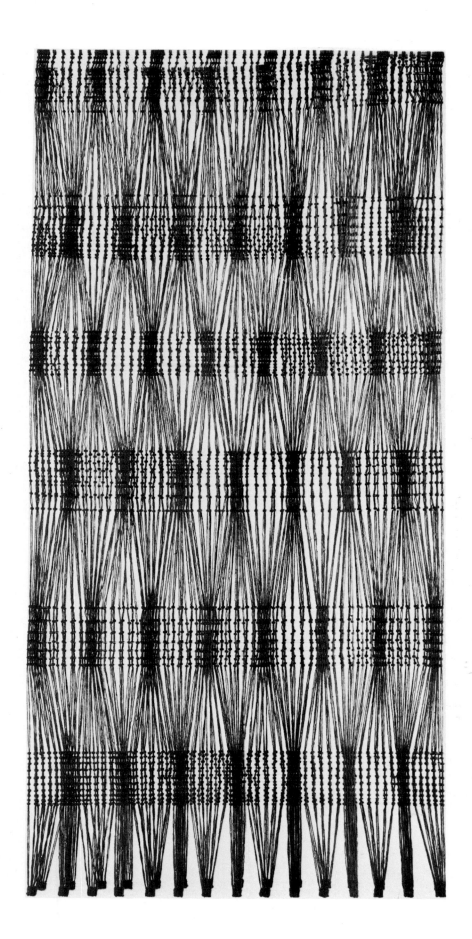

AKIKO SHIMANUKI Japan
Untitled 1970
knotting; wool, acrylic

Here the vertical yarns are knotted onto fine acrylic rods. Three
inches apart, the two layers combine in a multicolored translu-
cency.

Color Systems

Of those artists who use color systematically, perhaps no one is as consistent or refined as Richard Landis. In the 60's he wove double cloths of smooth, plied linen. Some of the most successful played small rectangular blocks in geometric color progressions against a solid ground or matrix. More recently the matrix has also been broken into a color system; the juxtaposition and combination of the two multiply the color relationships (p. 198). Even with the aid of elaborate charts and diagrams, only some of the admixed colors can be preplanned; others evolve in the weaving.

In the early 70's, while searching for a new yarn predyed in many graduated shades, Landis experimented unhappily with threads of fine wool, then was persuaded to consider the hundreds of colors available in sewing thread. Even though weaving a double cloth with so fine a material is painstakingly slow, the resulting fusion of crossover colors is smooth, not grainy. When, in the mid 70's, he collaborated with painter Craig Fuller, a more varied palette in diagonal composition was the result (p. 199).

As a series with variations is woven on each warp setup, Landis' vision extends into color fields unchartered even by him. Newer compositions, such as those shown on pages 198, 199, also tend to be highly developed in image and composition. Often these compositions contain an implied frame.

When, in the mid-70's, Margot Rolf undertook the challenge of color, it was not as an addition or ornament; rather, the color system became her *raison d'etre* (p. 195). She chose the primaries—red, yellow, blue—and added to them green (complement of red) plus white or ecru as the field on which the colors play.

Strands. The particular use of gravity as a design element that began in the 60's has grown in sophistication and frequency of use in the 70's. Many strands are not interwoven; of those who use interwoven strands, no one is as conspicuously important as Masakazu Kobayashi. Throughout the 70's he has allowed gravity to form the soft cascades of heavy weft that, like an Austrian shade, drapes downward between the narrow verticals of supporting warp (p. 197).

As shown on page 218, Lenore Tawney, in the late 70's, created very large translucent "volumes" by suspending thousands of linen strands from an overhead canvas rectangle. The insistent order of her square grid knotting plan contrasts with the free falling slubby yarn.

About the same time a Japanese and two Europeans experimented with vertical strands. Mario Yagi's adventure led to glamorous lighting fixtures for a Milanese producer. Bandiera Cerantola and Moik Schiele developed strand systems to exploit new potentials for chromatic iridescence. As shown on page 196, both artists have developed an ordered color sequence; both realize the kinetic vibrations resulting from moving past series of verticals. Schiele's color system is as directly stated as the straight falling strands themselves. Hard and dense, her rayon filaments readily respond to gravity. Their high luster electrifies the full-intensity color.

Cerantola describes her *Tessuto del Colore* in terms of "space experienced as the discovery

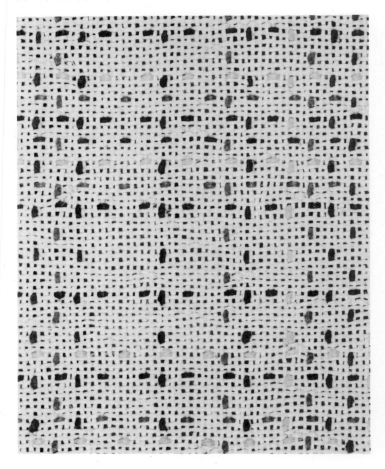

MARGOT ROLF Holland
Starting from 4 colors, series 2–III–I *(detail)* 1978
compound brocade; linen
78 6/8" × 78 6/8"

of color in fabric.'' Its three-meter cube is formed by hundreds of suspended strands—each a tube knit of yarns in a set proportion of primary colors. This proportion gradually progresses from red to orange or blue to green. A walkway diagonally across the cube divides it into two triangles. Saturate, full intensity color on these long sides of the triangles is more and more diluted with white as it progresses toward the apex. The concept is scientific; the result, sensual.

Marika de Ley's systemic color explosion is knit as a rhombus, then formed into a sweater. As shown on page 160, the horizontal and vertical stripes are achieved by carrying the yarn in dozens of individual balls. Akiko Shimanuki and Nancy Guay have both worked with color systems in lustrous filaments. The work of the former is described in page 192; Guay's *Arpeggio,* shown on page 236, is a striped progression of strands suspended between two wands. Highlights magnify the drama; with movement, the effect is fantastic.

MARGOT ROLF Holland
Starting from 4 colors XVI 1978
plain weave; linen
3 1/2" × 5 1/2" × 5 1/2"

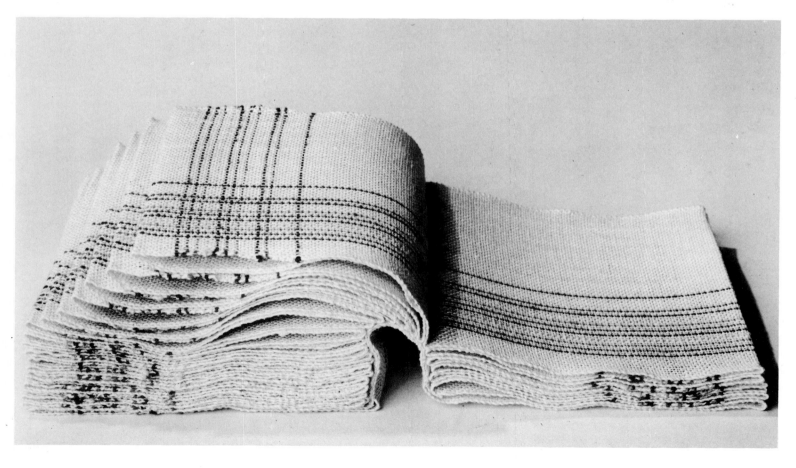

AKIKO SHIMANUKI *Japan*
Reflection No. 2 (detail) 1976
embroidery; acrylic sheet, man-made filament
7 7/8" × 7 7/8"
(for description see p. 188)

Of more than passing interest to those concerned with Art Fabric is the contemporary movement among painters devoted to pattern making. The common aesthetic among this group includes an essentially geometric vocabulary as well as the broadest range of color and color modulation used to produce interlocking, overlapping, and counterbalancing networks. Why are so many artists looking at pattern now? It has been acknowledged that decorative painting appropriates from other sources what is sensuous, repetitive, and completely identifies color with form.

There are parallel currents in all the arts; there is a rediscovery of principles underlying early art. The artists creating Art Fabric in the New Classicism know well their allegiance to textile traditions and the enrichment of these by the artists' unbounded vision.

WARREN SEELIG   U.S.A.
White Plus *(detail)*   *1976*
double plain weave; cotton
3'5" x 6'9"

Folded Cloth #2   *1975*
warp face repp; cotton
27" x 22"

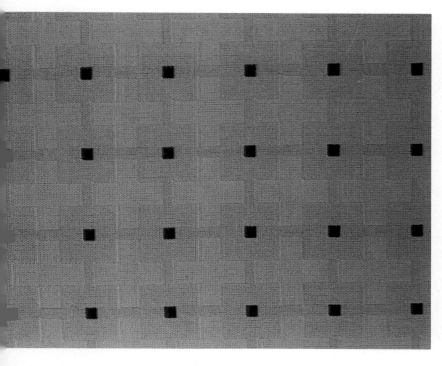

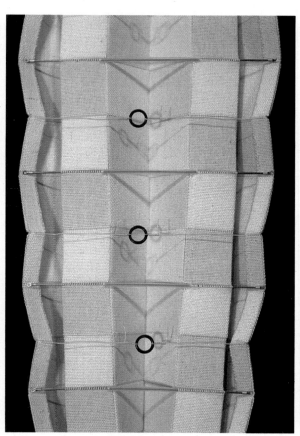

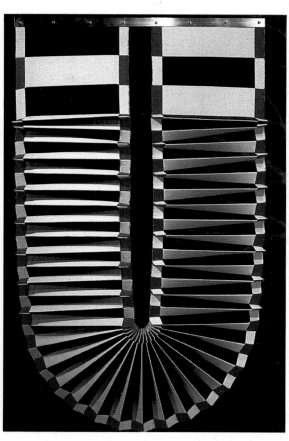

Vertical Shield #1 *(detail)*   *1976*
double plain weave;
cotton, rigid vinyl
81" x 12" x 2½"

Vertical Relief #6 *(back detail)*   *1974*
double plain weave; cotton, viscose, vinyl skeleton
84" x 17"

Accordion Relief #2   *1974*
double plain weave; cotton, rigid vinyl insert,
vinyl skeleton
40" x 30"

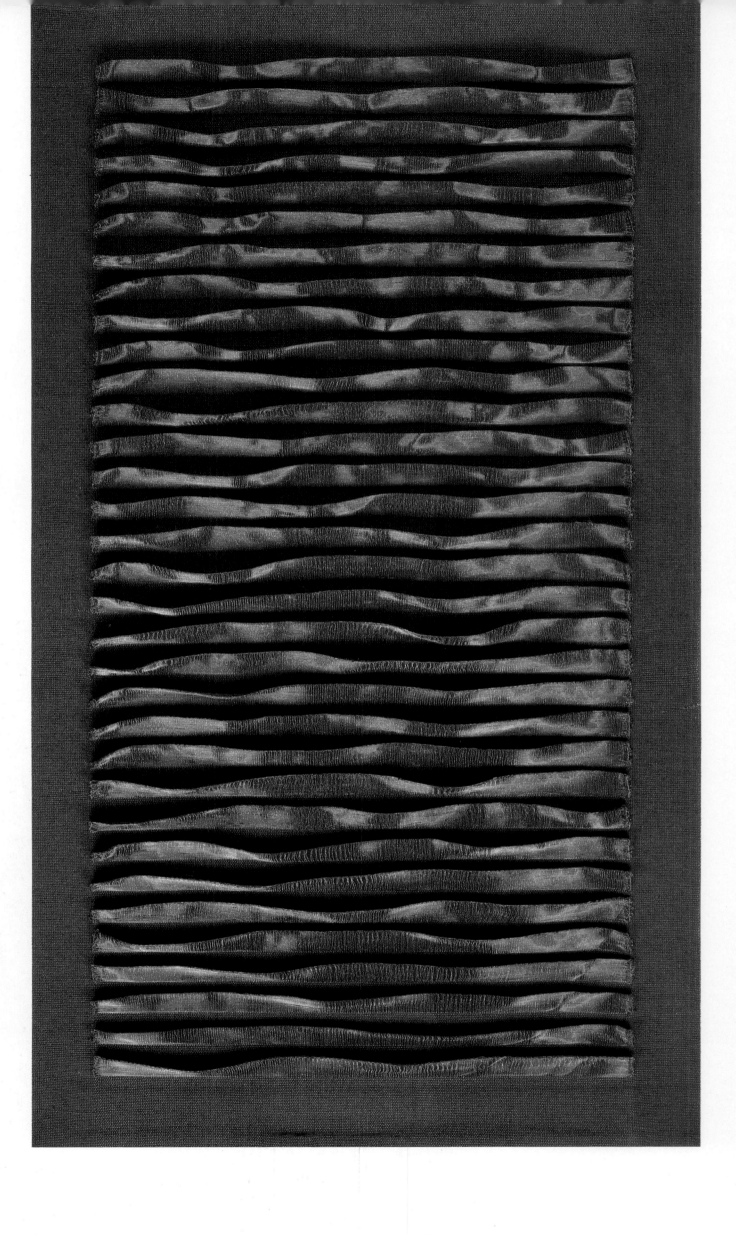

194

NANCY GUAY   U.S.A.

facing page
Untitled   1978
pleat weave; wool, viscose, copper gimp, copper wire
57" x 37"

*Collection: Ry-Co Corporation,
Hingham, Massachusetts*

right
Solstice   1979
twill weave; viscose film, Lurex, wool
55" x 55"

MARGOT ROLF   *Holland*
Starting from 4 Colors VIII-1   1976
*warp brocade with warp and weft face repp frame;
wool, linen*
6'6" x 6'6"

detail of corner

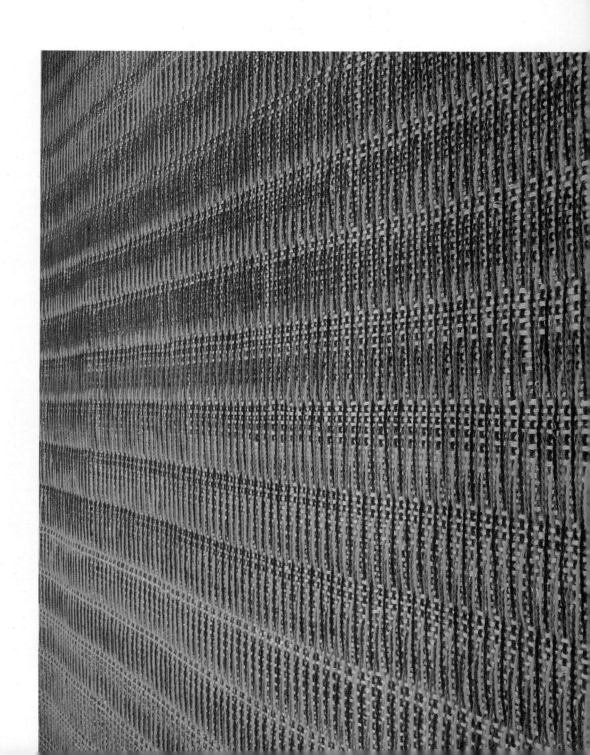

right

MOIK SCHIELE   Switzerland
Himmel   1975
tapestry with weft fringe; viscose
9'4" x 2'7" x 3'

below

MARISA BANDIERA CERANTOLA   Italy
Chromatic Structure   1976-77
tubular knit strands; acrylic fiber, mesh
12' x 12' x 12'

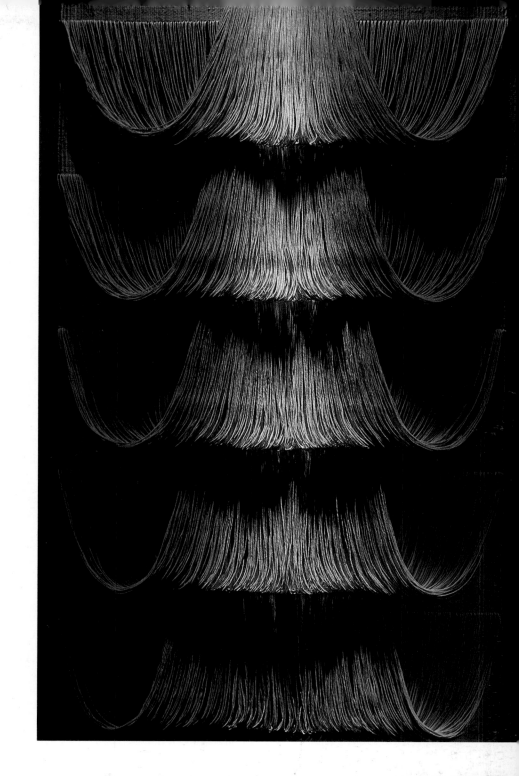

MASAKAZU KOBAYASHI   Japan

top
White Waves   *1974*
plain weave; cotton
66⅞" x 39⅝"

bottom
Waves 3   *1976*
plain weave; cotton
6'7" x 6'7"

RICHARD LANDIS   U.S.A.

facing page
The Passion   *1978*
double plain weave; cotton
15" x 12"

right

top
Cathedral   *1976*
double plain weave; cotton
18½" x 13"

bottom
Twelve Tone Study   *1976*
double plain weave; cotton
36" x 33"
In collaboration with Craig Fuller

HERMAN SCHOLTEN   *Holland*

Ruit   *1977*
tapestry over twill and rib weaves; wool, linen
8'6⅜" x 8'2" (turned c. 30°)

MICHELLE HEON Canada
Fragments 1979
plain weave; linen, silk
122 7/8″ × 96 1/8″

Collection: Museum of Contemporary Art, Montreal

6 ART FABRIC IN ARCHITECTURE

The clients for Art Fabric are business, government, and—by the late 70's—collectors, including museums. Still, the chief support comes from the architect and designer who consider works of art as an aspect of interior design. The architectural designer, his advisors, and gallery resources account for most sales and most commissions awarded. Since the mid-60's this patronage has been sufficient for our critical evaluation.

We acknowledge that hangings in architectural spaces are not new. Although the very nature of fiber means that few ancient examples remain, we have numerous descriptions in Biblical and classical writings. Coptic and Sassanian examples exist, as well as a few pre-Columbian pieces, such as the feather mosaic hanging (below). From the late Inca period in Peru, these large hangings were probably used as banners hung on special occasions. It would seem that most ancient hangings had ceremonial or associative use. Some distinguished rank and royalty, others the seat of power or religion. Unlike the apparel and accoutrements buried with the noble dead, ancient Art Fabrics were only occasionally preserved.

From the Middle Ages of Europe there remain fine tapestries that once hung on the walls of churches and castles. Usually figurative and illustrative, their color and pattern served as much to relieve the hard monotony of stone walls as to divide space or reduce drafts. In any case these old tapestries are not only remarkably successful in their power but also in an architectonic organization consistent with both the order of the spaces in which they were hung and in relation to the sculpture, stained glass, and forged metals within these spaces. That they related so well to architecture is ascribed to their being a weaver's art: through the use of a few rich colors and by subordinating their flat images to the horizontal/vertical structure of cloth, these weavers achieved solidly architectonic compositions. Their development of hatched color transitions and eccentric wefting is extraordinary. Only with the Renaissance were weavers reduced to following cartoons drawn by painters more concerned with modeling and perspective, and with movement and likeness than with gut expression of materials and structure.

facing page
OLGA DE AMARAL Colombia
El Gran Muro (detail) 1976
plain weave; horsehair, wool
64' × 4'

Commissioned by John Portman for the atrium lobby of the Peachtree Plaza Hotel, Atlanta

The thousands of tabs in weft-face repp were woven, then interlaced into 16 large panels to create this six-storey hanging. (See pre-installation color photograph on page 217.) The circular parapets are sufficiently distant from the hanging to protect it from the curious.

below
Mantle or Wall Hanging, Peru c. 1500 A.D.
wrapping and stitching; feathers, cotton, bast.
27 3/8" × 78 2/8"

Collection: Robert Woods Bliss Collection of Pre-Columbian Art, Dumbarton Oaks, Washington, D.C.

Although few pre-Columbian hangings remain, the Inca feather "banners" are spectacular. Their simple imagery is relieved by the mosaic-like iridescence of blue and gold feathers. The symbol can be seen for a great distance and its visual impact grows with close observation.

The early modern movement of the 20th Century embraced a broad range of hangings, some in tapestry technique, others in double cloth and still others pieced and sewn. One of the best overviews of this period is Sonia Delaunay's compilation of international Art Fabrics, *Tapis et Tissu,* published in 1929. But the works more often belonged to the Studio Craft Movement than to commissions for specific buildings.

In our interiors and especially in the city environment where the dynamic rightness of nature is lamentably absent, the structure and materials expressed in buildings today make the Art Fabric of the 70's a welcome relief. In fact, such large, relatively empty spaces as lobbies and reception areas, banking halls and passages are natural settings for Art Fabric. They offer organic relief to hard, monotonous surfaces. The lush materials provide color and focus for the eye and help to solve difficult acoustical problems. And they are less a security risk than many other art forms—it isn't easy to go off with a ten-foot hanging!

During the 60's and 70's, particularly in North America, architectural commissions have been the mainstay of the artists and dealers involved with Art Fabric. Some of the work produced has been successful in all respects; that is, in relation to site, in its aesthetics and presence, in scale, and in relationship to security and maintenance. Other commissions have failed in one or more respects. Sometimes this is the selection of the work or of the artist. Commercial studios and charlatan producers have been among the most aggressive in gaining commissions. Then, too, there are the foibles of a commission. It is not easy in any medium to buy a work still in the mind's eye. There is always the chance of a disruption in the studio or some shortsightedness in vision on the part of the specifier, dealer, or artist. Scaling for yet to be built spaces is difficult. One must also envision vista, light, and surrounding surfaces. Frequently fire codes become a factor. Sometimes flameproof materials are required; in other cases, flameproof treatment of materials is necessary; either may affect color or colorfastness or have potential degradation in light. With more and more frequency artists or dealers have been invited to the site to arrange the installation. This is useful. Artists have also become more skillful in their consideration of installation and hanging in relation to the art itself. (See opposite.)

Too often, and particularly in lobbies, work is installed without adequate protection. Means of keeping people away from the work are all too infrequently employed. Adequate maintenance and conservation are virtually nonexistent. There are certainly instances for types of work that should be screened by glass or hung over a dias or other horizontal surface that would keep people away. Still too little is known about cleaning and restoration. Of course, Art Fabric is only one among the new media endangered by placement in public spaces. But the problems point up the success and durability of gobelin tapestry, which is relatively impervious to handling, and can be cleaned, rolled, and easily stored or shipped.

facing page

top
AURELIA MUNOZ Spain
Aguila Beige 1977
knotting; jute, sisal
99" × 127" × 63"

This composition of four sail-like sheets is the first in which Muñoz integrated hanging devices as part of the whole. In the final installation she planned to refine the connections.

bottom
DANIEL GRAFFIN France
The Passage of Ramses (detail) 1976
(for description see p. 63)

To keep the great weight of his plaited leather frieze under tension, Graffin engineered special square-sectioned guys and turnbuckles.

BARBARA SHAWCROFT U.S.A.
model for Legs *1978*
macramé; waxed nylon, synthetic raffia
25″ × 9″

Commissioned for BART station, San Francisco

This model (1/2″ = 1′) realistically conveys the gargantuan scale of two fifty-foot columns, each six feet in diameter. Particularly useful for the artist, architect, and client in envisioning scale are miniaturized studies for monumental pieces.

Often the artists have developed a very reasonable sense of vigilance in the selection of materials, in the prevention of early default. While acceptance of commissions may impede their stylistic expressions—only occasionally can the unknown and unseen be commissioned—the artists have learned how to work with their clients. Some have engaged engineers and consulted industry in choosing materials. For example, Barbara Shawcroft explains that in the period of more than a year between being awarded the commission for *Legs* from the BART Art Council in San Francisco she engaged in the following processes:[1]

"The BART Engineers stated that my materials would have to undergo a test for non-flammability that would place the ropes in an extremely high heat for a period of four hours. The ropes had to pass the test by not burning, smoking, or melting. This testing created a period of one year of researching a fiber that would pass this test and a period of processing this fiber into rope.

"The nature of the non-flammable material presented some technical problems. The original vision of the fishing net and the more recent vision of the temple ropes in Japan created a 'fit' together that I used to conquer my technical difficulties with the non-flammable material. I exposed the ends of the splices and elongated the fringes at every new rope connection. This gave a more textured overall surface design than I had originally conceived. To balance off this new necessity I also hung the original loose-hanging ropes that I had planned to use in a more overall surface texture. I had originally planned to make use of a wind reversal caused by the subway train rushing through the station into the tunnel. I liked the idea of the surface texture moving and creating a kinetic feeling. This wind reversal worked as well with the overall surface texture and gave a flutter of movement as the train rushed through. The difference in the textural surface is that, originally, I planned to keep all of the texture along the inside of one leg in order to give it a sort of deep foliage kind of feeling (see model on p. 206). Dimension-wise, the BART engineers asked that I place the legs closer together. They wanted a certain amount of footage away from the edge of the platform because of the sculpture being made out of fiber. This involved a small replanning of the

top central section so that the legs would hang closer together. I originally thought that my sculpture would be, for the most part, orange with a touch of ochre on the left leg. The long hanging ropes were to be jet and greenish blacks with touches of different blues ranging from light to dark, and there were to be touches of white rope here and there. The non-flammable rope was so expensive that I was forced to use the available colors. Fortunately for me the fleece was made in orange. Unless I added to the expense of the rope by dyeing the white fleece into the jet and greenish blacks and the differing blues, I must settle for a khaki green. My commission budget would not handle this extra dye expense. I had calculated that all of the $50,000 would go directly back into the processing of the piece. The use of the khaki green presented a new design problem in that I felt that I must blend this dark colour with the orange.''

LENORE TAWNEY U.S.A.
Cloud VI *1979*
knotting; linen, cotton duck
191 3/4" × 191 3/4" × 191 3/4"
shown at ''Soft Exhibition,'' Kunsthaus, Zurich, 1979

The magic of Tawney's Cloud Series *is kinetic. In* Cloud VI *the strands flicker with air movements, creating a constantly changing range of densities. In this work, which hangs above a white platform, the shadows produced are like the pale caligraphic paintings of Mark Tobey, but they are ever-changing. All works in the* Cloud Series *are composed of thousands of linen strands knotted into an overhead tarpaulin. The rigid grid of the hanging pattern is modified by the organic slub and crimp of the linen. The* Cloud *for the Santa Rosa commission (p. 218) is protected by its well-chosen site, above and beyond inquisitive hands or careless maintenance.*

In Europe, the East European and Dutch governments, particularly, have bought and commissioned works for public buildings. In North America, passage into law of art budgets for major government buildings has encouraged many commissions. The U.S. General Services Administration funds have supported art in a broad range of media, with the Art Fabric becoming widespread. Many states have Art in Public Building Programs and none more successful than in California, which has commissioned works by Lia Cook and Kris Dey, among others.

One of the major commissions is Lenore Tawney's *Cloud Series* in the lobby of the Santa Rosa Federal Building in California (p. 218). Sixteen-foot long strands, dyed and painted in several shades of blue, hang from a painted canvas mounted on the ceiling. Although Tawney's acceptance of this first commission and move into architectural scale was a new challenge, the linear systemic construction she employed hearkens back to her early drawings (p. 187). There is a purity and nobility in her hanging strands that, in contrast with the concrete and glass, produces a sense of exhiliration.

Also related to the ceiling, but in quite another mood, is the fiber work by Gerhardt Knodel in the lobby of the M. D. Hunt Library at the University of Houston, Texas (p. 218). What is called an "interaction area," is filled with trees, intimate furniture groupings, and Knodel's 110-foot long composition of panels woven in Kentucky on production handlooms. This commission soars kite-like over the space. Mylar yarns provide an iridescent shimmer; by sheer size and movement the whole becomes a focal point even from the exterior. The work is tensioned and positioned by means of stainless steel cables and marine hardware attached at pre-engineered structural locations specified by the artist. The visual excitement lies in the scale, the planes of lively color, and the relation to the architectural environment.

Equally well integrated is Knodel's enormous *Free Fall* for the Detroit Plaza Hotel (p. 219). The artist describes it as a "vertical passage defined by light and color." It utilizes a series of forty fabric planes to create an animated sequence extending from the reflecting pool at its base to the skylight above. Conceived to accompany architecture, it responds to the impulses that the architecture initiates; the objective is a vital interaction. The fabrics billow, ripple, and sway with air currents. The reflective qualities of the work change with the light and with every new viewpoint that the spectator discovers in this active architectural setting. It is valid to point out that both the Houston and Detroit works can be dismantled, cleaned, and reinstalled.

Sheila Hicks has done more of her great works for the interiors of major buildings than almost any other contemporary artist working in the medium. She has led the way in the United States, Europe, and the Third World, working closely with the client—be it architect, government, or industry. She has traveled extensively and the varied cultures and experiences she has absorbed make each commission relative to a specific place and environment.

For the headquarters of the American Telephone and Telegraph Company in Basking Ridge, New Jersey (1976) she created two pieces: *The Green Silk Forest* in the executive area and *A Communications Labyrinth* in the commons space of the building. While each relates to earlier work, in both instances the environmental factors lend themselves to a new fulfillment and perfection.

We are familiar with Hicks' circles which are hierarchical—with them she brings everything together; construction and formal order anchor the thicknesses of her cords and her colors, from warm to cool. In the disk commissioned for the King of Saudi Arabia (p. 221), she uses gold gimp to create a cluster of date-like forms bound by cords. Unhappily, we might never have an opportunity to see the jeweled completeness of this piece; it is installed in the King's private loge at the Conference Center in Ryhad.

In New York in 1976, Hicks returned to modular elements but with the difference that she was working with cloth. The wall in the entrance hall of the luxurious Galleria cooperative is a silk bas-relief. In iridescent colors, lustrous silk sewn into tubes of varying thicknesses but uniform in length are wrapped at intervals with silk yarns so that they appear to be long, soft, horizontal pillows nestling together to form a dimensional wall (p. 220). It is fascinating to note the variations of technique within her cord compositions: wrapped, hanging, stacked, braided and woven cords.

A departure from the wrapped cords that
have become her hallmark since her first
work in 1968, a total wall in the Paris Roths-
child Bank (1970), her 1979 commission for
the Compagnie de Sain–Gobain proves
that, to her, the cord motif is without limit.
In this work her cords become twisted ropes of
linen, nylon, wool, and cotton yarns, the
mixing of colors enhanced through loosely
twisting the threads.

SHEILA HICKS U.S.A. (lives in Paris)
Untitled 1979
wrapping, plying, twisting; linen, wool, cotton
9′11″ × 35′5″
A fusion of circular motif and vertically striated relief.

Commissioned by Hellmuth, Obata & Kassabaum, Inc., St. Louis,
Missouri, for the Sheraton-Washington Hotel, D.C.

HELENA HERNMARCK *Sweden (lives in New York)*
Blue Bonnet *1979 (above);* Poppies *1979 (facing page)*
discontinuous brocade, soumak; wool, linen
11' × 20' (turned 90°)

Commissioned for Dallas Center, Dallas, Texas

This enormous "flower" commission is perhaps the most developed of Hernmarck's large series of hangings woven with blown-up photographs as the cartoon. The half-tone gradations are masterful. The very large scale is heightened by the extreme enlargement; the tiny flowers dwarf even the people viewing them. Brilliant oranges and violets are relieved by hundreds of green shades.

Helena Hernmarck is almost entirely engaged in working for architectural spaces. She uses Swedish wools—thick and thin yarns which she weaves on her four-harness looms. The surface richness of the grouped wefts enhances the integration of all elements. Image, materials, and process are never surrendered to the demands of her composition. She explains:[2] "I have tended to call the work I do 'Decorative Art,' with a European understanding of that term. My feeling is that there is still room for this art form . . . to fill a need and it has some clear limitations for which the most suitable solution is found." As some of her titles indicate, her work almost always entails pictorial representation. *The Journey* was commissioned by George Nelson & Company for the lobby of the Aid Association for Lutherans in Appleton, Wisconsin (p. 222).

The Nelson office, in full control of each detail of their job, allowed nothing to interfere with the visibility of her long rambling landscape. Larger than life, the piece combines illusion and reality.

One of the more fascinating of her earlier works is the two-sided, semitransparent hanging, *Carp,* where the images on one side play against the shadow of the images of the reverse. Her use of strips of perforated mirror Mylar film in the body of the work gives it transparency as well as high reflectivity.

Hernmarck's last work of the 70's, flower tapestries for the Dallas Centre were designed and woven so that the images produce in and out of focus effects. Originally inspired by a photographic technique, the increase of scale in the tapestry enhances the original beauty of the images.

HELENA HERNMARCK *Sweden (lives in New York)*
Carp 1973 (above and facing page top; detail facing page bottom)
discontinuous brocade (two-sided); linen, perforated plastic strips
5′3″ × 5′6″

*Commissioned by Eero Saarinen for John Deere and Co., Moline,
Ill.*

*Hernmarck's use of plastic strips cut from reject sequin stock to
achieve a reflective transparency is described on page 66. Her
two-sided panel is so effective that in either view the nearby fish
seem to be swimming at some distance from the others. The
placement in a glass pavilion is probably optimum. The detail
shows the rich combination of materials and the brocading technique. Close inspection will reveal double strips of mirror Mylar,
perforated to become at once reflective and transparent. The dark
areas (fish) are opaque and brilliantly colored—the lighter ones
translucent and watery.*

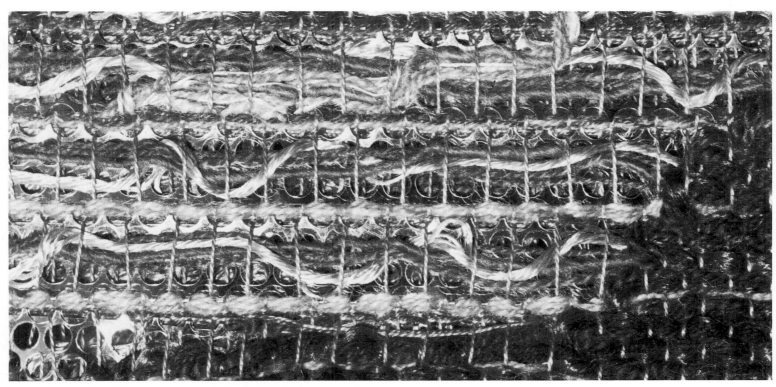

Blacks, browns and greys were the preferred colors in Jagoda Buic's work in the 60's; only occasionally did she venture into red for smaller pieces. Early in the 70's, red reappeared in a major piece (p. 233) and unrelieved white became a dominant choice for large works. We see her at work on the theatre curtain in the Museum of the Revolution in Sarajevo. A similar work, *Le Paysage Blanc*, is in the Archeological Museum in Split. A strong synthesis with the surrounding architecture provides embellishment and it is so comfortably conditioned by the space it inhabits that it creates a rich ambience.

Equally ubiquitous for over a decade are the architectural commissions by Olga de Amaral. Scale and variations in color and texture work wonderfully in *El Gran Muro* in the Peachtree Plaza Hotel in Atlanta. Real communion between art and architecture has been realized —these immense pieces ornament the mechanical core that is the central element of the interior. The cascade of yellow, orange, and beige leaf-like elements projects a strong decorative quality, while the wool and horsehair fiber contrasts with the raw concrete. The pieces are visible from any level of the atrium: as one exits from the elevators, from the rooms and hallways, and, of course, from the ground level. Because it cannot be handled by the passerby, it is protected from soil, as can be seen in the illustration on page 216.

(This, of course, brings up the question of art in our time: how important exactly is permanence. For certain works of art planned obsolescence seems acceptable. In history extraordinary cloths were created for coronations and other specific times. They were not meant to be permanent; sometimes the buildings that housed them were not either. But when this is the case, the artist, dealer, architect, and client must all have this understanding.)

OLGA DE AMARAL Colombia
El Grand Muro 1976
8 panels each 7' x 1'2"

facing page
Shown on a street in Bogota, Colombia
Commissioned for: Peachtree Center Plaza Hotel, Atlanta
Architect: John Portman & Associates, Atlanta

LENORE TAWNEY   U.S.A.

left
Cloud Series   1979
strands suspended from canvas; dyeing, painting
16' x 30'

Commissioned for: Federal Building, Santa Rosa, California

GERHARDT G. KNODEL   U.S.A.

below
Gulf Stream   1977
plain weave; wool, Mylar, metal
120' wide

Commissioned for: M. D. Anderson Library, University of Houston
Architect: ISD Inc., with Kenneth Bentsen & Associates, Houston

facing page
Free Fall   1977
plain weave; Mylar, metallic gimp, wool; with plexiglas tubes, nylon rope, stainless steel rods, cable
70' x 8' x 15'

Commissioned for: Detroit Plaza Hotel & Renaissance Center
Architect: John Portman & Associates, Atlanta

facing page
Rain Forest Tree   1971
supplementary weft joining; wool
9½' x 14'

Collection:
Weyerhaeuser Company, Tacoma

below
Journey   1977
supplementary weft joining; wool
4½' x 47'

Collection: Lutheran Insurance Co., Appleton, Wisconsin

right
Journey *(detail)*

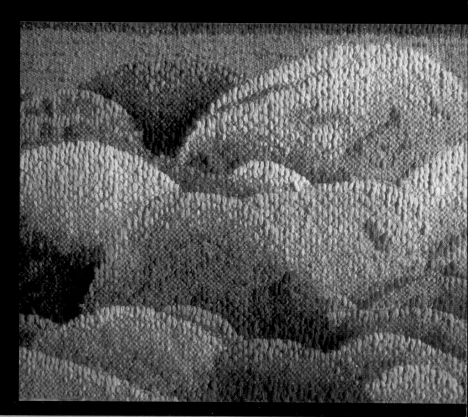

BARBARA SHAWCROFT   U.S.A.

above left
Legs   *1978*
knotless netting, splicing; Nomex nylon
50' x 20' x 6'

Commissioned for: BART Embarcadero Station,
San Francisco
by BART Art Council
above right
Legs *(detail)*

Blue Circles to See Through   *1977*
wrapping with bowline knot; synthetic rope
27' x 31' x 9' deep

Shown at The National Museum of Modern Art,
Kyoto & Tokyo

224

MARIETTE ROUSSEAU-VERMETTE *Canada*
Blancs Brillants *1974*
pleat weave; wool
7' × 21'

Collection: *Administrative Office, National Museum, Ottawa*

Woven in three long panels, the enormous relief achieves its strong, rounded ribs through a pleat weave technique. The bleached white wool is made the more brilliant by virtue of movement within the piece and the clear highlights on the rib.

7 ART FABRIC IN ENVIRONMENT, LANDSCAPE, AND THEATRE

It all started with Happenings. Allen Kaprow's first public Happening occurred in 1958 and was aptly called "Communication." His interest in environment and Happenings spurred an entire movement in the 60's. His concern was for an art that "must become preoccupied with and even dazzled by the space and objects of our everyday life, either our bodies, clothes, rooms, or if need be the vastness of 42 Street." He invented the term *Happenings* in reference to an art form related to theatre, performed in a given time and space.

So it appears to be entirely natural that Art Fabric should have its place in environment, in landscape, and in theatre: it functions not as a backdrop to a tableau; it is living material, part of the action, the experience; it exists in space related to other objects in a sequence of time.

ENVIRONMENTS

In the 60's painting went out of studios and museums and onto city walls. Sculpture embellished parks and plazas. The late Frederick Kiesler, a leader in many aspects of the avant-garde for five decades, had made us aware of sculpture to be in, providing a total experience that combined nature, ritual, and involvement—a sense of being, a sense of spirit and place.

Isolated works taken out-of-doors do not always contribute to the environment, nor are they, in themselves, always compatible. However, the number of "environmental" exhibitions and special installations in the 70's served to prove certain environmental qualities of work within enclosing walls and out-of-doors.

EWA PACHUKA Poland (lives in Australia)
Arcadia (detail) 1977
crochet; polypropylene, coir
c. 120" × 197" × 157"

Collection: New South Wales Art Gallery, Sydney, Australia

trees, foodstuffs and flowers. She senses the fiber of our hair, skin, and tissues. And she forcibly projects these insights into both individual works and the collective, environmental statements.

In Amsterdam in 1974, Sheila Hicks' one-person exhibition at the Stedelijk Museum, Amsterdam, included several environmental works. The mended sheets and darned socks she displayed at the same time in the window of de Bijenkorf Department Store represented a radical departure from the refinement of her silky surfaces and sensuous color. It was here that she started her transition from single works to environmental concerns.

She had been invited some time before to a convent of French Carmelite nuns near the Bois de Boulogne—they were weaving and wanted her to weave with them. She was struck by the densely darned wool sheets revealing an intimate handwriting and modest patience that later became documents for her own work. From this came her first presentation, at the 1977 Biennale in Lausanne, of darned sheets hanging together with eight tons of freshly washed and ironed laundry borrowed from the local hospital. In "Fiber-works" at The Cleveland Museum she presented *Reprise Repertoire* (p. 43): four linen dropcloths darned in diamond grids.

As her repertoire grew, the exhibition format was determined by the site. The illustrations on pages 44 and 45 from "Tons and Masses" shown in the Konsthall in Lund indicate one focus. When invited to exhibit by the Municipality of Montreuil, Hicks was given the fullest freedom to create her own environment. She based her presentation on thread to make a powerful statement accessible to all the people who live and work in Montreuil. She defined her purpose in planning the environment:[2] "[I] will deal with creation by thread. In the heart of the ateliers in the different parts of Montreuil I will introduce, with the help of animators, methods and ideas which will allow us to discover how to create with thread; Thread, Color, Texture. How to transform a flexible and linear element, a 'thread,' into an alphabet of forms in order to formulate a tactile language. *To give substance to ideas.*

"[It] will concern itself with communication through the language of textiles, to conceive and to realize a certain number of practical and personal objects. This could lead to the creation of original works which could be shown, and even to the development of forms and materials which are reproducible in large or small quantities. The effort will consist in making those people who work with thread, textiles and tapestries to be conscious of the great number of possibilities which need to be explored and to help strengthen their experiences and their capacity for expression.

"[I] will approach a delicate problem: how to earn a living with thread. Those people who create with thread, who weave and embroider, must all struggle to find the way to work and live from the activity they have chosen. Their work may well be expressive, inventive and striking, but there exist few social structures which permit the textile artist to realize his work. In spite of his desire to offer his work to society and to live from his activity, there are barriers which prevent him from expressing himself and from realizing his ideas. I will attempt to share my twenty years' experience in the field, in hope that the dialogue will lead to new developments.

"Why thread? Why Montreuil? Why autumn-winter 78–79? Times have changed and times continue to change. We are participating in the marked growth of interest in the quality of life, on all levels. Everyone wishes to select, to obtain for himself and to make the materials in which he dresses, sleeps and with which he surrounds himself.

"Between the simple domestic textile and the complex art textile, a whole labyrinth from which can spring an infinity of miracles remains to be discovered."

JAGODA BUIC *Yugoslavia*
Formes Mouvantes sur l'Eau et sur le Vent *1973*
tapestry with weft fringe; wool

233

CHRISTO (JAVACHEFF)   U.S.A.
Running Fence   1976
nylon canvas
18' x 24½ miles long

Installed in Sonoma and Marin Counties, California

facing page

DANIEL GRAFFIN   France
Sail   1977
sewing; polyester cloth, aluminum poles
49'2" x 49'2"

Commissioned for: Hotel Camino Real, Cancún, Mexico
Architect: Ricardo Legorreta, Mexico, D.F.

Columns   1976
sprang; nylon rope
15' x 90' x 12'

Installed in corridor of Romanesque church, Angers, France

NEDA AL-HILALI   U.S.A.
Tongues   1975
plaiting; industrial paper
17 elements, each 12' to 18' long

Shown on beach at Venice, California

FREDERIC AMAT   Spain
Series of Vestidures   1978
mixed media
each c. 66⅞" x 25⅝"

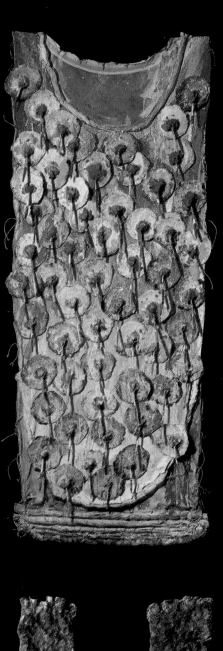

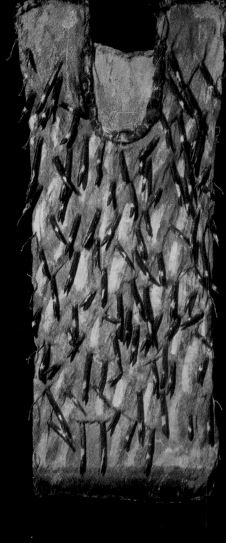

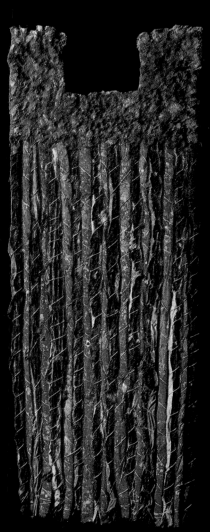

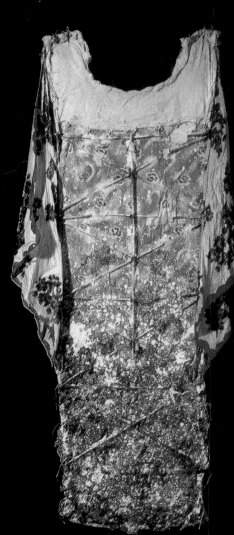

FREDERIC AMAT   Spain
Series of Vestidures   1978
mixed media
each c. 66⅞" x 25⅝"

COLETTE Tunis (lives in New York)
My Living Environment 1973

This is the artist's home environment, which she changes from
time to time. She is the doll in the photography.

above and facing page
URSZULA PLEWKA-SCHMIDT Poland
Cemetery and Biological Destruction *1979*

*The spatial compositions are open-work constructions of such
rigid materials as wicker and metal; these are plaited all around or
filled in with fabric of soft crochet or knitted texture.*

In a completely different mode of expression also in crochet—another Polish artist has created environments that are also social commentaries. Urszula Plewka-Schmidt, since her first works in the late 60's, has gone through several evolutions and transformations. Her small-scaled graveyards are a symbol and a synthesis of man's persistence. There are vestiges of a presence within nature, a fascination with the artifacts that express personal needs, work, beliefs, and everyday life, and a coexistence with nature up to the moment of returning to the soil.

Her commentaries on biological destruction —as she puts it "human wrecks, wounded and intoxicated without orientation, engaged in dancing the dance of death"—illustrate the control and restraint with which she meshes her materials and imagination. In the photographs shown here and on pages 239, 246 and 247, one can see that the obvious youth and vigor of her humans assert life and defy destruction.

above and facing page
URSZULA PLEWKA-SCHMIDT Poland
Cemetery and Biological Destruction *1979*

THEATRE

Historical and cultural circumstances give rise to innovations in all the arts. When the Diagilev's Ballet Russe first performed *Parade* in Paris in 1917, Picasso had already designed the sets and costumes. As early as 1912 Oscar Schlemmer had designed costumes for the Triadic Ballet in Stuttgart and later at the stage workshop at the Bauhaus in 1922. In Paris, in 1923, Sonia Delaunay was responsible for the costuming of the famous dancer Lizica Codreant.

Isamu Noguchi's sets for Martha Graham, Robert Rauschenberg's sets, and Andy Warhol's props for the Merce Cunningham Dance Company are well known internationally. As indeed are the 'Art Fabric' costumes for the Broadway production of *Lenny* and the innovations of Alwin Nikolais for his own dance company. For years, several of the artists working in fiber have been involved with theatre—Jagoda Buic worked with the Dubrovnik Theatre Festival: her costumes for Hamlet are shown on pages 252, 253. We are familiar with the early body coverings of Debra Rapaport shown in *Beyond Craft*.

Frederic Amat of Barcelona creates costumes, backdrops, and props for theatre as well as for his "celebrations of fiestas": he does this not for a specific fiesta but for those that might have existed in the past and those that he hopes might still occur (p. 240). His objects— vestments, utensils, ceremonial instruments —are created of mixed media but with fiber as a recurrent and dominant material. The sets and costumes shown here are for the performance, *Accio - Zero* in the Palau de Congressos, Montjuic, Barcelona (1974–76). His materials are varied: cloth, twigs, grasses, bones, paper, skins of animals, many-colored threads—an inventory of markets and fiestas. This young artist has captured the admiration of critics and public in his own country, in Switzerland, and in Mexico.

facing page
FREDERIC AMAT *Spain*
Accio-Zero y Accio-U *1974–76*

A Pantomime-Ballet conceived by Amat, who also designed the mise-en-scène *and costumes. It was presented at the Sala Vincon in Barcelona.*

GLEN KAUFMAN U.S.A.
above
Mino Study/White *1979*
weft twining; polypropylene twine
72″ × 24″ × 12″

facing page
Polycloak *1979*
tapestry, weft pile; polyethylene film, nylon
78″ × 48″ × 26″

The heroic proportions of each of these pieces would suggest that they must have been crafted for science fiction creatures.

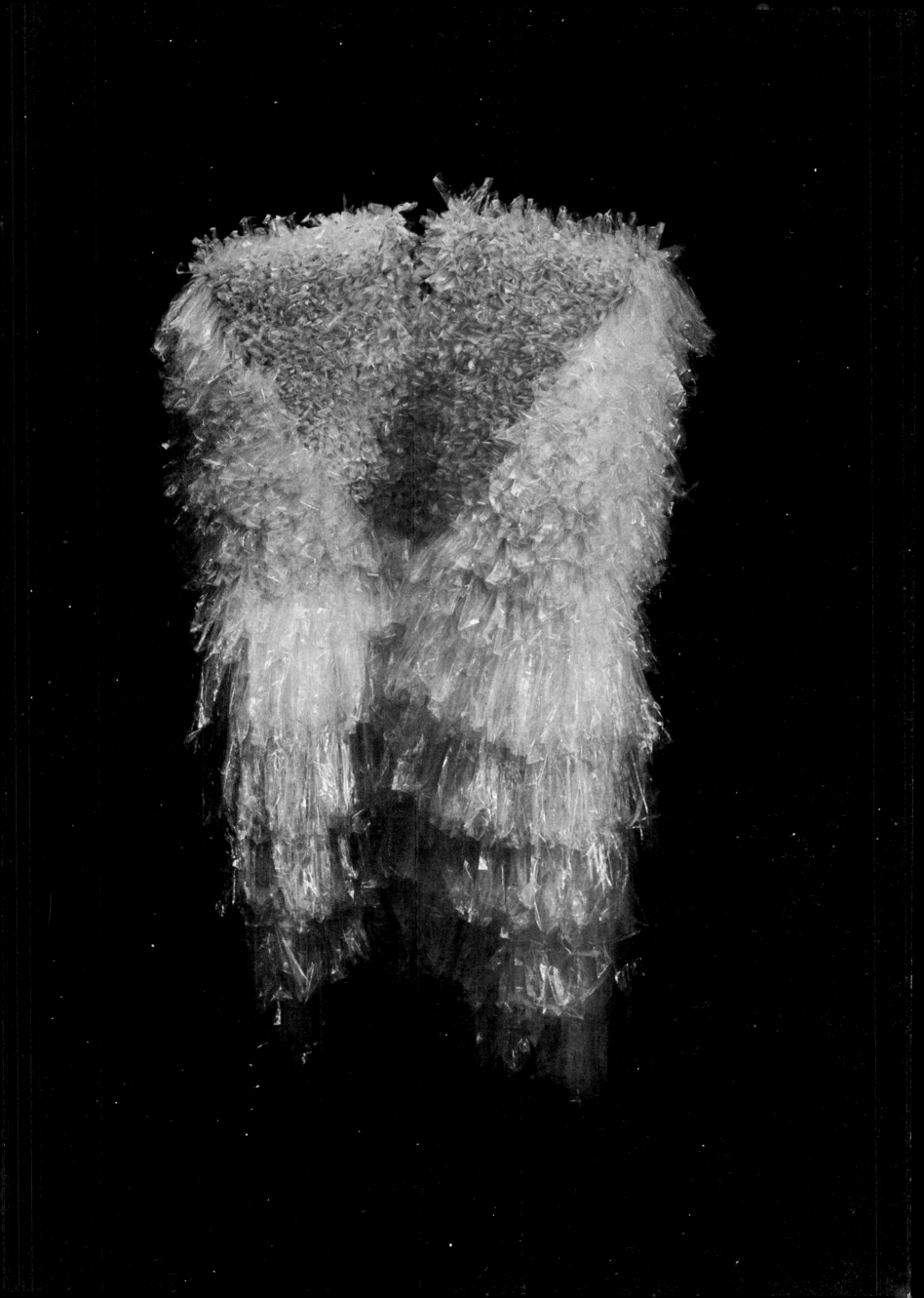

GLOSSARY

BATIK—Refers to the application of liquified wax, paste, starch, resin, or clay to cloth so as to resist dyes.

BROCADE—A woven cloth in which a supplementary element is introduced onto the two-element ground: brocades may be in the filling or the warp of both.

CABLE PLY YARN—A firm, round yarn usually of eight or more strands twisted together.

COILING—In basketry the process of concentrically stitching the element of each new course to the element(s) below it.

COUCHING—An embroidery technique in which one element is laid over the cloth then stitched to it by another, usually finer, element.

DAMASK—Twill or satin woven cloths with pattern areas created by warp-face and weft-face areas.

DISCONTINUOUS BROCADE—A free weaving technique in which the brocade yarn does not run from selvage to selvage but is laid-in according to the requirements of a figure or motif.

DOUBLE CLOTH—A four-element weaving technique using two sets of warp and two sets of weft, producing two interwoven cloths, one over the other.

ECCENTRIC—Term applied to woven elements deviating from the horizontal-vertical definition of textiles.

EGYPTIAN CARD WEAVING—Narrow goods woven to pattern by the manipulation of a series of punched cards through which the warp is threaded rather than by harnesses.

ELEMENT—In the construction of fabric, a component or set of components: knitting is a typical single-element technique; most weaving is two-element; pile fabrics and brocades are three-element; double cloth is four-element, etc.

ENDS—See *warp*.

FABRIC—A pliable plane of any material or technique. Most fabrics are constructed of fibrous yarns.

FILAMENT—A single fiber, usually extruded continuously as in silk and man-made fiber production.

FILLING—In weaving, the crosswise element which interlaces at right angles with the warp; synonymous with weft and woof (archaic).

FILLING-FACED—Term applied to cloth in which the filling picks predominate over the warp ends; the filling may conceal the warp completely.

FILM—A thin, pliable layer of dense, homogeneous material such as plastic. Slit film may be used as a fabric element.

FLOSS—A yarn in which the several strands or plies are not twisted together but lie loose and parallel.

FREE WEAVING—Weaving in which pattern is not controlled by the loom but through manipulation by the weaver, usually with a discontinuous weft; examples are tapestry, soumak, and knotted pile.

GAUZE—A loosely woven cloth often stabilized by twisting the warp or wrapping with the weft.

GIMP—A yarn in which one strand is spirally wrapped around a core of yarn or yarns.

GOBELIN—Derived from the famous French tapestry center of Gobelin, the word is now used as the generic term for the technique of tapestry joinings in which wefts of adjacent areas are looped around each other.

HARNESS—In the loom, a frame from which are suspended the heddles, through which the warp yarns are threaded.

HEDDLE—In the loom, one of a set of cords or wires, suspended from a harness, with heddle eyes through which warp ends are threaded.

HIGH WARP *(haute lisse)*—A tapestry loom in which the warp yarns are vertical so that the weft yarn is pushed downward.

IKAT—The process of wrapping-to-pattern, then dyeing, segments of yarn before cloth construction begins. Those parts of the yarn that are to remain undyed are covered with a resist material impermeable to the dye.

INTERLACING—To engage the warp ends with filling yarns to make a web or woven cloth.

JACQUARD—A pattern-controlling device composed of punched cards and individual heddles suspended on long cords. It may be attached to looms, knitting, or lace machines to allow extremely complex constructions in long pattern repeats.

KILIM—A flat, woven rug, cover, or hanging, originally oriental and often reversible. Often kilims employ a tapestry joining of unsewn slits, sometimes called kilim slits.

LAID-IN—See *discontinuous brocade*.

LENO—A technique for woven fabric in which pairs of warp ends are twisted between each insertion of weft.

LOOM CONTROLLED—Woven patterns created by manipulating the harnesses. Compare with *free weaving*.

LOW WARP *(basse lisse)*—A tapestry loom in which the warp yarns are horizontal so that the beat-up weft yarn is pushed forward, toward the weaver.

MONOFILAMENT—A yarn composed of one continuous fiber. (Except for silk and horsehair, all are man-made.)

MULTIFILAMENT—A yarn composed of several continuous (usually coarse) filaments.

MULTIPLE HARNESS—A loom with six or more harnesses; a cloth woven on a loom with multiple harnesses, such as an eight-harness twill or satin.

MYLAR—A trade name registered by E. I. DuPont for certain nylon films. These may be laminated to a thin layer of aluminum to form mirror Mylar. Mylar yarns are laminates of Mylar and aluminum slit and sometimes wrapped with a filament yarn.

NARROW GOODS—Plaited or woven tapes, ribbons, and straps with selvages, generally eight inches or less in width.

PICK—A single shot of weft yarn.

PLAITING—A fabric technique employing one, two, or more sets of elements interlaced over and under in the manner of braiding or plain weaving. Elements run on the diagonal. Prime technique of basketry.

PLANGI—Also called tie-dye, it is accomplished by raising portions of an open cloth and resist-tying them with thread or bast. True plangi always involves some crimping or folding of the material.

RESISTS—All resist techniques are based on the principles of folding or covering. In the first case, parts of the fabric or yarn itself serve as resists; in the second, another material covers parts of the fabric.

ROPING—Plying fiber or yarn bundles into a rope. These may be looped at the outer end in the manner of a fringe.

RYA—The Finnish designation for a woven rug with a long, hand-knotted pile.

SATIN—One of three basic woven constructions (the other two are plain weave and twill) with long, regularly spaced floats on face and back.

SCAFFOLD WEFTING—An obscure, difficult technique used in a few cultures other than pre-Columbian Peru. Literally, a supplementary weft is used as a frame or scaffold to wind a small warp on. When this warp is interlaced with weft, the scaffold is removed.

SELVAGE (literally, self-edge)—In a woven cloth, the warpwise edges at which the weft wraps around the outermost warps as it reenters the web. The selvages prevent raveling. A few handwoven cloths, especially those woven on a frame or backstrap loom, have horizontal selvages as well, and so are four-selvaged.

SETT (also set)—Usually refers to the disposition of the warp ends in the dents of the reed, determining the density of the cloth. Cloth sett includes the closeness of the weft as well.

SHAPED WEAVING—Cloth in which the selvages are not parallel but angled or curved, usually achieved by relaxing warp tension and pulling in on the weft yarn.

SHED—The space between sets of warp ends made by the raising or lowering of harnesses, so that the filling can be passed through.

SINGLE-ELEMENT—Fabric constructions based on a single component or set of components; typical are knitting, crochet, knotting, and—in braiding—a single set of elements.

SOUMAK—A technique of wrapping wefts around two or more warp ends to produce a surface similar to chain stitch.

STRAIGHT DRAW—In weaving, warp repeatedly threaded in progression such as a 1, 2, 3, 4.

TAPESTRY—Any of several free weaving techniques for joining (or separating) wefts that are horizontally adjacent. In slit tapestry the separation is made by consistently turning the wefts around adjacent warp ends so as to produce a vertical slit. A tapestry is a fabric woven with tapestry joinings.

TEXTILE—A woven fabric with two or more sets of elements.

TURK'S CAP—A spherical form plaited with a single element, usually of rope and connected with maritime trades.

TURNED 90°—Term applied to a finished piece hung with the warp not vertical as woven, but horizontal.

TRITIK—The needle technique of stitching through the cloth a thread or bast element which is then drawn so tightly that the resulting folds resist dye penetration and produce a line of undyed dots.

TWILL—A basic weave in which the filling yarns pass over one or more and under two or more warp yarns in successive progression to create the appearance of diagonal lines.

TWINING—A construction older than weaving which is based on twisting pairs of elements. Weft twining involves a warp plus pairs of wefts. Warp twining may have a weft or be single-element (sprang). Twining is one of the three basic techniques of basketry.

WARP—In woven cloth, the lengthwise or vertical element that is threaded into the loom. The warp is composed of many yarns, individually called "ends."

WARP-FACE—Cloth in which the warp or vertical element dominates over the weft.

WEB—While still on the loom, the woven cloth resulting from the interlacing of warp and weft.

WEFT—Horizontal or crosswise element(s) in woven cloth; also called filling (see also *pick*).

WRAPPING—Refers to spiral winding, in which one yarn element is wound around another element or core.

REFERENCE NOTES

Chapter 1

1. D'HARNONCOURT, René, Director, The Museum of Modern Art, New York, 1949–1968. Discussion at an informal acquisitions committee meeting in the 1960's at which Mildred Constantine was present.

2. ROSENBERG, Harold, "The Art World," *New Yorker,* p. 103, February 20, 1978.

3. ALLOWAY, Lawrence, "The Artist Count: In Praise of Plenty," *Art in America,* September–October 1977.

4. ALLOWAY, Lawrence, Letter to Mildred Constantine, April 9, 1978.

5. PEVSNER, Nikolaus, *Pioneers of Modern Design,* The Museum of Modern Art, New York, 1949, pp. 18, 19.

6. BAUHAUS, Weimar, Germany 1919–1925.
   BAUHAUS, Dessau, Germany 1925–1928.

7. COHEN, Arthur A., *Sonia Delaunay,* Harry N. Abrams Inc., New York, pp. 80–81.

8. Wright's respect for crafts was manifest in his inclusion of weaving and pottery studios in Taliesin West and in his plan for an arts and crafts school. (Wright, Frank Lloyd, *Manifesto,* 1932.)

9. "Good Design" exhibitions, directed by Edgar Kaufmann, Jr., The Museum of Modern Art, 1949–55.

10. "Textiles U.S.A.," exhibition, The Museum of Modern Art, 1956.

11. SLIVKA, Rose, "American Craft," *American Craft Council,* New York, June/July 1979, p. 88.

12. BILLETER, Erika, Catalogue for *Claire Zeisler—A Retrospective,* The Art Institute of Chicago, 1979, p. 9.

13. TAYLOR, Joshua C., *America As Art,* National Collection of Fine Arts, Smithsonian Institution Press, Washington, D.C., 1976, p. 289.

14. LURCAT, Jean, Catalogue for the *1re Biennale Internationale de la Tapisserie,* Musee Cantonal des Beaux-Arts, Lausanne, Switzerland, 1962, p. 8.

15. TUCKER, William, "The Road to Tirgu Jiu," *Art in America,* New York, November/December 1976, pp. 96–101.

16. GIEDION-WELCKER, Carola, *Constantin Brancusi,* Schwabe Publishers, Basel, Switzerland, 1958.

Chapter 2

1. *Beyond Craft,* Fabrics International 1960; Lenore Tawney 1962; Woven Forms 1963; Wallhangings 1969.

2. WIGHT, FREDERICK S., Catalogue for *Deliberate Entanglements,* published by UCLA Art Galleries, University of California, Los Angeles, 1971.

3. Description of plates
   p. 42
   ALICIA PENALBA   France
   Chuchicamata
   tapestry; sisal, cotton, plastic
   142" × 55" × 15"
   Collection: Mobilier National, Paris
   MASAKASU KOBAYASHI   Japan
   W³–W To The Third Power
   plain weave; vinylon
   118" × 71" × 39"
   DEBBE MOSS   U.S.A.
   Fiber Tile Wall
   crochet; wool
   61" × 81" × 10"

RENATA BONFANTI   Italy
Algeria 5
discontinuous weft brocade; wool, hemp, cotton
75" × 67"
LENORE TAWNEY   U.S.A.
Waters Above the Firmament
slit tapestry, collage; linen, paper, pigment
153" × 144"
WARREN SEELIG   U.S.A.
Triple Planar Fold 2
plain weave, folded; cotton
56" × 84"
GERHARDT G. KNODEL   U.S.A.
Act 8
resist dyeing, fabrication; silk, nylon
94" × 118" × 169"
MARIYO YAGI   Japan
Gen Ou- B
roping, plying; hemp and aluminum
66" × 68" × 4"
JEAN STAMSTA   U.S.A.
Tarzan's Rope
crochet; wool and synthetics
472" × 10"
JAGODA BUIC   Yugoslavia
Variabil Noir
tapestry; sisal, goat hair
138" × 256" 7 units
SHERRI SMITH   U.S.A.
Overhang
waffleweave; mohair
89" × 94" × 11"
OLGA DE AMARAL   Colombia
Equilibrio en Rojo y Azul
wrapping, double weave; horsehair, wool
91" × 75" × 6"
p. 43
SHEILA HICKS   U.S.A.   (lives in Paris)
Reprisage Repetoire
darning, stitching; silk, linen, wool, cotton
177" × 354" (3 units)
HILDA SCHREIER   Canada
Triangle 2
knotting, wrapping; sisal
177" × 98" × 39"

4. LEE, Sherman E., *Fiberworks,* published by The Cleveland Museum of Art, 1977. Foreword to catalogue.

5. *Structuur in Textiel,* Stedelijk Museum, Amsterdam, 1976.

6. *Weich und Plastich* (Soft Art), Kunsthaus, Zurich, 1979.

Chapter 3

1. CAMPBELL, Pat, excerpt from *Statement of Concerns,* May 9, 1979.

2. Description of plates on pp. 152–53.
   Pyramid #6: Hand-formed paper (rag and pernambuco), hawthorne wood, raffia, New Zealand fleece, owl and emu feathers.
   Manuscript #12: Hand formed rag paper, New Zealand fleece, hawthorne wood, raffia, silk, beads.
   Oblation #1: Hand formed rag paper, hawthorne wood, glass beads, raffia.
   Manuscript #11: Hand formed rag paper, New Zealand fleece, hawthorne wood, raffia, silk and linen thread.
   Shadow Oblation: Hand formed rag paper, hawthorne wood, silk and linen thread, leather.
   Letter Bundle #4: Rag and composite hand formed paper, hawthorne wood, raffia, New Zealand fleece, ink and colored pencils.

Ancient Tide/1932: Hawthorne wood, rag paper formed directly on wood structure, spun gampi paper, carved bone, ink, pastel, linen, silk thread.

Blue Line Bundle: Handmade paper (linen), hawthorne wood, metallic thread, rag paper formed directly on knotted element, silk and linen thread.

Curtain/Olio/Act Six: Handmade rag paper, spun gampi paper, hawthorne wood, carved bone, silk, colored pencil, ink.

3. Excerpt from letter to Jack Lenor Larsen, November 9, 1976.
4. PINCUS-WITTEN, Robert "Winsor Knots: the Sculpture of Jackie Winsor," *Arts Magazine,* New York, June 1977, pp. 127–133.
5. BUHLER, Alfred, *The Dyer's Art, ikat, batik, plangi,* Van Nostrand Reinhold, 1976.
6. SCHIRA, Cynthia, excerpt from letter to Jack Lenor Larsen.

Chapter 4

1. Letter to Mildred Constantine, January 12, 1980.
2. Symposium held at The Museum of Modern Art, New York, 1951.
3. LARSEN, Jack Lenor, from "Fiber Works in Miniature," *Craft Horizons,* February 1975.
4. ODDY, Revel, Introduction to catalogue of *1st International Exhibition of Miniature Textiles,* September 1974.

Chapter 5

1. BIRD, Junius, Introductory Comments excerpted from "Technology and Art in Peruvian Textiles," Lecture at the Museum of Primitive Art, New York, 1963, in *Motive,* November 1965, p. 22.
2. ALBERS, Anni, *On Weaving,* Wesleyan University Press; Middletown, Conn., 1965, p. 15.
3. Statement on "Pressed Twills," March 1980.
4. Letter to Jack Lenor Larsen, April 30, 1979.
5. Excerpt from statement in *Structuur in Textiel,* Stedelijk Museum, Amsterdam, 1977.
6. Excerpt from Lenore Tawney: *A Personal World,* Brookfield Craft Center, Conn., 1978.

Chapter 6

1. Excerpt from statement to Mildred Constantine, July 14, 1979.
2. Letter to Mildred Constantine, July 17, 1979.

Chapter 7

1. ABAKANOWICZ, Magdalena, *Organic Structures,* Malmö Konsthall, 1977, p. 37.
2. HICKS, Sheila, *Buttonhole 2,* Paris, July 1978.
3. AL-HILALI, excerpt.
4. FRANKENSTEIN, Alfred, "Report from California, Christo's Fence Beauty or Betrayal," *Art in America,* November/December, 1976.
5. Letter to Jack Lenor Larsen, September 12, 1976.
6. Letter to Mildred Constantine, September 24, 1979.

BIBLIOGRAPHY

Works Consulted or Cited

Books

ALBERS, ANNI. *On Designing.* New Haven, Connecticut: Pellango Press, 1959.

————. *On Weaving.* Middletown, Connecticut: Wesleyan University Press, 1965.

Art Nouveau. Edited by Mildred Constantine and Peter Selz. New York: The Museum of Modern Art, 1959.

Bauhaus 1919–1928. Edited by Herbert Bayer. New York: The Museum of Modern Art, 1938.

BEUTLICH, TADEK. *The Technique of Woven Tapestry.* New York: Watson Guptill, 1971.

CASSOU, JEAN, LANGUI, EMIL, and PEVSNER, NIKOLAUS. *Gateway to the 20th Century.* New York: McGraw-Hill, 1962.

COHEN, ARTHUR A. *Sonia Delaunay.* New York: Harry N. Abrams Inc., 1975.

CONSTANTINE, MILDRED and LARSEN, JACK LENOR. *Beyond Craft: The Art Fabric.* New York: Van Nostrand Reinhold, 1973.

EMERY, IRENE. *The Primary Structures of Fabrics, An Illustrated Classification.* Washington, D.C.: The Textile Museum, 1966.

D'HARCOURT, RAOUL. *Textiles of Ancient Peru and Their Techniques.* Edited by Grace G. Denny and Carolyn Osborne; translated by Sadie Brown. Seattle: University of Washington Press, 1962.

KUENZI, ANDRE. *La Nouvelle Tapisserie.* Geneve: Les Editions de Bonvent, 1973.

LARSEN, JACK LENOR. *The Dyer's Art, ikat, batik, plangi.* With Alfred Bühler, Bronwen & Garrett Solyom. New York: Van Nostrand Reinhold, 1976.

LARSEN, JACK LENOR with JEANNE WEEKS, *Fabrics For Interiors, A Guide For Architects, Designers, and Consumers.* New York: Van Nostrand Reinhold, 1975.

PEVSNER, NIKOLAUS. *Pioneers of Modern Design.* New York: The Museum of Modern Art, 1949.

ROSSBACH, ED. *Baskets as Textile Art.* New York: Van Nostrand Reinhold, 1973.

WIEBEL, ADELE COULIN. *Two Thousand Years of Textiles.* New York: Pantheon Books, 1952.

Weich und Plastich (Soft Art) Zurich: Kunsthaus, 1979.

WINGLER, HANS M. *The Bauhaus.* Cambridge, Massachusetts, and London, England: MIT Press, 1969.

Catalogues and Periodicals

BIENNALE INTERNATIONALE DE LA TAPISSERIE. Catalogues of the exhibitions. Lausanne, 1962, 1965, 1967, 1969, 1971, 1973, 1975, 1977, 1979.

DELIBERATE ENTANGLEMENTS. Catalogue of the exhibition at the UCLA Art Galleries. University of California, Los Angeles, 1971.

FABRICS INTERNATIONAL. An exhibition catalogue reprinted from *Craft Horizons.* New York, September–October, 1961.

FIBERWORKS. Foreword to catalogue. Published by The Cleveland Museum of Art, 1977.

LES ANNEES "25." Catalogue published by Musée des Arts Decoratifs. Paris, 1966.

PERSPECTIEF IN TEXTIEL. Catalogue of the exhibition at the Stedelijk Museum. Amsterdam, 1969.

SLIVKA, ROSE. *American Craft,* American Craft Council. New York, June/July 1979, p. 88.

STRUCTUUR IN TEXTIEL. Stedelijk Museum. Amsterdam 1976.

LENORE TAWNEY: A PERSONAL WORLD, Brookfield Craft Center. Connecticut, 1978.

WALL HANGINGS. Catalogue of the exhibition at The Museum of Modern Art. New York, 1969.

BIOGRAPHIES

Abbreviations:

BIT *Biennale Internationale de Tapisserie, Lausanne*
IEMT *International Exhibition of Miniature Textiles, London*

ABAKANOWICZ, Magdalena   Poland   b. 1930
Studied at Fine Arts Academy, Warsaw. Associate Professor, Fine Arts Academy, 1965 to present. 38 one-person exhibitions since 1960. Exhibitions: BIT, all since 1962; Bienal of Art, São Paulo, Brazil; Biennale of Art, Venice, 1965; "Wallhangings," The Museum of Modern Art, N.Y., 1969; "Perspectief in Textiel," Stedelijk Museum, Amsterdam, 1969; "Experiencias Artistico Textiles," Museo Español de Arte Contemporaneo, Madrid, 1971; "Soft Sculptures," Camden Art Centre, London; Edinburgh Festival of Arts, Edinburgh, 1971, 1972; "Deliberate Entanglements," Art Galleries, Univ. of California, Los Angeles, 1971–72; "Textile Objekte," Kunstgewerbemuseum, Berlin, 1975; "Fiber Works:Europe and Japan," Kyoto and Tokyo, 1976; "Fiberworks," The Cleveland Museum of Art, Cleveland, 1977; "Weich und Plastisch," Zurich, 1979. Collections: Museums in Warsaw, Lodz, Poznan, Slupsk, Poland; Amsterdam, Haarlem, Holland; Mannheim, Dortmund, Germany; São Paulo, Brazil; Lund, Stockholm, Göteborg, Malmö, Sweden; Zurich, La Chaux-de-Fon, Lausanne, Switzerland; Oslo, Norway; Prague, Czechoslovakia; The Museum of Modern Art, N.Y.; Detroit Institute of Art, Mich.; AT&T, Basking Ridge, N.J.; Sydney, Australia; Kyoto Japan. Awards: Gold Medal, VIII São Paulo Bienal of Art, 1965; Prize, Polish Minister of Culture, 1965; Prize, Polish Minister of Foreign Affairs, 1970; State Prize, 1972; Doctor Honoris Causa, Royal College of Art, London, 1974; Prix Herder, Univ. of Vienna, 1977.

ALBERS, Anni   U.S.A.   b. 1899, Germany
Studied at Bauhaus, Weimar and Dessau, 1922–30. Assistant Professor of Art, Black Mountain College, N.C., 1933–49. One-person Exhibitions: Baltimore Museum of Art, Md.; Bauhaus-Archiv, Berlin; Carnegie Institute, Pittsburgh; Colorado Springs Fine Arts Center; Contemporary Arts Museum, Houston; Honolulu Academy of Arts; Kunstmuseum der Stadt Dusseldorf; Massachusetts Institute of Technology, Cambridge; The Museum of Modern Art, N.Y.; Wadsworth Atheneum, Hartford; Yale Univ. Art Gallery, New Haven; Brooklyn Museum, N.Y.; Katonah Gallery, N.Y.; Queens College Library, N.Y.; Monmouth Museum, Monmouth; University of Hartford, Conn. Collections: Art Institute of Chicago; Baltimore Museum of Art; Bauhaus-Archiv, Berlin; Busch-Reisinger Museum, Cambridge, Mass.; Cranbrook Academy of Art, Bloomfield Hills, Mich.; The Currier Gallery of Art, Manchester, N.H.; The Jewish Museum, N.Y.; The Johnson Wax Collection, Racine, Wisc.; Kunstgewerbemuseum, Zurich; Kunsthalle Nuremberg; The Metropolitan Museum of Art, N.Y.; The Museum of Modern Art, N.Y.; Neue Sammlung Museum, Munich; Stadtische Kunstsammlungen, Darmstadt, Germany; Victoria and Albert Museum, London; Yale Univ. Art Gallery, New Haven. Has devoted many years to graphic work and has shown throughout the U.S.A. and abroad. Awards: Honorary Degree of Doctor of Fine Arts, University of Hartford, Conn., 1979; Medal of American Institute of Architects in the Field of Craftsmanship, 1961; Citation, Philadelphia Museum College of Art, 1962; Tamarind Lithography Workshop Fellowship, 1964; DABA Citation, The Decorative Arts Book Award, 1965; Degree, Doctor of Fine Arts, Honoris Causa, The Maryland Institute College of Art, 1972; Degree, Doctor of Laws, Honoris Causa, York Univ., Toronto, Ontario, 1973; Degree, Honorary Degree of Doctor of Fine Arts, Philadelphia College of Art, 1976; Degree, Honorary Degree of Doctor·of Fine Arts, Univ. of Hartford, 1979.

AL-HILALI, Neda   U.S.A.   b. 1938, Czechoslovakia
Studied at Univ. of California, Los Angeles, M.A. Exhibitions: "Deliberate Entanglements," Los Angeles, 1971; "Sculpture in Fiber," Museum of Contemporary Crafts, N.Y., 1972; "Three Dimensional Fibre," Govett-Brewster Gallery, New Plymouth, New Zealand, 1974; The National Art Galleries in Wellington, Hamilton, Auckland, Christchurch, and Dunedin, Australia; "California Design '76," Pacific Design Center, Beverly Hills, Calif., 1976; Museum of Contemporary Art, Chicago; "Fiberworks," The Cleveland Museum of Art, 1977; "Fiber Works: Americas and Japan," Kyoto and Tokyo, Japan, 1977; "Current Directions in Southern California Art," Los Angeles Institute for Contemporary Art, 1978; 3rd Textile Triennale, Lodz, Poland; "Diverse Directions," Museum of Art, Washington State University, Pullman, Wash. Collections: Queen Elizabeth II Arts Council of New Zealand, New Plymouth; Johnson Collection of Contemporary Crafts; Marine Midland Center, Knox-Albright Collection, Buffalo, N.Y.; Tishman Corporation, Los Angeles, Calif.; Owens-Corning Collection, Bonaventure Hotel, Los Angeles, Calif.; Hyatt Regency, Chicago; Security Pacific National Bank (numerous branches); Bank of San Antonio, Texas; Shaklee Corporation, San Francisco, Calif.; Uniplan Corporation, Burlingame, Calif.; Itel Corporation, San Francisco, Calif.; Bank of California, San Francisco, Calif.; North Western National Bank, St. Paul. Minn.; Centralny Muzeum Wlokiennictwa, Lodz, Poland.

de AMARAL, Olga   Colombia   b. 1932
Studied at Colegio Mayor of Cundinamarca; Cranbrook Academy of Art, Mich. Taught at each of these institutions as well as at Haystack Mountain School of Crafts, Maine; Penland School of Crafts, N.C.; San Jose State College, Calif.; Arts and Crafts, Berkeley, Calif. One-person exhibitions since 1958 in major cities internationally. Exhibitions: "Wallhangings," The Museum of Modern Art, N.Y., 1969; 1973 Trienalle, Milan; 1975, 1977 BIT; "Fiberworks," The Cleveland Museum of Art, 1977; "Fiber Works:Americas and Japan," Kyoto and Tokyo, 1977; "Deliberate Entanglements," Univ. of California, Los Angeles, 1971. Collections: Dreyfus Corp., N.Y.; Regency Hyatt House, Chicago, Ill.; First National City Bank, Chicago, Ill.; Embarcadero Center, San Francisco, Calif.; Fort Worth National Bank, Texas; Museo de Arte Moderno, Bogota, Colombia; The Chicago Art Institute; Peachtree Plaza Hotel, Atlanta, Ga.; Omaha Public Library, Nebr. Award: First Prize, III Biennal, Medellin, Colombia.

AMAT, Frederic   Spain   b. 1952
Studied architecture and scenography. One-person Exhibitions: Galeria Trece, Basle, Switzerland and Barcelona, Spain, 1979; Museo P.A., Monterey, Mexico, 1978; Museo Regional De Oaxaca, Mexico, 1978; Galeria Ponce, Mexico, 1978; "Homage to Joan Miro," Mallorca, 1977; Galeria Juana Mordo, Madrid, 1977; Galeria Harry Janlovici, Paris, 1976; Galeria Trece, Barcelona, 1976; Petita Galeria, Lerida, Spain, 1972; Galeria Redor, Madrid, 1972; Galeria Aquitania, Barcelona, 1971; Galeria Trece, Barcelona, 1970. Exhibitions: "L'Avaguardia Catalana Contemporanea," Museos de Viaregio and Pistoia, Italy, 1979; "Artists Catalans" Centre Georges Pompidou, Musée National d'Art Moderne, Paris, 1978; "Pintura Española Contemporanea," Foundation Galouste Gulbenkian, Lisbon, 1978; "Amnistia Drets Humans Art," Foundation Joan Miro, Barcelona, 1976; "Primera Antologia Catalana de l'Art i l'Object," Foundation Joan Miro, Barcelona, 1976; "23 Artistas Catalanes," Galeria Ponce, Mexico, 1975; "Ultima Pintura Catalana," Gallery Juan Mas, Barcelona, 1975; "Grafica Española Contemporanea," Buenas Aires, 1975; "Ma de Pintura," Colegio de Arquitectos, Barcelona, 1971. Performances: "Accio Zero," Gallery Juana Mordo, Madrid; Teatre Lliure, Barcelona; Cunningham Studio, N.Y., 1979; "Accio U," Grand Palais, Paris, 1976.

ANDERSON, Jan   U.S.A.   b. 1952
Studied at Univ. of California, Los Angeles, M.F.A. 1979.
Taught at Univ. of California, Los Angeles, Art Dept.,
Teaching Associate 1978–79, Teaching Assistant, 1977–1978.
Scholarships: Handweavers Guild of America Scholarship,
1978; Univ. of California, Los Angeles Dean's Discretionary
Scholarship, 1977.

ANDERSON, Marilyn   U.S.A.   b. 1941
Studied at Occidental College, Los Angeles, Calif., B.A. 1963,
Psychology; School of Theology at Clarement, Calif., M.Th.,
1968, thesis in European church history; M.A. in Histeri-
ography, California State College, Los Angeles; also studied
with Neda Al-Hilali at Univ. of California, Los Angeles. Exhibi-
tions: Fairtree Gallery, N.Y., 1972; Fiberworks, Berkeley, 1977;
Los Angeles Municipal Art Gallery, 1978; Riverside Museum,
Collaborative installation with Neda Al-Hilali, Maryann
Glantz, and John Garrett, Dunaway O'Neill Gallery, Los
Angeles, 1979. Awards: 1977, 1979 N.E.A. Fellowship.

ASHBY, Mary   U.S.A   b. 1937
Studied at Oberlin College, Ohio, B.A. 1959; Simmons Col-
lege, School of Library Science, Boston, Mass., M.S. 1978.
Teaches at Brookfield Craft Center, Brookfield, Conn. and
Wadsworth Atheneum, Hartford, Conn., 1969 to present.

BANDIERA, Cerantola, Marisa   Italy   b. 1934
Studied at Fine Arts Academy, Venice, Diploma. Exhibitions:
1973, 1975, 1977, 1979 BIT; "Structuur in Textiel," Stedelijk
Museum, Amsterdam, 1977. Collection: Museum de la
Tapisserie de Lausanne.

BASSLER, Jim   U.S.A.   b. 1933
Studied at Univ. of California, Los Angeles, M.A. 1969. Assis-
tant Professor of Art, Univ. of California, Los Angeles; taught at
1974, 1975, 1976 Workshop in Sante Fe, N.M.; 1974
Workshop, San Diego State Univ.; 1972 Workshop, Cranbrook
Academy of Art; 1972 Workshop, Los Angeles Handweaver
Assoc.; 1972 Workshop, National Handweavers Assoc., Detroit,
Mich. Exhibitions: "Transformation: UCLA Alumni in Fiber,"
1979; The Dyer's Art, N.Y., 1976.

BEUTLICH, Tadek   Great Britain   b. 1922, Poland
Studied in Poland, Germany and at the Sir John Cass School of
Art and Camberwell School of Arts and Crafts, England.
Taught weaving at Camberwell, 1951–74. Exhibitions: 1963,
1967, 1969, 1972, 1974, Grabowski Gallery, London; 1967 BIT;
Smithsonian Institution, Washington, D.C., 1970; Los
Angeles, 1971; Denver Art Museum, 1972; Victoria and Albert
Museum, London 1973; IEMT 1974, 1976, 1978.

BIRSTINS, Inese   Canada   b. 1942, Latvia
Studied at Sydney University, Australia, B.A. 1963. Working in
fiber art and jewelry since 1973. Participant in Fibre Interchange, Banff Centre for the Arts, Alberta, 1979. Teaching
weaving and design in Vancouver since 1965. Curator of the
Minotaur Studio Gallery, 1977–1978. One-person Exhibition:
Place des Arts, Vancouver, 1978. Exhibitions: "Habitat," Vancouver, 1976; Capilano College, Vancouver; The Fraser Valley
College and other public galleries in British Columbia. Collections: External Affairs Collection, Ottawa; private collections in
Canada, U.S.A., Australia, and Germany.

BOHDZIEWICZ, Emilia   Poland   b. 1941
Studied at Academy of Fine Arts in Warsaw (Interior Architecture). Now painting and working in tapestry. Exhibitions: 1977,
1979 BIT.

BOOM, Harry   Holland   b. 1945
Studied at Academie Voor Beeldende Kinst St. Joost, Breda,
1963–68; Akademie Sztuk Pieknych, Warsaw, 1963–69.
Teaches at Akademie voor Beeldende Kunst, Enschede; Guest
Teacher at several academies of art in the Netherlands and

elsewhere, 1974. Collection: Bank Giro, Amsterdam; Villa,
Bergen op Zoom; Verzameling van het Rijk, The Hague; Dege-
meente Hengelo, Hengelo; Licht Rekleme van Herk, Krimpen
a/d Y sel; Rotterdamse Kunst Stichting, Rotterdam.

BOSSCHER, Madeleine   Holland   b. 1942
Studied at Akademie voor Industriele Vormgeving, Eindhoven.
Exhibitions: Stedelijk Museum, Amsterdam, 1972; 1973 BIT;
1976 IEMT; "Structuur in Textiel," Stedelijk Museum,
Amsterdam, 1977; "Wallhangings: The New Classicism," The
Museum of Modern Art, N.Y., 1977. Collections: Stedelijk
Museum, Amsterdam; Hedendaagse Kunst, Utrecht.

BRANCUSI, Constantin   Romania (lived in Paris)
1876–1957
Trained in local carpentry school; awarded scholarship to Art
Academy, Bucharest. Arrived in Paris 1904, where he remained
for the rest of his life. His work has had a profound effect on the
development of modern sculpture and is represented in major
museums throughout the world.

BRANDFORD, Joanne Segal   U.S.A.   b. 1933
Studied at Univ. of California, Berkeley, M.A. 1969, Decorative
Arts; B.A. 1955, Design. Taught at Montclair State College,
Upper Montclair, N.J., 1979; Fiberworks Center for the Textile
Arts, Berkeley, Calif., 1977; Rhode Island School of Design,
Providence, R.I. 1977; Wheelock College, Boston, Mass.
1975–76; Radcliffe Seminars, Cambridge, Mass. 1972–76;
Massachusetts College of Art, Boston, Mass. 1971–74; Cam-
bridge Center for Adult Education, Cambridge, Mass. 1970–72;
Project, Inc., Cambridge, Mass. 1970–72; Univ. of California,
Berkeley, 1967–69. Exhibitions: Herbert F. Johnson Museum,
Ithaca, N.Y.; "The Dyer's Art," Museum of Contemporary
Crafts, N.Y. Awards: Research Fellow in Textile Arts, Peabody
Museum of Archaeology and Ethnology, Harvard Univ., Cam-
bridge, Mass., 1972–78; Fellow of the Radcliffe Institute, Cam-
bridge, Mass., 1971–1973.

BRENNAND-WOOD, Michael   Great Britain   b. 1952
Studied at Bolton College of Art and Design, 1969–72; Embroidery, Manchester Polytechnic B.A. 1975; Embroidery, Birmingham Polytechnic M.A. 1976. Part-time Lecturer, Em-
broidery/Textiles, Goldsmith College, University of London
1977 to present. Exhibitions: Peterloo Gallery, Manchester,
1975, 1976, 1977; 1978 IEMT. Collections: Metropolitan
Borough of Wigan; Ilkestone County Law Courts, Derbyshire.

BUIC, Jagoda   Yugoslavia   b. 1930
Studied at Academy of Applied Arts, Zagreb; later in Rome and
Vienna. Since 1965 one-person exhibitions in museums in Split,
Dubrovnik, Belgrade, Ljubljana, Buenos Aires, Paris,
Bordeaux, Nantes, São Paulo, Stockholm, Dusseldorf, Amster-
dam, Rosc, Dubin. Exhibitions: 1965 to 1977 BIT; 1976 IEMT;
"Wallhangings," The Museum of Modern Art, N.Y., 1969;
"Fiberworks," The Cleveland Museum of Art, 1976. Collec-
tions: Museums in Zagreb, Sarajevo, Split, Amsterdam,
Lausanne, Nuremberg, Paris, Bordeaux, Stockholm; AT&T,
Basking Ridge, N.J.; John Deere, Ill.; Kennedy Center,
Washington, D.C.; Dreyfus, N.Y. Awards: Silver Medal, Trien-
nale Milan, 1955; 1979 Grand Prix of the XIII Bienal de São
Paulo; 1976 Prix Herder, University of Vienna.

CAMPBELL, Patricia   U.S.A.   b. 1943
Studied at Cranbrook Academy of Art, Bloomfield Hills, Mich.
M.F.A. 1978; Fashion Institute of Technology, N.Y., 1971–73;
1969–71 Univ. of Georgia, Athens, Ga., M.F.A. 1971, Fabric
Design; 1961–65 Colby College, Waterville, Maine, B.A.
Degree in Art History, 1965. Taught at Tyler College of Art,
Temple Univ., Philadelphia, Pa., 1977, 1978, 1979;
Philadelphia College of Art, Philadelphia, Pa., 1978; Kansas
City Art Institute, Kansas City, Mo., 1973–76; Peace Corps,
Paraiba, Brazil, 1966–68. Collections: Hyatt Regency Hotel,
Memphis; H&R Block National Headquarters, Kansas City.

CARAU-ISCHI, Marguerite   Switzerland   b. 1928
Self-taught weaver. One-person Exhibition: Hadler-Rodriquez
Gallery, N.Y., 1979. Exhibitions: "Wallhangings," The
Museum of Modern Art, N.Y., 1969; "Perspectif in Textiel,"
Stedelijk Museum, Amsterdam, 1969; Nice; Paris; The Hague;
1967, 1969, 1971, 1979 BIT.

CESAR (Baldaccini)   France   b. 1924
Studied at the Ecole Beaux-Arts, Marseille. Has exhibited in the
United States, in South America, in Japan, in the 1957 São
Paulo Bienal, "Documenta," Kassel, 1969, "Weich und
Plastisch," Zurich, 1979.

CHAPNICK, Karen   U.S.A. (Lives in Canada)   b. 1950
Studied at Univ. of California, Los Angeles, M.A. 1976. Exhibi-
tions: "Emerging Artists," Master of Arts Exhibition, Frederick
S. Wight Gallery, Univ. of California, Los Angeles, 1979;
"Selections from Design '76," The Allrich Gallery, San Fran-
cisco, Calif. 1978; "Nora Blanck and Karen Chapnick: A
Presentation of Current Work" (two-person show), Surrey Art
Gallery, Surrey, B.C.; "Transformation: UCLA Alumni in
Fiber," University of Calif., Los Angeles, 1979; 1979 BIT; "Na-
tional Miniature Fiber Exhibition," Sante Fe, N.M. Commis-
sions and Collections: U.S. Government General Services Ad-
ministration, Federal Building, Oklahoma City, Okla.; The
Canada Council Art Bank, Art Collection of the Canadian
Government, Ottawa, Ontario; Fluor Corp., Irvine, Calif.;
Shiley Laboratories, Irvine, Calif.; Arthur Elrod Associates,
Palm Springs, Calif. Award: Grant from the Canada Council,
1979.

CHRISTO (Javacheff)   U.S.A.   b. 1935, Bulgaria
Studied at Fine Arts Academy, Sofia 1952-56; work-study at
the Burian Theatre, Prague. Exhibitions: First "Packages" and
"Wrapped Objects," Paris, 1958; "Packaging of a Public
Building," "Stacked Oil Drums," and "Dockside Packages,"
Cologne Harbor, 1961; "Iron Curtain-Wall of Oil Drums,"
Paris, 1962; "Stacked Oil Drums," Gentilly, 1962; "Wrapping
a Girl," London 1962; "Showcases," 1963; "Store Fronts,"
U.S.A., 1964; "Air Package" and "Wrapped Tree," Stedelijk
van Abbemuseum, Eindhover, 1966; "42,390 Cubic Feet
Package," Walker Art Center, Minneapolis School of Art, 1966;
"Packed Fountain" and "Packed Medieval Tower," Spoleto,
1968; "Packed Kunsthalle," Berne, 1968; "5,600 Cubic Meters
Package," for Documenta 4, Kassel, 1968; "Project for a
Wrapped Coast," 1968; "1,240 Oil Drums Mastaba,"
Philadelphia Institute of Contemporary Art, 1968; "Packed
Museum of Contemporary Art," Chicago, 1969; "Wrapped
Floor," 2,800 square feet drop cloths, Museum of Contem-
porary Art, Chicago, 1969; "Wrapped Coast-Little Bay-One
Million Square Feet," Sidney, Australia, 1969; Project for
"Valley Curtain," Colo., 1971; "Valley Curtain, Grand
Hogback, Rifle, Colorado," 1971-72; Project for "Running
Fence," California, 1973; "The Wall," wrapped Roman wall,
Rome, 1974; "Ocean Front," New Port, R.I. 1974; "Running
Fence, Sonoma and Marin Counties, California, 1976.

CLAYDEN, Marian   Great Britain (Lives in California)
b. 1937, England
Studied at Kesleven College, England, 1955-57; Nottingham
School of Art, England, 1957-59; self-taught in resist dyeing
technique. Exhibitions: "Fabric Vibrations," Museum of Con-
temporary Crafts, N.Y., 1972; "In Praise of Hands," World
Crafts Council, Toronto, 1973; San Diego Art Museum, Calif.
1973; "California Design '76," Pacific Design Center, Los
Angeles, 1976; "Fiber Structures," Museum of Art, Carnegie
Institute, Pittsburgh, 1976; "The Dyer's Art," Museum, 1976;
"Diverse Directions," Museum of Art, Washington State
Univ., Pullman, Wash. 1978. Collections: San Jose State Univ.,
Calif.; Cooper-Hewitt Museum, Smithsonian Institution, N.Y.;
The Johnson Collection of Contemporary Crafts.

COLETTE   Tunis (lives in New York)   b. 1947
Has lived in New York since 1969. Studied painting and has ex-
hibited in New York as well as in countries of Europe (including
"Weich und Plastisch," Zurich, 1979) since 1970.

COLLINGWOOD, Peter   Great Britain   b. 1922
Qualified in medicine at St. Mary's Hospital Medical School,
1946; 1950, began training in the weaving studios of Ethel
Mairet, Barbara Sawyer and Allistair Morton; 1952, set up own
workshop in Highgate. Teaching visits to U.S.A. in 1962, 1964
and 1968. Exhibitions: Crafts Centre, London, 1964; Building
Centre, London, 1966; "Structuur in Textiel," Stedelijk
Museum, Amsterdam, 1977. Collections: City Art Gallery,
Bristol, and Victoria and Albert Museum, London. Award:
Gold Medal, International Handicrafts Exhibition, Munich,
1963.

COOK, Lia   U.S.A.   b. 1942
Studied at Univ. of California, Berkeley, M.A. 1973; Associate
Professor, Univ. of California, Davis; California College of Arts
and Crafts, Oakland. Exhibitions: 1973, 1975, 1977 BIT; 1976,
1978 IEMT; "Fiber Works: Americas and Japan," Kyoto and
Tokyo, 1977. Collections: AT&T, Basking Ridge, N.J.; 2 Embarcadero Center, San Francisco; Univ. of Texas, Austin; City
Hall, Fairfield, Calif. Awards: N.E.A. Fellowship, 1974, 1977,
1978.

COOPER, Rochella   U.S.A.   b. 1933, South Africa
Studied at Univ. of Cape Town, School of Music, B. Mus. 1954;
music student, Royal Academy of Music, London, 1955; since
1973 at Museum of Fine Arts School, Houston, Texas. Exhibitions: Contemporary Arts Museum, Texas; Abilene Museum,
1974; Gallery, Houston, 1975; "Weavers I," Houston, 1976;
Texas Craft Triennial, Dallas Museum of Fine Arts; 1977, 1978
IEMT.

COENEN, Linda   U.S.A.   b. 1947
Studied at Univ. of Wisconsin, B.A. 1969, Art Education; Art
Education, Florida State University, M.A. 1971. Exhibitions:
Stonybrook Museum, N.Y. 1978; "Intent '78 Fabrics," Edin-
boro, Pa.; Fall River 20th National Exhibition, Mass., 1978;
1978 IEMT.

DE BOER, Corrie   Holland   b. 1932
Studied at the Rietveld Academy, Amsterdam, 1953-57. Ex-
hibitions: Amsterdam, 1973; The Hague; Haarlem; Cologne;
Paris; 1975 BIT; 1978 IEMT. Collections: Stedelijk Museum,
Amsterdam; National Collection of the Netherlands; AT&T,
Basking Ridge, N.J.

DE LEY, Marijke   Holland   b. 1943
Studied at the Gerrit Rietveld Academy in Amsterdam,
1964-68. Co-assistant to the Benno Premsela design-team,
1969-74. Exhibitions: "Inter Decor," Netherlands; Frankfurt,
Germany; Euro Domus, Italy; "Interieur," Belgium; Vincent
van Gogh Museum, Amsterdam, 1976; "Total Design,"
Amsterdam, 1977; "Atelier 14," Stedelijk Museum, Amsterdam, 1977; 1978 Pieter Brattinga Print Gallerie, Amsterdam.

DEY, Kris   U.S.A.   b. 1949
Studied at Univ. of California, Los Angeles, M.F.A. 1976.
Teaching Associate in Design, Univ. of California, Los Angeles,
1974-76; Teaching Assistant in Design, Univ. of California, Los
Angeles, 1973. Exhibitions: "Emerging Artists," M.F.A. Ex-
hibition, Frederick S. Wight Gallery, Los Angeles, Calif., 1974;
"Tapestry and Other Fiber Forms," Fine Art Gallery; California
State Univ., Northridge; University Gallery, Univ. of North
Dakota, Grand Forks, 1975; Art Fabrics Gallery, Los Angeles,
Calif.; "Eight Soft Artists," Long Beach City College, Long
Beach, Calif., 1976; "California Design '76," Pacific Design
Center, Los Angeles, Calif., 1977; "Wallhangings: The New
Classicism," The Museum of Modern Art, N.Y., 1977; "Proto
Fibers," Lowe Art Gallery, Syracuse Univ., N.Y.; "California
Women in Crafts," Craft and Folk Art Museum, Los Angeles.

DI MARE, Dominic   U.S.A.   b. 1932
Self-taught. One-person Exhibitions: Braunstein Gallery, San Francisco, 1979; Florence Duhl Gallery, N.Y., 1977, 1978; Anneberg Gallery, San Francisco, 1973, 1975, 1979; Museum West, San Francisco, 1966; Museum of Contemporary Crafts, N.Y., 1965. Exhibitions: Milan Triennale, 1964; Museum of Contemporary Crafts, N.Y., 1966; "Objects USA," 1966; Vatican Museum, Rome, 1978; 1979 BIT; "Paper Sources," The Allrich Gallery, San Francisco, 1978; 1976, 1978 IEMT; "Object As Poet," Renwick Gallery, Smithsonian Institution, Washington, D.C., 1977; "Recent Media," Brooks Memorial Art Gallery, Memphis, Tenn., 1977; "Paper Art," Claremont College, Los Angeles, 1977; "Usable Art," Braunstein Gallery, San Francisco, 1977; "Handmade Paper Object," Santa Barbara Museum of Art, Calif., 1977; "American Crafts '76," Museum of Contemporary Art, Chicago, Ill., 1976; "California Design," Los Angeles, 1976. Collections: Museum of Contemporary Crafts, N.Y.; St. Paul Art Center, Minn.; Portland Art Museum, Oreg.; Brooks Memorial Art Gallery, Memphis, Tenn.; Johnson Wax; Collection Lannan Foundation, N.Y. and Fla. Award: N.E.A. Grant, 1977.

DZAMONJA, Dusan   Yugoslavia   b. 1928
One-person exhibitions since 1954 in Yugoslavia, Italy and Switzerland; XXXV Venice Biennal. Collections: The Museum of Modern Art, N.Y.; Tate Gallery, London; Galerie Nationale d'Art Moderne, Rome; Kunsthalle, Mannheim; Rijksmuseum Kroller-Muller, Otterlo; Museu National d'Art Moderne, São Paulo; Museum Boymans-van Beuningen, Rotterdam; Collection Peggy Guggenheim, Venice; Musée National d'Art Moderne, Prague; public collections in Yugoslavia. Awards: prizes in Yugoslavia; 1977 Rembrandt Prize, Goethe Foundation, Basle.

FERGUSON, Tamiko Kawata   U.S.A.   b. 1936, Japan
1956–66 worked in sculpture and product design in Japan. Now working as a jeweler.

FISCH, Arline   U.S.A.   b. 1931
Studied at Skidmore College, N.Y., B.S. 1952; Univ. of Illinois, M.A. 1954; School of Arts and Crafts, Copenhagen, Denmark, 1956–57; Apprentice School for Gold- and Silversmiths, Copenhagen, 1966–67. Professor of Art, San Diego State Univ., Calif. Exhibitions: "Californian Design," Los Angeles, 1976; Electrum Gallery, London; Florence Duhl Gallery, N.Y.; Basle, Switzerland; "Miniature Textiles," Melbourne, Australia; Southwest Missouri State Univ.; Museum of Contemporary Art, Chicago; Sheldon Memorial Art Gallery, Nebr.; Phoenix Art Museum, Seattle; Humboldt State Univ., Calif; Craft and Folk Art Museum, Los Angeles; Adelaide Festival Centre, Australia; International Jewelry Exhibition, Design Centre, Phillippines; "Trends 77," Jewelry Museum, Pforzheim. Collections: Museum of Contemporary Crafts, N.Y.; Minnesota Museum of Art; Worshipful Company of Goldsmiths, London; Johnson Wax Collection; Western Illinois Univ.

FRUYTIER, Wilhelmina   Holland   b. 1915
Self-taught. Exhibitions: 1974, 1976, 1978 IEMT; 1965, 1967, 1969 BIT; "Wallhangings," The Museum of Modern Art, N.Y., 1969; Museo de Arte Contemporaneo, Madrid, 1969. Public Collections and Buildings: KLM-hoofdkantoor, Amstelveen; Delta-Lloyd-hoofdkantoor, Amsterdam; Hotel Hilton-Schiphol and Nederlandse Bankhoofdkantoor, Amsterdam; CIBA/GEIGY-Nederland, Arnhem; New England Merchant National Bank, Boston; Technische Hogeschool, Delft; Technische Hogeschool, Eindhoven; Organisation Mondial de la Sante, Geneva; Crematorium Ockenburg and Ministerie van Economische Zaken, The Hague; PTT Collection; Rijkswaterstatt-hoofd-kantoor; Shell-hoofdkantoor; s'Hertogenbosch; Provinciehuis Noord Brabant; Rice University, Houston; Jutphaas, SKF, European Research Center; Rotterdam, Museum Boymans-van Beuningen; OGEM-hoofd-kantoor; Holland-

Amerika Lijn-s.s. Statendam; Bank of America, San Francisco; Stadhuis, Tilburg; SHV-hoofd-kantoor, Utrecht.

GARRETT, John   U.S.A.   b. 1950
Studied at Claremont Men's College, Calif. B.A. 1972; Univ. of California, Los Angeles, M.A. 1976. Teaches at Scripps College, Claremont, Calif. One-person Exhibitions: Riverside Art Center and Museum, Calif., 1976; Griswold's Art Gallery, Claremont, Calif., 1977. Exhibitions: "Master Fiber Works," Kansas City Art Institute, Mo., 1974; "Fine and Applied Fiber," Santa Barbara Art Institute, Calif., 1974; "Six Fiber Artists," Kaplan-Baumann Gallery, Los Angeles, 1975; "A Mano," New Mexico State Univ., Las Cruces, N.M., 1976; "Gallery Artists Plus," Kaplan-Baumann Gallery, Los Angeles, 1976; "From the Textile Tradition," Escondido Regional Art Center, Calif., 1977; Second Annual Textile Invitational, Weber State College, Ogden, Utah, 1978.

GILBERT, James R.   U.S.A.   b. 1949
Studied at Cranbrook Academy of Art, M.F.A. 1975. Collections: Renaissance Center, Detroit; The Edmonton Plaza Hotel, Edmonton, Alberta; Iowa State Univ.

GRAFFIN, Daniel   France   b. 1938
Studied at Ecole des Metiers d'Art, Paris, 1957; Polytechnic School of Art, London, 1958; Université d'El Azhar, Egypt, 1962–63. One-person Exhibitions: Gallery Suzy Langlois, Paris, 1974; Musée des Arts Decoratifs, Nantes, 1976; La Cite, Luxembourg Maison de la Culture, Rennes, 1976; Stedelijk Museum, Amsterdam, 1977; Allrich Gallery, San Francisco, 1979; 1974 IEMT; Galery Cora Devries, Amsterdam, 1975; 1973, 1975, 1977, 1979 BIT; "Fiber Works:Europe and Japan," Kyoto and Tokyo, 1976; "Fiberworks," The Cleveland Museum of Art, 1977; "Fil," Montreuil, 1978. Collections: Musée des Arts Decoratifs, Nantes; Stedelijk Museum, Amsterdam; AT&T, Basking Ridge, N.J.

GROSSEN, Françoise   Switzerland (lives in U.S.A.)   b. 1943
Studied textile design at Gewerbeschule, Basle; Univ. of California, Los Angeles, M.A. 1968. One-person Exhibitions: Jack L. Larsen, Inc., The Hadler Galleries, N.Y.; Bellerive Museum, Zurich; Reed College, Portland; 1973, 1975, 1977 BIT; 1974, 1976, 1978 IEMT; "Fiber Works:Americas and Japan," Kyoto and Tokyo, 1977. Represented in Hotel Hyatt Regency, O'Hare, Chicago; Embarcadero Center #1, San Francisco; Hotel Hyatt Regency, San Francisco; Bank of Texas, San Antonio; North Texas State Univ., Denton; Hotel Hyatt Regency, Montreal.

GUAY, Nancy Allen   U.S.A.   b. 1945
Studied at Haystack Mountain School, 1963–67; Univ. of Wisconsin, Madison, M.F.A. 1976. Studio assistant for Jack Lenor Larsen, N.Y. Exhibitions: "Reflections/Fiber," Wm. Underwood Co., 1979; "10 Boston Fiber Artists," Northeastern Univ., 1978; Skidmore College Invitational, Saratoga Springs, N.Y., 1978; Clark Gallery, Lincoln, Mass., 1978; "Contemporary Weaving," The Boston Athenaeum, 1977; "Wallhangings: The New Classicism," The Museum of Modern Art, N.Y., 1976. Represented in: Fidelity Group Renovation of New England Merchants Bank Bldg.; Boston Federal Home Loan Bank Board, Washington, D.C.; The United Nations, N.Y.; Ry-Co Corp., Hingham, Mass.; Calvary Lutheran Chapel, Madison, Wisc.; Flad and Associates, Architects, Madison, Wisc.; Offices Unlimited Incorporated, Boston; AT&T, N.J. Awards: Massachusetts Council on Arts and Humanities, Artists Foundation Fellowship, 1979; American-Scandinavian Foundation, 1975; grant from the Finnish Government, 1975; grant from the League of Finnish-American Societies, Helsinki, 1975; Dennis Award, Univ. of Wisconsin Crafts Show, 1974; Marguerite Mergentime Award for Textile Design, Skidmore College, 1967.

GUERMONPREZ, Trude   U.S.A.   19 ?-1975
Born in Austria. Studied at Municipal School of Arts, Halle,
Germany; Textile Engineering School, Berlin; also in Finland,
Sweden, and Czechoslovakia. Taught at Black Mountain Col-
lege, N.C., 1947–49; California College of Arts and Crafts,
Oakland; San Francisco Art Institute. Award: Gold Medal,
American Institute of Architects, 1970.

HALLMAN, H. Theodore   U.S.A. (lives in Toronto)
b. 1933
Studied at Tyler School of Fine Arts, Philadelphia; Fontanbleau
School of Fine Arts, France; Cranbrook Academy of Art,
Bloomfield Hills; Univ. of California, Berkeley. Exhibition:
1964 Milan Triennale. Collections: Addison Gallery of
American Art, Andover, Mass.; Victoria and Albert Museum,
London; Brooklyn Museum of Art, N.Y.; Cooper-Hewitt
Museum, N.Y.; Museum of Contemporary Crafts, N.Y.;
Oakland Museum of Art, Calif.; Philadelphia Museum of Art;
Smithsonian Institution, Washington, D.C.

HEON, Michele   Canada   b. 1948
Studied at Univ. of Montreal, M.F.A. 1978; Jagiellon Univ.,
Poland, 1972–73; Superior School of Fine Art, Poznan,
1973–74; Studied experimental tapestry with Magdalena
Abakanowicz and Ursula Plewka-Schmidt; study tour for
theatre design and costume in France, 1975; Banff Centre for
the Arts, Fibre Interchange, 1977, 1978, 1979. Teaches at the
Univ. of Quebec, Chicoutimi, Quebec. One-person Exhibition:
Pod Jaszezury, Poland, 1974 and 1979. Exhibitions: "Fibre,"
Powerhouse Gallery, Montreal, 1977; First Biennale
Quebecoise, Montreal, 1977; First Biennale of New Tapestry in
Quebec, Museum of Contemporary Art, Montreal, 1979; Col-
lection: Museum of Contemporary Art, Montreal. Scholarships:
Ministry of Art and Culture, Warsaw, Poland, 1972–73 and
1973–74; Government of Quebec, 1976 and 1977.

HERNMARCK, Helena   Sweden (lives in New York)   b.
1941
Studied at Swedish State School of Art, Craft and Design,
1959–63. One-person Exhibitions: The Museum of Modern Art,
N.Y., 1973; Los Angeles County Museum of Art, 1974; The
Danish Museum of Decorative Arts, Copenhagen, 1977. Collec-
tions: National Museum, Stockholm; National Gallery of Vic-
toria, Melbourne; The Swedish State Council for the Arts,
Stockholm; The Museum of Modern Art, N.Y.; Los Angeles
County Museum of Art. Commissions: Cunard Steamship Co.,
London, 1968; Weyerhaeuser Co., Tacoma, Washington,
1970–71; First City National Bank, Dayton, Ohio, 1973; Deere
& Co., Moline, Ill., 1973; Bethlehem Steel Corp., Pa., 1973;
John Hancock Mutual Life Insurance Co., Boston, Mass.,
1973–75; Olympic Tower Association, N.Y., 1975; Aid Associa-
tion for Lutherans, Appleton, Wisc., 1977; Dallas Centre,
Texas, 1978–79. Award: American Institute of Architects
Craftsmanship Medal, 1973.

HICKS, Sheila   U.S.A. (lives in Paris)   b. 1934
Studied at Yale Univ., New Haven, Conn., M.F.A. 1959.
Taught at Universidad Catolica, Santiago, Chile, 1958; Univer-
sidad de Mexico, Mexico City, 1962. Design Consultant,
Ministry of Artisanat, Rabat/Sale, Morocco, 1973; Director,
Commonwealth Trust Handweaving Workshop, Calicut, India,
1970–77; Atelier des Grands Augustins, Paris, founded 1967;
Atelier Cour de Rohan, Paris, founded 1977. One-person Ex-
hibitions: Galerie Bab Rouah, Rabat, 1971; Stedelijk Museum,
Amsterdam, 1974; Musée des Arts Decoratifs, Nantes, 1974;
Modern Masters Tapestry, N.Y., 1974; Galerie Alice Pauli,
Lausanne, 1975; Konsthall, Lund, Sweden, 1978; "Fil," Mon-
treuil, 1979; Musée des Tapisserie, Aix-en-Provence, 1979. Ex-
hibitions: "Woven Forms," Museum of Contemporary Crafts,
N.Y., 1963; 1967, 1969, 1971, 1973, 1975, 1977 BIT;
"Perspectief in Textiel," Stedelijk Museum, Amsterdam, 1969;
"Wall Hangings," The Museum of Modern Art, N.Y., 1969;

"Deliberate Entanglements," Art Galleries, Univ. of Califor-
nia, Los Angeles, 1971–72; 1974 IEMT; "Des Tapisseries
Nouvelles," Musée des Arts Decoratifs, Paris, 1975; "Fiber
Works:Europe and Japan," Kyoto and Tokyo, 1976; "Fiber-
works," The Cleveland Museum of Art, 1977. Public Collec-
tions: AT&T, Basking Ridge, N.J.; National Assembly, Paris;
Stedelijk Museum, Amsterdam; The Ford Foundation, N.Y.;
The Museum of Modern Art, N.Y.; Art Institute of Chicago;
Musée des Arts Decoratifs, Nantes; Cooper-Hewitt Museum,
N.Y.; Kunstgewerbemuseum, Zurich; National Museum,
Prague; Rochester Institute of Technology, N.Y.; Wilmington
Trust Bank, Del.; IBM, LaDefense, Paris. Award: Crafts-
manship Medal, American Institute of Architects, 1975.

HOPE, Polly   Great Britain   b. 1933
Studied at Chelsea Polytechnic and Slade Schools of Art, London. Exhibited painting and sculpture in one-person and group
exhibitions in Europe and U.S.A. One-person exhibition at
Kornblee Gallery, N.Y., 1978; 1977 BIT. Since 1974 has
worked in soft art.

HORIUCHI, Toshiko   Japan   b. 1940
Studied at Cranbrook Academy of Art, Bloomfield Hills, Mich.,
M.F.A. 1966. Taught at Teachers' College, Columbia Univ.,
N.Y., 1967; Bunka Institute, Tokyo, 1968–69, 1970–75; Univ.
of Georgia, Athens, 1969–70. Exhibitions: "Wallhangings,"
The Museum of Modern Art, N.Y., 1969; "Birds-eye View of
Contemporary Handicrafts," Central Museum, Tokyo, and Na-
tional Museum of Modern Art, Kyoto, 1973; "Japan Tradition
Vivante," Museum of Modern Art, Kyoto, 1976;
"Fiberworks," The Cleveland Museum of Art, 1977; "Fiber
Works:Americas and Japan," Kyoto and Tokyo, 1977. De-
signer: Boris Kroll, N.Y., 1966–67; Toppan Printing Co.,
Tokyo 1971–75; Design Assistant, Tsuneko Yokota, 1963–64;
Pacific House Fabric Company, Tokyo, 1964; TAMA Fine Art
College, Tokyo.

INGRAM, Judith   U.S.A.   b. 1926
Studied at Philadelphia College of Art. Exhibitions: Gallery
252, Philadelphia, 1967, 1969, 1971, 1973, 1975; Philadelphia
College of Textile and Design; Muse Gallery, Philadelphia,
1978; Philadelphia Art Alliance; Philadelphia Print Club;
Philadelphia Museum of Art; Tokyo Central Museum of Arts,
Japan. Collections: Philadelphia Museum of Art; Delaware Art
Museum; RCA Executive offices throughout U.S.A. and Puerto
Rico; First Pennsylvania Bank; Westinghouse; BMW of North
America, Inc.

ISOBE, Harumi   Japan   b. 1941
Studied at Hiyoshigaoka Art and Craft School, Kyoto, Japan,
1957–60; State School of Art and Design, Sweden, 1968–70.
Teaches at Kawashima Textile School, Kyoto, Japan. Exhibi-
tions: Gallery St. Goran and Draken, Stockholm, 1974; "Fiber
Works:Europe and Japan," Kyoto and Tokyo, Japan 1976.

ITTER, Diane   U.S.A.   b. 1946
Studied at Univ. of Pittsburgh, Pa., B.A. 1969; Indiana Univ.,
Bloomington, M.F.A. 1974. Exhibitions: "Beaux Arts De-
signer/Craftsman," Columbus, Ohio, 1975, 1977; 1976 IEMT;
"American Crafts," Museum of Contemporary Art, Chicago,
1976; "Young Americans," Museum of Contemporary Crafts,
N.Y., 1977; "New Dimensions in Fiber Design," Md., 1977;
Allied Craftsmen of San Diego, Calif., 1977; "Basketry,
Selected Artists," The Hadler Galleries, N.Y., 1977. Collec-
tions: Columbus Gallery of Fine Arts, Ohio; Univ. of Texas Art
Museum, Austin. Award: N.E.A. Craftsman's Grant, 1977–78.

JACOBS, Ferne   U.S.A.   b. 1942
Studied at Claremont College, Calif., M.F.A. 1976; Art Center
College of Design, Los Angeles, 1960–63; Pratt Institute, N.Y.,
1964–65; California State College, Long Beach, 1966–67.
Taught at California State Univ., Los Angeles, 1972. Exhibi-
tions: "Fiber Structures," Denver Art Museum, 1972;

"Sculpture in Fiber," Museum of Contemporary Crafts, N.Y., 1972; "In Praise of Hands," World Crafts Council, Toronto, 1974; 1974 IEMT; The Hadler Galleries, N.Y., 1975; "American Crafts 1976," Museum of Contemporary Art, Chicago. Collections: Royal Scottish Museum, Edinburgh.

JACOBI, Ritzi   Germany   b. 1941, Romania
Studied at Fine Arts Institute, Bucharest, 1966 (tapestry techniques).

JACOBI, Peter   Germany   b. 1935, Romania
Studied at Fine Arts Institute, Bucharest, 1961 (sculpture). Exhibitions: Biennale of Middelheim-Anves, Belgium, 1968; International Exhibition of the Scottish Royal Academy, 1969; "Interfauna," Dusseldorf, 1968; Triennale, Milan, 1969; "Deliberate Entanglements," Art Galleries, Univ. of California, Los Angeles, 1971–72; 1969, 1971, 1973, 1975, 1977, 1979 BIT; Maison de la Culture, Grenoble, 1970; as well as in Chicago, Washington, D.C., Prague, Copenhagen, Alexandria, Berlin, Budapest, Belgrade, Moscow, Warsaw, Mexico; National Museum of Modern Art, Kyoto and Tokyo, 1976; First Bienial of German Tapestry, 1978; Personal exhibitions in Kunsthalle, Mannheim; Kunsthalle, Baden-Baden. Collections: National Gallery, Bucharest; Museum of the XX Century, Vienna; Museum für Kunst und Gewerbe, Hamburg; Museo di Arte Moderno, Rome. Awards: Bienal de São Paulo, Art and Communications Award, 1973; Louis Tiffany Foundation, 1974; State Prize of Baden-Wurttemberg, 1976.

JAMART, Susan   U.S.A.   b. 1942
Studied at Univ. of California, Berkeley, Calif., M.A., 1974; Haystack Mountain School of Crafts, Maine, 1974 (scholarship student and teaching assistant). Taught at Fiberworks, Berkeley, 1973, 1974, 1976; Yarn Depot, San Francisco, 1973; San Francisco Adult School, 1973; Berkeley Adult School, Berkeley, 1973; California College of Arts and Crafts, Oakland, 1973. Exhibitions: 1976 IEMT; "California Design '76," Pacific Design Center, Los Angeles, 1976; Cypress College Fine Arts Gallery, Cypress, Calif., 1976; Allrich Gallery, San Francisco, 1975.

KAUFMAN, Glen   U.S.A.   b. 1932
Studied at Cranbrook Academy of Art, M.F.A. 1959; Certificate State School of Arts and Crafts, Copenhagen, Denmark, 1959–60. Teaches at Univ. of Georgia, Athens. Exhibitions: Museum of Contemporary Crafts, N.Y., 1967; "Objects USA," 1969; American Crafts Council, N.Y., 1977; "Modern American Textiles, Sculptures and Tapestries," Oslo, Copenhagen, Brussels, 1972–73; "Fiber," Wisc., 1974; 1974, 1976, 1978 IEMT. Collections: Museum of Contemporary Crafts, N.Y.; Rockford Art Association, Ill.; S.C. Johnson Collection; Univ. of Wisconsin. Awards: Fulbright Grant to Denmark, 1959; grant for research and travel in Europe, Univ. of Georgia, 1973; N.E.A., Craftsmen's Grant, 1976–77.

KNODEL, Gerhardt   U.S.A.   b. 1940
Studied at California State Univ., Long Beach, M.A. 1970; Univ. of California, Los Angeles, B.A. 1961. Taught at Los Angeles City Schools, 1962–68; California State Univ., Long Beach, 1969–70; Artist in Residence and Director, Fiber Dept., Cranbrook Academy of Art, Bloomfield Hills, Mich. 1970 to present. Exhibitions: Pasadena Art Museum, 1971; Detroit Institute of Arts, 1973; 1975, 1977 BIT; Museum of Contemporary Craft, Chicago, 1976; "Fiberworks," The Cleveland Museum of Art, Ohio, 1977, "Diverse Directions," Univ. of Washington, Pullman, 1977. Collections: Univ. of Houston, Texas; Detroit Plaza Hotel, Mich.; U.S.A. Federal Building, Oklahoma City; Xerox Corp., Stamford, Conn. Award: N.E.A. Grant, 1976.

KOBAYASHI, Masakazu   Japan   b. 1944
Studied at Kyoto Univ. of Arts, 1963–66. Designer, Kawashima Textile Mills, Kyoto. Exhibitions: 1973, 1975, 1977, 1979 BIT; First International Textile Triennale, Lodz, Poland; 1976, 1978

IEMT; Angers Tapestry Festival, France, 1976; "Fiber Works: Europe and Japan," Kyoto and Tokyo, 1976; "Fiberworks," The Cleveland Museum of Art, 1977. Collections: Takamathu Imperial Residence, Japan; City of Lausanne, Switzerland; National Museum of Modern Art, Kyoto.

KOBAYASHI, Naomi   Japan   b. 1945
Studied at Musashino Art Univ., 1969. Exhibitions: Tokyo Craft Exhibition, 1969, 1970, 1972; "Textile Sculpture," Kyoto, 1971; Kyoto Craft Exhibition, 1973, 1975; 1976, 1978 IEMT; 1977, 1979 BIT; "Fiber Works:Europe and Japan," Kyoto and Tokyo, 1976.

KREJCI, Luba   Czechoslovakia   b. 1925
Studied at School of Art Industry, Brno, 1945–49; Taught in Brno, 1949–50. Designer, Textilni Tvorba, Brno, Prague, 1949–55; Institution of Folk Art Production, 1955–60. Exhibitions: 1969 BIT; 1974 IEMT; "Lace Hangings," Jindrichuv Hradec, 1976; "Fiber Works:Europe and Japan," Kyoto and Tokyo, 1976; "Fiberworks," The Cleveland Museum of Art, 1977. Collections: Slovak National Gallery, Bratislava; The Institution of Ethnography, Brno; Institution of Folk Art Production, Brno; The Museum of Applied Arts, Brno; The Czech Ministry of Culture, Prague; Institution of Folk Art Production, Prague; The Museum of Applied Arts, Prague; Stedelijk Museum, Amsterdam; Bellerive Museum, Zurich; Museum of Contemporary Crafts, N.Y.

KUO, Suzanna   U.S.A.   b. 1941
Informal study of batik during residence in Japan 1971–72; Indiana Univ., Bloomington, Ind., Ph.D. English, 1971. Taught at Univ. of Oregon, Eugene, 1978, 1979; Marylhurst College, Lake Oswego, Oreg., 1977; School of the Arts and Crafts Society, Portland, 1972–74. One-person Exhibition: Contemporary Crafts Gallery, Portland. Exhibitions: "Portland-Sapporo Crafts Exhibition," Marui-Imai, Sapporo, Japan; Renshaw Gallery, Linfield College, McMinnville, Oreg.; Northwest Artists' Workshop, Portland; "Mountain High," Timberline Lodge, Mt. Hood, Oreg.; Seattle Center, Seattle; Portland Art Museum. Award: Cash Award, Oregon Artists' and Craftsmen's Exhibition, Oregon State Fair, Salem. Commissions for two kiosk designs, Portland Transit Mall.

KUSAMA, Yayoi   Japan (lives in New York)   b. 1941
Studied at the Arts and Crafts School, Kyoto. Has been living in the United States since 1968. Began his work with environments in 1965. Collections: Museum Ludwig, Cologne; Dartmouth College Museum, Hanover, N.H.

KUSAMA, Tetsuo   Japan (lives in U.S.A.)   b. 1946
Studied at Musashino Art Univ., Tokyo; Cranbrook Academy M.F.A. 1973. Teaches at Utah State Univ. Exhibitions: 1977 BIT; 1976 IEMT; "Fiberworks," The Cleveland Museum of Art, 1977; "Fiberworks:Americas and Japan," Kyoto and Tokyo, 1977; "International Directions in Fiber," California State Univ., 1978. Collections: Salt Lake Art Centre, Utah; Pacific Design Centre, Calif.; SSI Container Corporation, Calif.

KUTNICK, Malka   U.S.A.   b. 1946, Germany
Studied at Wayne State Univ., BFA 1969, MA 1970. Taught at Massachusetts Institute of Technology, 1975–76; Jewish Community Center, Brighton, Mass., 1974–76; Royal Oak and Oak Park Adult Education, Detroit, 1969. Director, Massachusetts Institute of Technology Student Art Association, 1979 to present. Exhibitions: "Cotton Comes Home," International Fiber Competition, Southeastern United States Museum Tour, 1976; Massachusetts Institute of Technology, 1975; Rotch Library, 1974.

KWAK, Kae Jung   Korea
Director, Kae Jung Kwak's Handicrafts Experimental Laboratory, 1963 to present. Lecturer at Hongik Graduate School (crafts), 1970–72; Lecturer at Duksung Women's Col-

lege (applied art), 1971. Exhibitions: National Art Exhibition, Korea, 1968–75; "Expo '70," Osaka, Japan, 1970; "In Praise of Hands," Toronto, Canada, 1974; "Grass Exhibition," Los Angeles County Museum of Art, 1976.

LAMBRECHT, Bernadette   Belgium   b. 1929
Exhibitions: 1975 BIT; 1978 IEMT. Represented in Belgian State Collections.

LANCASTER, Lois   U.S.A.   b. 1932
Studied at Stanford Univ., B.A. Anthropology 1954; graduate work in Ceramics, Univ. of California, Los Angeles, 1955–56; studied painting, Univ. of Hawaii, 1960; graduate work in ceramics, Univ. of Wisconsin, 1963–64; studied painting and art history, Univ. of Washington, 1965; graduate work in textile art, Univ. of California, Berkeley, 1975; Univ. of California, Berkeley, M.A. Visual Design (Textile Art) 1979. Exhibitions: "Elevator Environment," Univ. of California, Berkeley, 1977; "The Dyer's Art," Fiberworks Gallery, Berkeley, 1977; "Recent Photo Sculpture," Camerawork Gallery, San Francisco, 1977; "Fiber Works:Americas and Japan," Kyoto and Tokyo, 1977; Group Show, the Textile Museum, Washington D.C., 1978; "A Valentine Surprise," Fiberworks Gallery, Berkeley, 1978; The Fine Arts Museums of San Francisco, Downtown Center, 1979; National Miniature Exhibition, Santa Fe, N.M., 1979.

LANDIS, Richard   U.S.A.   b. 1931
Studied at Arizona State University; studied weaving with Mary Pendelton and art with photographer Frederick Sommer. Traveled in Europe and Japan. Exhibitions: Prescott College, Ariz., 1969; Laguna Beach Art Association, Calif., 1971; "Structuur in Textiel," Stedelijk Museum, Amsterdam; "The New Classicism," The Museum of Modern Art, N.Y., 1976; Washington State Univ., Pullman, 1978; National Miniature Exhibition, Sante Fe, N.M., 1979. Collections: The Museum of Modern Art, N.Y.; Stedelijk Museum, Amsterdam; Cooper-Hewitt Museum, N.Y.; Detroit Institute of Art, Mich.

LIVINGSTONE, Joan E.   U.S.A.   b. 1948
Studied at Portland State Univ., Oreg. B.A. 1978; Cranbrook Academy of Art, Bloomfield Hills, Mich., M.F.A. 1974. Graphic and stage designer, The Portland Shakespeare Company, 1969–72; Hillside Center for the Arts, Portland, Oregon, 1970–72. Instructor, Kansas City Art Institute, 1975 to present. Exhibitions: 14th Annual Mid-Michigan Exhibition, 1973; Kemper Gallery, Kansas City, Mo., 1975; "Artists in the Schools," Delaware Art Museum Traveling Exhibition, 1975–76; "Three Spatial Attitudes," Central Michigan State Univ., Mt. Pleasant, 1976; The Hadler Galleries, N.Y., 1975, 1976.

LUNDBERG, Thomas   U.S.A.   b. 1953
Studied at Univ. of Iowa, B.F.A. 1975; Indiana Univ., M.F.A. Textiles 1976. Exhibitions: First Biennial Thread and Fiber Competition, Alexandria Museum, La., 1978; Indianapolis Museum of Art, 1978; 1978 IEMT.

MAN RAY   U.S.A. (lived in Paris)   1890–1978
Studied at the National Academy of Design and at the Ferrer Center, N.Y. In 1921 left for Paris; worked in Rayogramme, photography and film. Embraced Surrealism. Has shown worldwide since 1915. *Enigma of Isidore Ducasse* shown in "Weich und Plastisch," Zurich, 1979.

McQUEEN, John   U.S.A.   b. 1943
Studied at Tyler School of Art, Temple Univ., Philadelphia, Pa., M.F.A. 1975. Exhibitions: "Fiber Works:Americas and Japan," Kyoto and Tokyo, 1977; "Baskets," San Francisco, 1978; Recent Acquisitions, 1979, Philadelphia Museum of Art, Philadelphia, Pa. Awards: Federal Parks Service Grant, 1976; N.E.A. 1977, 1979.

MORINO, Sachiko   Japan   b. 1943
Studied at Kyoto Art Univ. Exhibitions: since 1967, Japan Art Exhibition, Museums of Tokyo and Kyoto, Japan Contemporary Craft Exhibit, Kyoto City Exhibition, Kyoto Craft Exhibition, 1976 IEMT; 1977 BIT. Award: Prize of Merit, Kyoto City Exhibition.

MOSS, Debbe   U.S.A.   b. 1948
Studied at California State Univ., Northridge, B.A. 1970; Univ. of California, Los Angeles, M.A. 1973. Exhibitions: "Fiber Environments," Univ. of California, Los Angeles, 1973; "Fiber Works," Scripps College, Calif., 1973; "Pliable Structures," Ross-Freeman Gallery, Northridge, Calif., 1974; 1975 BIT; 1976 IEMT; "Fiberworks," The Cleveland Museum of Art, 1977.

MUNOZ, Aurelia   Spain   b. 1926
Studied at School of Applied Arts, Barcelona. Exhibitions: 1965, 1969, 1971, 1973, 1977 BIT; 1974, 1976 IEMT; "Fiber Works: Europe and Japan," Kyoto and Tokyo, 1976; "Fiberworks," The Cleveland Museum of Art, 1977; "Convergence 76," Pittsburgh. One-person Exhibitions: New York, Barcelona, Czechoslovakia, Switzerland, Holland, Edinburgh. Collections: AT&T, Basking Ridge, N.J.; Contemporary Art Museums of Madrid, Villafames, and Seville, Spain; Umelocko Prumislove Museum of Prague; Provinciehuis Noord Brabant, Holland; Stedelijk Museum, Amsterdam; Edificios Industriales and Banco Condal, Barcelona; Royal Scottish Museum, Edinburgh; Spanish Tourist Office, N.Y.; Museum of Modern Art, Kyoto. Awards: Paris Silver Medal, 1968; "Foundation March," Scholar in Textile Research, 1968.

MUNSTERS, Carla   Holland   b. 1939
Studied painting at Jan van Eyck Academy, Maastricht, 1961–66. Since 1970 has worked with plastics. Exhibitions: 1975 BIT; in Holland and abroad. Collections: in State collections and museums.

NEMES, Maria   Hungary   b. 1935
Studied at Budapest University, 1953–58. Exhibitions: 1976 IEMT.

O'BANION, Nance   U.S.A.   b. 1949
Studied at Univ. of California, Berkeley, M.A., Design. Assistant Professor, Textile Dept., California College of Arts and Crafts, Oakland, Calif. 1974 to present. One-person Exhibition: Fiberworks Center for the Textile Arts, Berkeley. Award: N.E.A. grant for Artist in Residence, Fiberworks Center for the Textile Arts, Berkeley.

ONAGI, Yoichi   Japan   b. 1931
Studied painting at Kyoto Gakugei University, 1954–56. Worked at Tatsumura Textile Institute, Kyoto, 1959–64. Exhibitions: 1973 BIT; 1976 IEMT.

OWIDZKA, Jolanta   Poland   b. 1927
Studied at the Krakow Academy of Fine Arts and Warsaw Academy of Fine Arts. Taught at Institute of Applied Art and Design. Designer of Textiles. Was an active member of the Studio of Experimental Artistic Weavers for ten years. Exhibitions: 1st Polish Interior Architecture Exhibition, National Museum, Warsaw, 1952; Museums of Applied Arts, Zurich and Geneva, 1957; XII Triennale of Art, Milano, 1960; 1962, 1965, 1971 BIT; "Polish Modern Art in Buenos Aires," Mexico, Havana, and Montevideo, 1965–67; "Wallhangings," The Museum of Modern Art, 1969. Collections: Continental Bank, Chicago; Museum for History of Textiles, Lodz; New Art Center, Ottowa; National Museums of Wroclaw, Warsaw, Poznan; North Central Museum, Slupsk; Museum of Warsaw History; National Theatre, Warsaw; Lot Airlines, Frankfurt, Amsterdam, Berlin; Tribrook Corp., Oakbrook, Illinois; Hotel Regence Hyatt, Montreal; Central Railroad Station, Warsaw; Hotel Victoria, Warsaw.

PACHUCKA, Ewa   Poland (lives in Australia)   b. 1936
Studied sculpture at Catholic Univ., Lublin; Lodz School of
Fine Arts, specializing in tapestry. One-person Exhibitions:
"Landscape and Bodies," 1977; "Arcadia," 1977. Exhibitions:
Zamek Group Gallery, Lublin, 1958; Writers Club, Warsaw,
1958; "Wallhangings," The Museum of Modern Art, N.Y.,
1969; Norrkopings Museum, Sweden, 1969; Grabowski
Gallery, London, 1970; Triennale of Contemporary Art, New
Delhi, India, 1974; "Twentieth Tasmanian Art Gallery Exhibi-
tion—Sculpture," 1976. Collections: National Gallery of Victoria and New South Wales Art Gallery, Sydney, Australia,
1978.

PENALBA, Alicia   Argentina (lives in Paris)   b. 1913
Studied sculpture at Buenos Aires Academy; Zadkin Studio,
Paris, 1948. One-person Exhibitions: Galerie Claude Bernard
and Galerie du Dragon, Paris. Exhibitions: Salon de la Jeune
Sculpture and Salon des Realities Nouvelles, Paris; 1975, 1979
BIT; "Fiberworks," The Cleveland Museum of Art, 1977. Col-
lections: School of Economic and Social Studies, St. Gallen,
Switzerland; The Cleveland Museum of Art, Ohio.

PIXLEY, Anne Flaten   U.S.A.   b. 1932, Paris
Studied at St. Olaf College, B.A.; studied art in New York
City; Graduate School, Claremont, California, M.F.A. Taught
in Ohio and Massachusetts. Has exhibited since 1972; 1979 BIT.
Commissions in Boston, Mass.

PLEWKA-SCHMIDT, Urszula   Poland   b. 1939
Studied at the Academy of Art, Poznan. Lecturer at the
Academy of Art, Poznan, 1967 to present. Fifteen one-person
exhibitions. Exhibitions: 1971, 1973, 1975, 1979 BIT; "In
Praise of Hands," Toronto, 1975; "A Voyage to the Source of
Time," Sopot, Poland, 1979. Collections: Museum of the
History of Weaving, Lodz; National Museums, Poznan and
Slupsk; National Museum, Berlin-Charlottenburg; Museum
Bellerive, Zurich.

POLLACK, Mark   U.S.A.   b. 1954
Studied at Rhode Island School of Design, B.F.A.; Tyler School
of Art. Exhibitions: "Focus on Fiber," 1978; "Paint and Fiber:
Recent Works," Goldie Paley Design Center Gallery,
Philadelphia, 1979; National Fiber Invitational, Woods Gerry
Gallery, Providence, 1977; "Selected International Artists,"
The Hadler Galleries, N.Y., 1976.

RAUSCHENBERG, Robert   U.S.A.   b. 1925
Studied at Kansas City Art Institute, Mo.; Academie Julien,
Paris, France; Black Mountain College, N.C.; The Art Students
League, N.Y. Major One-person Exhibitions: Italy, Germany,
France, England, Canada, Israel, Sweden, as well as major cities
in the United States. Major Retrospective: National Collection
of Fine Arts, Washington, D.C., 1977. Collections: The
Museum of Modern Art, N.Y.; The Whitney Museum of
American Art, N.Y.; Moderna Museet, Stockholm, Sweden;
Kunstsammlung Nordrhein-Westfalen, Dusseldorf, Germany;
Stedelijk Museum, Amsterdam, The Netherlands; Philadelphia
Museum of Art, Pennsylvania; Albright-Knox Art Gallery, Buf-
falo, N.Y.; Tate Gallery, London, England; Pasadena Art
Museum, Calif.; The Baltimore Museum of Art, Md.; Museum
of Contemporary Art, Chicago, Ill.; The Wadsworth
Atheneum, Hartford, Conn. Collection: Peter Ludwig, Wallraf-
Richartz Museum, Cologne, Germany; Neue Galerie, Aachen,
Germany; Minneapolis Institute of Arts, Minneapolis, Minn.;
Hirshhorn Museum, Washington, D.C. Award: Grand Prize,
Venice Biennale, 1964. Designed sets for Merce Cunningham
Dance Company.

ROLF, Margot   Holland   b. 1940
Studied tapestry weaving "de Uil," Amsterdam, 1962; Gerrit
Rietveld Academie, Amsterdam, 1967–70. Instructor, Haystack
Mountain School of Crafts, Deer Isle, Maine, 1975; Textile
Dept., Gerrit Rietveld Academie, Amsterdam, 1974 to present.

One-person Exhibitions: Kunstkring Haaksbergen, Holland,
1972; Kunsthandel Ina Broerse, Amsterdam, 1973; Municipal
Art Centre "De Vaart," Hilversum, 1975; Amro-Bank Gallery,
Amsterdam, 1975. Exhibitions: Textielmuseum, Tilburg, 1969;
"De Wevende Kring," Amsterdam, 1971; "Variaties in Tex-
tiel," 1974–75; "Werken in textiel III," Frans Hals Museum,
Haarlem, 1974; Galerie Nouvelles Images, The Hague; 1977
BIT; 1978 IEMT. Award: Travel Grant, Ministry of Culture,
The Hague, 1975.

ROSANJIN, Kitquoi   Japan   1883–1959
Worked as a calligrapher, sign board carver, engraver. Started to
work in pottery in 1915; first exhibited in 1925. Exhibitions:
The Museum of Modern Art, N.Y., 1954; Japan House Gallery,
N.Y., 1972

ROSSBACH, Ed   U.S.A.   b. 1914
Studied at Univ. of Washington, Seattle; Columbia Univ.,
N.Y.; Cranbrook Academy of Art, Bloomfield Hills, Mich. Pro-
fessor Emeritus, Univ. of California, Berkeley. Exhibitions:
Triennale, Milan, 1964; "Museum West," San Francisco, 1965;
Museum of Contemporary Crafts, N.Y. 1968; University Art
Collections, Arizona State Univ., Tempe, 1968; "Wallhang-
ings," The Museum of Modern Art, N.Y. 1969; Brooklyn
Museum; "Wallhangings: The New Classicism," The Museum
of Modern Art, 1977; "Structuur in Textiel," Stedelijk
Museum, 1977; Honolulu, 1978; Athens, Ga., 1979; "Fiber
Works:Americas and Japan," Kyoto and Tokyo, 1977. Collec-
tions: Women's College, Univ. of North Carolina, Greensboro;
California State Fair, Sacramento; Univ. of Indiana, Bloom-
ington; Univ. of Illinois, Urbana; Mansfield State College,
Mass.; The Johnson Collection; The Museum of Modern Art,
N.Y.

ROUSSEAU-VERMETTE, Mariette   Canada   b. 1926
Studied at Ecole des Beaux-Arts, Quebec; Oakland College of
Arts and Crafts, Calif. Head, Fiber Department, Banff Centre,
Alberta. Exhibitions: 1962, 1965, 1967, 1969, 1971 BIT;
"Wallhangings," The Museum of Modern Art, N.Y., 1969;
Jack Lenor Larsen Showroom, N.Y., 1970; New Design Gallery,
Vancouver, 1964; Université de Sherbrooke, Quebec, 1965.
Collections: National Gallery of Canada, Ottawa; Museum of
Contemporary Art, Montreal; Vancouver Art Gallery; Kennedy
Center for the Performing Arts, Washington, D.C.; Esso World
Headquarters, N.Y.; Canadian Embassies in foreign countries;
Palais de Justice, Montreal; Buffalo Savings Bank; National
Bank of Canada, Place d'Armes, Montreal; Royal Bank, Mirabel
Airport; Alcoa, Pittsburgh, Pa. Award: Officier de l'Ordre du
Canada, 1976.

RUDDICK, Dorothy   U.S.A.   b. 1925
Studied at Radcliff College and Black Mountain College. One-
person Exhibitions: Issacson Gallery, 1957; Weyhe Gallery,
1959, 1961, 1963; Graham Gallery, 1967, 1969, 1971, 1973;
Fischbach Gallery, 1976. Exhibition: 1977 BIT.

SADLEY, Wojciech   Poland   b. 1932
Studied at Academy of Fine Arts, Warsaw, 1949–59; Institute
of Industrial Design, Warsaw, 1960–68. Head of Faculty of
Tapestry, Academy of Fine Arts, Warsaw. Exhibitions:
"Wallhangings," The Museum of Modern Art, N.Y., 1969;
1962, 1965, 1967, 1969, 1971, 1973, 1975 BIT; 1974, 1976,
1978 IEMT. Collections: Muzeum Narodowe, Bydgoszcz,
Poland; Historical Textile Museum, Lodz; Osaka Museum,
Japan; Galerie "F," Ulm, Germany; Museum of Physical
Culture and Tourism, Warsaw; Muzeum Narodowe, Warsaw;
Museum Bellerive, Zurich; also museums in Canada,
Copenhagen, Paris, Stockholm, and U.S.A. Awards: State
Award, 1969; Special Prize, Exempla Exhibition, Munich,
1970.

SAMARAS, Lucas   U.S.A.   b. 1936, Greece
Came to the United States in 1948. Studied at Rutgers Univ.;

Columbia Univ. (Art History under Meyer Schapiro). One-person Exhibitions: Rutgers Univ., 1955, 1958; "Dinners, Liquid Aluminum Pieces, Pastels and Plasters," Green Gallery, N.Y., 1961; "Bedroom, Boxes, Plastics," Green Gallery, N.Y., 1964; "Boxes, Wall Pieces," Dwan Gallery, Los Angeles, 1964; "Mirror Room, Transformations, Boxes, Skull Drawings," The Pace Gallery, N.Y., 1966; "Mirrored Room No. 3," Galerie der Spiegel, Cologne, 1969; "Chair Transformations," The Pace Gallery, N.Y., 1970; "Mirrored Room No. 3," Kunstverein Museum, Hannover, Germany, 1970; "Stiff Boxes and Autopolaroids," The Pace Gallery, N.Y., 1971; "Box Retrospective," Museum of Contemporary Art, Chicago, 1971; "Retrospective," The Whitney Museum of American Art, N.Y., 1972; "Pastels," The Museum of Modern Art, N.Y., 1975; "Photo Transformations," California State Univ., Long Beach, 1975; "Photo Transformations," Institute of Contemporary Art, Boston, 1976; "Photo Transformations," Zabriskie Gallery, Paris, 1977; "Photo Transformations," Walker Art Center, Minneapolis, 1977; "Reconstructions," The Pace Gallery, N.Y., 1978. Collections: Buffalo, N.Y.; Ridgefield, Conn.; Chicago, Ill.; Canberra, Australia; St. Louis, Mo.; Dallas, Texas; Cambridge, Mass.; Ft. Worth, Texas; Washington, D.C.; Bloomington, Ind.; Los Angeles, Calif.; Minneapolis, Minn.; New Orleans, La.; Philadelphia, Pa.; San Francisco, Calif.; Seattle, Wash.; Hartford, Conn.; in Europe as well.

SANDOVAL, Arturo Alonzo   U.S.A.   b. 1942
Studied at California State College, Los Angeles, B.A. 1964, M.A. 1969 Cranbrook Academy of Art, Bloomfield Hills, Mich., M.F.A. 1971. Head of Weaving Program, Univ. of Kentucky, Lexington, 1974 to present. One-person Exhibitions: Rasdall Gallery, Univ. of Kentucky; Krannert Gallery, Univ. of Evansville, Ind.; Art Gallery, Cornell College, Mount Vernon, Iowa. Exhibitions: Museum of Contemporary Crafts, N.Y.; Fine Arts Galleries, State Univ. College, Oneonta, N.Y., 1971; Detroit Institute of Art, Mich.; Kent State Univ., Kent, Ohio; Rich's Department Store, Atlanta, Ga., 1973; Evansville Museum of Arts and Sciences, Evansville, Ind. (Museum Merit Award), 1972; 1977 BIT; "Wallhangings: The New Classicism," The Museum of Modern Art, N.Y., 1977. Award: N.E.A. Creative Research Grant, 1973.

SAUER, Dick   U.S.A.   b. 1942
Studied at Univ. of Wisconsin, Milwaukee, M.F.A. 1969. Teaches at Mount Wachusett Community College, Gardner, Mass. Collections: Jack Lenor Larsen, Inc., N.Y.; British Embassy, Washington, D.C.; Kawashima Textiles, Kyoto; Milwaukee Art Center, Univ. of Wisconsin; Univ. of Minnesota. Awards: American Crafts Council Grant, 1977; N.E.A. Grant, 1974.

SCHIELE, Moik   Switzerland   b. 1938
Studied at Kunstgewerbeschule, Zurich. Exhibitions: 1969, 1971, 1973, 1975, 1977 BIT; 1974, 1976, 1978 IEMT; "Wallhangings," The Museum of Modern Art, N.Y., 1969. Collections: First National Bank, Chicago; Cemetery Chapel, Uetliberg; Bellerive Museum, Zurich; The Museum of Modern Art, N.Y.; Catholic Churches Urdorf and Witikon; Museum of Applied Art; Reform Church Neu-Affolten; Hospitals Bombach and Triemli, Zurich; AT&T, Basking Ridge, N.J.

SCHIRA, Cynthia   U.S.A.   b. 1934
Studied at Rhode Island School of Design, B.F.A.; Aubusson School of Decorative Art, Univ. of Kansas, M.F.A. Teaches at Univ. of Kansas. Exhibitions: 1973, 1975, 1977 BIT. Awards: 1967 Tiffany Foundation Fellowship; 1974, N.E.A. Fellowship.

SCHOLTEN, Desirée   Holland   b. 1920
Born in Indonesia. Studied at Royal Academy, The Hague, 1942–43; School of Arts and Crafts, Amsterdam, 1948–51. Exhibitions: 1967, 1969, 1977, 1979 BIT; Prague, 1970; Lodz, 1972–73; 1976, 1978 IEMT; Stedelijk Museum, Amsterdam,

1976–77; Boymans-van Bueningen Museum, Rotterdam, 1977; Muzea Jindrichuv Hradec, Prague, 1978. Collections: Stedelijk Museum, Amsterdam; Boymans-van Beuningen Museum, Rotterdam; Galerie Nouvelles Images, The Hague; P.T.T. Collection, The Hague; Gebouw Gemeentewaterleidingen, Amsterdam-Sloterdijk; Provinciehuis Gelderland, Arnhem; Bleuland Ziekenhuis, Gouda; Dienst's Rijk Verspreide Kinstvoorwerpen, The Hague; Gewestelijk Arbeidsbureau, Heerenveen; Rijksmuseum Kroller-Muller, Otterlo; Landhuis Architect G. Rietveld, Santpoort; Amrobank, Rotterdam; Dienst Esthetische Vormgeving P.T.T., The Hague.

SCHOLTEN, Herman   Holland   b. 1932
Studied at Instituut voor Kunstnijverheidsonderwijs, Amsterdam, 1948–52. Lecturer at Akademie voor Kunsten Industrie, Enschede, 1961–65; Akademie voor Industriele Vormgeving, Eindhoven, 1966–69; Koninkijke Akademie voor Kunst en Industrie, Den Bosch, 1967–71; Teaches in Textile Dept., Gerrit Rietveld Academy, Amsterdam, 1971 to present. Exhibitions: "Wallhangings," The Museum of Modern Art, N.Y., 1969; 1965, 1967, 1969, 1971, 1973, 1975, 1977 BIT; Frans Hals Museum, Haarlem, 1971; Lenore Tawney's Landmark House, N.Y., 1972; Nederlandse Wandtapijten, Katowice, Lodz, Sopot, 1972–73; Frans Hals Museum, Haarlem, 1974; 1974, 1976 IEMT; Stedelijk Museum, Amsterdam, 1974–1975; Museum Boymans-van Beuningen, Rotterdam, 1977. Collections: Gebouw Gemeentewaterleidingen, Amsterdam-Sloterdijk; Stedelijk Museum, Amsterdam; Gebouw P.T.T., Telefoondistrict, Amsterdam; Provinciehuis Gelderland, Arnhem; The Royal Scottish Museum, Edinburgh; Dienst Esthetische Vormgeving P.T.T., The Hague; Galerie Nouvelles Images, The Hague; National Life Center, Nashville; Dreyfus Corporation, N.Y.; Ruth Kaufmann Gallery, Inc., N.Y.; SHV Holdings, Utrecht; J.C. Penney Company, Inc., N.Y.

SCHREIER, Hilde   Canada   b. 1926, Austria
Self-taught. Exhibitions: "In Praise of Hands," World Crafts Council, Toronto, 1974; "Textile into 3D," Art Gallery of Ontario, 1974; "Contemporary Crafts of the Americas," Colorado State Univ., Fort Collins, Colo., 1975; "Habitat," United Nations Conference on Human Settlements, Vancouver, 1976; "Spectrum Canada," Royal Canadian Academy, Montreal, 1976; "Fiberworks," The Cleveland Museum of Art, 1977. Collections: Univ. of Kingston, Ontario; Ontario Crafts Council, Jean A. Chalmers Collection of Contemporary Canadian Crafts, Toronto.

SEELIG, Warren N.   U.S.A.   b. 1946
Studied at Philadelphia College of Textiles and Science, B.S. 1972; Cranbrook Academy of Art, Bloomfield Hills, Mich., M.F.A. 1974. Assistant Professor, Colorado State Univ., Fort Collins, 1974; Philadelphia College of Art, 1979 to present. One-person Exhibitions: James Yaw Gallery, Birmingham, Mich., 1974, 1976; Sangre de Cristo Arts and Conference Center, Pueblo, Colo.; "Fabric Constructions," The Hadler Galleries, N.Y., 1975; "Contemporary Crafts of the Americas," Colorado State Univ., Fort Collins, 1975. Exhibitions: "Cranbrook Weavers: Pacesetters and Prototypes," The Detroit Institute of Arts, 1973; "Contexture," Fort Wayne, Ind., 1974; The Hadler Galleries, N.Y., 1975, 1976.

SEKIMACHI, Kay   U.S.A.   b. 1926
Studied at California College of Arts and Crafts, Oakland, 1946–49. Exhibitions: "Wallhangings," The Museum of Modern Art, N.Y., 1969; Camden Arts Centre, London, 1972; 1973 BIT; National Endowment for the Arts, 1974. Collections: Royal Scottish Museum, Edinburgh; Metro Media, Los Angeles; Dreyfus Corp., N.Y.; Oakland Museum, Calif.; Johnson's Wax Collection, Racine; Smithsonian Institution, Washington, D.C.; National Museum of Modern Art, Kyoto.

SEVENTY, Sylvia   U.S.A.   b. 1947
Studied at Lone Mountain College, San Francisco, M.F.A. 1978;

California State Univ., Northridge, B.A. 1973. One-person Exhibition: "Installations," Fiberworks Gallery, Berkeley, Calif., 1978. Exhibitions: "Design West," Museum of Science and Industry, Los Angeles, 1972, 1973; "Light and Substance," University Art Museum, Univ. of New Mexico, 1973; "Photography Unlimited," Fogg Art Museum, Harvard Univ., Cambridge, Mass., 1974; "Tapestry and Other Fiber Forms," Fine Arts Gallery, California State Univ., Northridge, 1974; "Heartfelt Hearts," Fiberworks Gallery, Berkeley, 1978; "The National Miniature Fiber Exhibition," Sante Fe, N.M., 1979.

SHAWCROFT, Barbara   U.S.A.   b. 1930, England
Studied at Central School of Arts and Crafts, London, 1952–53; Ontario College of Art, Toronto, 1957–58; North Carolina State College, Raleigh, 1960–61; California College of Arts and Crafts, Oakland, M.F.A. 1973. Instructor, California College of Arts and Crafts, San Francisco State Univ.; University of California, Los Angeles; College of Marin, Kentfield, Calif.; San Jose State Univ., Calif., 1972–76. Weaver: Lili Blumenau, N.Y., 1961–62; Jack Lenor Larsen, Inc., N.Y., 1962–65. One-person Exhibitions: Mills College, Oakland, Calif., 1974; College of Marin, Kentfield, Calif., 1970; Annenberg Gallery, San Francisco, 1969. Exhibitions: "Fabrications," Cranbrook Academy of Art, Bloomfield Hills, Mich., 1972; "Sculpture in Fiber," Museum of Contemporary Crafts, N.Y., 1972; Schenectady Museum, N.Y.; Oakland Museum, Calif.; 1973 BIT; "Three Dimensional Fibre," Govert-Brewster Galleries, New Plymouth, New Zealand, 1974; 1974 IEMT; "California Design '76," Pacific Design Center, Los Angeles, 1976. Collections: The 3 Embarcadero Center Building, San Francisco, 1976; BART "Embarcadero" Station, San Francisco, 1976.

SHIMANUKI, Akiko   Japan   b. 1930
Studied at Tokyo Univ. of Arts. Teaches weaving and textile design at Tokyo Zokei Univ. Numerous personal and group exhibitions in Tokyo; 1975, 1977 BIT; 1976 IEMT. Award: Japan Craft Exhibition, Tokyo, 1971. Member of the Japan Craft Design Association.

SIEBER-FUCHS, Verena   Switzerland   b. 1943
Studied at Kunstgewerbeschule, Basle, Zurich. Exhibitions: Kunstgewerbemuseum, Bern, 1968, 1969, 1970; Kunstgewerbemuseum, Zurich, 1973; Stadtische Kunstkammer Strauhof, Zurich, 1975; Kunsthaus, Zurich, 1975, 1978; The Hadler Galleries, N.Y., 1976; Florence Duhl Gallery, N.Y., 1978. Collections: Town of Zurich; Canton of Zurich; Canton of Thurgau. Award: Swiss Government Fellowship, 1968, 1969, 1970; (Leistungspreis), Kunstgewerbeschule, Zurich.

SIEGFRIED, Liselotte   Switzerland   b. 1935
Studied at School of Decorative Arts, Zurich; Instructor 1970–71. Exhibitions: "In Praise of Hands," World Crafts Council, Toronto, 1974; "Fiberworks," The Cleveland Museum of Art, 1977; 1974, 1976 IEMT; "Fadenfantasien," Museum Bellerive, Zurich, 1974; International Tapestry Exhibition, Crear, Gouvieux, Paris, 1975; 1975 BIT. Collections: Museum Bellerive, Zurich; City of Zurich; The Cleveland Museum of Art, Ohio.

SMITH, Sherri   U.S.A.   b. 1943
Studied at Stanford Univ., B.A. Art 1965, Phi Beta Kappa; Cranbrook Academy of Art, M.F.A. 1967. Assistant Professor, weaving and textile design, School of Art, Univ. of Michigan, Ann Arbor, 1974; Instructor, Colorado State Univ., Fort Collins, Colo., 1971–74; Head of Woven Design Dept., Boris Kroll Fabrics, N.Y.; Textile Designer, Dorothy Liebes, Inc., N.Y. One-person Exhibition: Colorado Springs Fine Arts Center, 1976. Exhibitions: "Wallhangings," The Museum of Modern Art, N.Y., 1969; Museum of Contemporary Crafts, N.Y., 1969; Colorado Springs Fine Arts Center, 1970; 1971, 1973, 1975, 1977 BIT; Cranbrook Academy of Art, Bloomfield Hills, Mich., 1972; Smith College Weaving Exhibition, 1972; Denver Art Museum, 1972; Univ. of Iowa Museum, Iowa City, 1973;

Jacques Baruch Gallery, Chicago, 1974; Kansas City Art Institute, Kansas City, 1976; "Fiberworks," The Cleveland Museum of Art, 1977; Cincinnati Art Museum, Cincinnati, Ohio, 1978; 3rd Tapestry Triennale, Lodz, Poland, 1978. Collections: The Art Institute of Chicago; Colorado Springs Fine Arts Center; Hackley Art Museum, Muskegon, Mich.; Borg-Warner, Inc.; AT&T; Hyatt Regency Hotel, Quebec; Detroit Plaza Hotel; Dubai Airport Hotel. Award: Silver Medal, 3rd Tapestry Triennale, Lodz, Poland, 1978.

STAEHLIN, Marlise   Switzerland   b. 1927
Studied at Kunstgewerbeschule, Zurich. Artist in residence, Sydney College of the Arts, Australia, 1979. Taught at workshops at Univ. of California, Los Angeles, Cranbrook Academy; Fiberworks. Collections: Ciba-Geigy, Basle; Collection Pro Helvetia, Zurich; Museum Bellerive, Zurich; Museum of Contemporary Crafts, N.Y.; CITAM, Lausanne.

STAMSTA, Jean   U.S.A.   b. 1936
Studied at Univ. of Wisconsin, Milwaukee, B. S. 1958. One-person Exhibitions: Univ. of Virginia, Blacksburg, 1973; Univ. of Wisconsin, Whitewater, 1974; Rochester Art Center, Minn., 1974; Bergstrom Art Center and Museum, Neenah, Wis., 1976. Exhibitions: 1971 BIT; "Fabrications," Cranbrook Academy of Art, Bloomfield Hills, Mich., 1972; "Beaux Arts Designer/Craftsman," Columbus Gallery of Fine Arts, Ohio, 1973, 1975; "Contexture," Ft. Wayne, Ind., 1974; VII National Crafts Invitational, Illinois State Univ., Normal, 1974; "Contemporary Crafts of the Americas," Colorado State Univ., Ft. Collins, 1975; "Wisconsin Directions," Milwaukee Art Center, Wis., 1975; 1976 IEMT; "Fiber Structures," Museum of Art, Carnegie Institute, Pittsburgh, 1976; "Fiberworks," The Cleveland Museum of Art, 1977. Collections: Public Library, Glenview, Ill.; Museum of Contemporary Crafts, N.Y.; Columbus Gallery of Fine Arts, Ohio; Univ. of Wisconsin, Kenosha; The Johnson Collection of Contemporary Crafts.

STEIN, Ethel   U.S.A.   b. 1917
Studied sculpture with Chaim Gross at Cummington Art School; color and form with Josef Albers, Hannes Beckmann; weaving with Klara Cherepov, Ia Lampe, Alberto Garcia (Mitla, Mexico), Edna Blackburn, Mary Walker Phillips, Milton Sonday, Peter Collingwood, Lewis Knauss; Navajo Community College. Exhibitions: Riverside Museum, N.Y.; Loeb Center, New York University; Katonah Gallery, N.Y.; 92nd Street Y.M.H.A., N.Y.; Donnell Library, N.Y.; Newark Museum, N.J.; "The Dyer's Art," Museum of Contemporary Crafts, N.Y.; National Miniature Fiber Exhibition, Santa Fe, N.M., 1979.

SUTTON, Ann   Great Britain   b. 1935
Studied at Cardiff College of Art, 1951–55. Exhibitions: British Craft Center, 1969, 1975; 1974, 1976, 1978 IEMT. Collections: National Museum of Wales, Cardiff; Victoria and Albert Museum, London; Oxford City and County Museum, Woodstock. Awards: Welsh Arts Council, 1970; Travel Scholarship, Worshipful Company of Weavers and Royal Society of Arts, London, 1971.

SZILVITZKY, Margit   Hungary   b. 1931
Self-taught. Exhibitions: "Folded Textiles," Kosneg, Swinger, 1976; Amos Anderson Museum, Helsinki, 1977; Textile Biennale, Szombathely, 1970, 1972, 1974, 1978; Textile Triennale, Lodz, 1975; Hungarian Miniature Textiles, 1975; Musée Chateau D'Annecy, 1976; Nordfylland Kunstmuseum, Aslborg, 1977; 1978 IEMT. Collections: Szombathely Savaria Museum; Museum of Applied Arts, Budapest; Museum Janus Pannonius, Pecs. Award: First Prize, Textile Biennale, Szombathely, 1974.

TATE, Blair   U.S.A.   b. 1952
Studied at Rhode Island School of Design, B.F.A. 1974; Haystack Mountain School of Crafts, with Jack Lenor Larsen,

1978; Massachusetts College of Art, 1979. Taught at Worcester Craft Center, 1978–79; Instructor, Clark Univ.; Worcester Art Museum School; Boston Center for Adult Education, 1978 to present; Univ. of Mass., Continuing Education, 1975; RISD, Summer Sessions and Workshops, 1974. Exhibitions: National Miniature Fiber Exhibition, Santa Fe, N.M., 1979; "Warp and Weft," Boston Athenaeum, 1978; American Academy in Rome, two-person exhibition, 1977; "Contemporary Crafts of the Americas," Colorado State Univ., Ft. Collins, 1975.

TAWNEY, Lenore   U.S.A.   b. 1925
Studied at Univ. of Illinois, Champaign-Urbana; Institute of Design, Chicago, weaving with Marli Ehrman; sculpture with Archipenko; tapestry with Marta Taipale. One-person Exhibitions: "Lenore Tawney: A Personal World," Brookfield Craft Center, Brookfield, Conn.; Willard Gallery and Hadler Gallery, N.Y.; "Weaving/Collage/Assemblage, 1962 to 1975," Art Gallery, California State University, Fullerton, 1975. Exhibitions: "Wallhangings," The Museum of Modern Art, N.Y., 1969; "In Praise of Hands," World Crafts Council, Toronto, 1974; "Coenties Slip," Whitney Museum, N.Y., 1974; 1975 BIT; "Fiberworks," The Cleveland Art Museum, 1977; GSA Commission, Santa Rosa, Calif., 1978. Collections: Kunstgewerbemuseum, Zurich; Museum Bellerive, Zurich; First National Bank of Chicago; Univ. of Southern Illinois, Edwardsville; Brooklyn Museum, N.Y.; Cooper-Hewitt Museum, N.Y.; Museum of Contemporary Crafts, N.Y.; The Museum of Modern Art, N.Y.; The Cleveland Museum of Art, Ohio. Fellow of American Crafts Council.

TOMASZKIEWICZ, Boleslaw   Poland   b. 1930
Studied at State Superior School of Plastic Arts, 1955; since 1975, Vice Chairman of the Clothing and Fabrics Dept. Participated in exhibitions in Poland and abroad.

TRENTHAM, Gary L.   U.S.A.   b. 1939
Studied at Indiana Univ., M.F.A. 1972. Associate Professor, Textile Design, Auburn Univ., 1977 to present; taught in experimental school for culturally deprived students, Jetton Junior High School, Paducah, Ky., 1968–69. Exhibitions: "Contemporary Basketry," Ft. Wayne Art Center, Fort Wayne, Ind., 1972; National Invitational Crafts Exhibition, Univ. of New Mexico, 1973; "Objects: Basketry Techniques," American Craftsman Gallery, N.Y., 1975; "Source Detroit," Cranbrook Academy of Art Museum, Bloomfield Hills, Mich., 1976; "Photofibers," Joe and Emily Lowe Art Gallery, Syracuse Univ., Syracuse, N.Y., 1977; Basket Invitational, Florence Duhl Gallery, N.Y., 1977; "Basket Makers Art" and "76 Elements," Gallery of Contemporary Crafts, Greenwich, Conn., 1979; 1975 BIT; "Fiber Structures," Museum of Art, Carnegie Institute, Pittsburgh, Pa., 1976; 1976 IEMT; Museum of Art, Univ. of Minnesota, Duluth, 1977; "Fiber Forms 78," Cincinnati Art Museum. Award: N.E.A. Craftsman Fellowship.

VAN BLAADEREN, Maria   Holland   b. 1944
Studied at the Rietveld Academy, Holland 1964–68. Worked at Jack Lenor Larsen, Inc., N.Y., 1970–71. Teaches in Textile Dept., Rietveld Academy, Amsterdam. Exhibition: 1975 BIT.

VAN DERPOOL, Karen   U.S.A.   b. 1946
Studied at Tyler School of Art, Temple University, Philadelphia, M.F.A. 1970. Currently teaching at Univ. of Washington, Seattle. One-person Exhibitions: Gallery of the Sun Valley Center for the Arts and Humanities, Sun Valley, Idaho, 1977; The Davis Gallery, Idaho State Univ., Pocatello, Idaho, 1979. Exhibitions: "Fiber Forms: Past and Present," Brookfield Craft Center, Conn., 1974; "Young Americans," Museum of Contemporary Crafts, N.Y., 1977; "The Mondale Show," Seattle Art Museum, 1978; IEMT 1978. Awards: Scholarship, Haystack Mountain School of Crafts, Deer Isle, Maine, 1969; First Award in Textiles, Idaho State Invitational Craft Show, Sun Valley, 1975; Fellowship, Penland School of Crafts, Penland, N.C., 1978.

WARD, Evelyn Svec   U.S.A.
Studied at Otterbein College, Westerville, Ohio, B.A.; Sorbonne, Paris, 1952. Textile Assistant, The Cleveland Museum of Art until 1955. Exhibitions: "Fiberworks," The Cleveland Museum of Art, 1977; National Miniature Fiber Exhibition, Santa Fe, N.M., 1979. Collections: The Cleveland Museum of Art; The Cleveland Trust Collection; numerous private collections. Award: Distinguished Alumni Award for Special Achievement in Fine Arts, Otterbein College, April 1979.

WILSON, Ann Gawthrop   U.S.A.   b. 1949
Studied at California College of Arts and Crafts, Oakland, M.F.A. Textiles 1976; Cranbrook Academy of Art, Bloomfield Hills, Mich., B.F.A. 1972. One-person Exhibitions: Robert L. Kidd Associates/Galleries, 1978; Pacific Basin School of Textile Arts, Berkeley, 1975. Exhibitions: Fiberworks, Berkeley, 1978; San Francisco Arts Festival, Civic Center Plaza, San Francisco, 1973. Awards: Curatorial Fellowship, N.E.A., 1978–79.

WINSOR, Jackie   Canada (lives in New York)   b. 1941
Studied at Yale Summer School of Art and Music, 1946; Massachusetts College of Art, B.F.A., 1965; Rutgers University, N.J., M.F.A. 1967. One-person Exhibitions: Canada, 1968, 1971; Contemporary Arts Center, Cincinnati, 1976; Museum of Modern Art, San Francisco, 1977; Wadsworth Atheneum, Hartford, 1978; The Museum of Modern Art, N.Y., 1979. Exhibitions: since 1968 in the United States, Hamburg, Paris, Denmark, Vancouver, Amsterdam, and Zurich.

WOOD, Don   U.S.A.   b. 1942
Studied at Northeastern Oklahoma State Univ., B.A.; Univ. of Tulsa, M.A.; Graduate work, Univ. of Kansas and Univ. of Arkansas. Exhibitions: National Miniature Fiber Exhibition, Santa Fe, N.M., 1979; "Oklahoma Designer Craftsmen Exhibitions"; 1976 IEMT; "Stitchery '77," Pittsburgh, Pa.; South West Crafts Biennial, Sante Fe, N.M., 1977; ODC Fiber Invitational; 32nd Annual American Indian Artists Exhibition. Collections: Williams Companies Collection; Hardesty Corp. Collection; Tulsa Performing Arts Center; Univ. of Tulsa Collection; First National Bank of Siloam Springs, Ark.

YAGI, Mariyo   Japan   b. 1948
Studied environmental design at Kyoto University of Fine Arts, 1966–70. One-person Exhibition: The Hadler Galleries, 1978. Exhibitions: "Fiberworks," The Cleveland Museum of Arts, 1977; "Fiber Works: Americas and Japan," Kyoto and Tokyo, 1977; 1975, 1979 BIT; 1976 IEMT.

ZEISLER, Claire   U.S.A.   b. 1903
Studied at Columbia Univ., N.Y.; Institute of Design, Chicago. One-person Exhibitions: Chicago Public Library, 1962; Renaissance Society, Univ. of Chicago, 1962; Art Institute of Chicago, 1964, 1966; Richard Feigen Galleries, Chicago and New York, 1968; Northern Illinois University, Dekalb, 1970; The Hadler Galleries, N.Y., 1977; Art Institute of Chicago, 1979. Exhibitions: "Woven Forms," Museum of Contemporary Crafts, N.Y., 1963; Collectors Show, 1965; "Perspectif in Textiel," Stedelijk Museum, Amsterdam, 1969; Kunstgewerbemuseum, Zurich, 1963; Indianapolis Museum, Ind., 1968; Kranert Museum, Urbana, Ill., 1969; Ravinia Festival, Highland Park, 1969; Ruth Kaufmann Gallery, N.Y., 1971; Denver Art Museum, Colo., 1971; "Deliberate Entanglements," Univ. of California, Los Angeles, 1971; museums in Zacheta and Warsaw, Poland, 1971; Utah Museum of Fine Arts, Salt Lake City; Museum of Contemporary Art, Chicago, Ill.; "Sculpture in Fiber," Museum of Contemporary Crafts, N.Y., 1972; 1973 BIT; Univ. of Texas at Austin, 1973; The Cleveland Museum of Art, 1974; Herbert F. Johnson Museum, Cornell Univ., Ithaca, 1974; 1974, 1976, IEMT; National Gallery of Art, Wellington, New Zealand, 1975; "Textile Objekte," Kunstgewerbemuseum, Berlin, 1975; "American Crafts '76, An Aesthetic View," Museum of Contemporary Art, Chicago, 1976; "The Object as Poet," Renwick Gallery, Na-

tional Collection of Fine Arts, Washington, D.C., 1977; "American Crafts 1977," Philadelphia Museum of Art, Phila.; "Fiber Works:Americas and Japan," Kyoto and Tokyo, 1977; "Fiberworks," The Cleveland Museum of Art, 1977; "Chicago: The City and Its Artists, 1945–1978," The Univ. of Michigan Museum of Art, Ann Arbor, 1978; "Diverse Directions," Museum of Art, Washington State Univ., Pullman, Wash., 1978. Collections: First National Bank, Chicago; First National Bank, Brussels; Dreyfus Fund Collection, N.Y.; Wisconsin Art Center, Milwaukee; Art Institute of Chicago; Univ. of Wisconsin, Madison; Stedelijk Museum, Amsterdam; Museum Bellerive, Zurich.

PHOTOGRAPHY CREDITS

The authors acknowledge with thanks the use of photographs provided by the artists themselves.

Page

2/3 Jacques Betant, Paris
6 Piotr S. Jankowski, Warsaw
8 The Museum of Modern Art, New York
9 Crankbrook Academy of Art, Bloomfield
Hills, Michigan
10 Sean Hudson, London
11 (top) Jan Nordahl, Södertälje, Sweden
(bottom) Jan Michlewski, Warsaw
12 Walter Dräyer, Zurich
13 (top) From *Rigour of Imagination,*
Arturo Schwarz, Milan
(bottom) Mathews, The Museum of Modern Art, New York
17 Rudolph Burckhardt, New York
18 Jerzy Sabara, Warsaw
19 Jerzy Sabara, Warsaw
20 (top) Robert Häusser, Mannheim
(bottom) Barcelo, Barcelona
21 (top) Y. Shiratori, Kyoto
(bottom) S. Murakaku, Kyoto
22 Jan en Fridtjof, Amsterdam
23 Jan en Fridtjof, Amsterdam
24 Andre Morain, Paris
26 Georg Rehsteiner, Switzerland
27 Cranbrook Academy of Art, Bloomfield Hills, Michigan
28 (top) Stedelijk Museum, Amsterdam
29 (bottom) David S. Watanabe, San Francisco
30 Jan Nordahl, Södertälje, Sweden
31 Nino lo Duca, Milan
32 (top) Jan Nordahl, Södertälje, Sweden
(bottom) Erazm Ciolek, Warsaw
33 Jan Nordahl, Södertälje, Sweden
34 Jerzy Sabara, Warsaw
35 Robert Häusser, Mannheim
37 (bottom) Truls Melin, Malmo, Sweden
38/39 Phillipe Deleport, Montreuil
40 Louis Allrich Gallery, San Francisco
41 Jonas Dovydenas, Chicago
42/43 H. C. Hlobeczy, Cleveland Museum of Art, Ohio
44 Truis Melin, Sweden
45 Andreassen, Sweden
46 (bottom left) Jerzy Sabara, Warsaw
(bottom right) Ritter Jeppesen Pty. Ltd., Doncaster, Australia
52 The Hadler-Rodriguez Gallery, New York

Page

61 E. A. K. Foto, Pforzheim, West Germany
62 Jonas Dovydenas, Chicago
63 (top) Jerzy Sabara, Warsaw
(bottom) Ray W. Jones, New Jersey
64/65 Mieke H. Hille, Amsterdam
67 (top) Stenor, Holland
(bottom) Stedelijk Museum, Amsterdam
69 (top) Aleksander Karolyi
70 Walter Dräyer, Zurich
71 (top) Claude le-Anh, Paris
73 Photo Graphic, Zurich
76 Stone and Steccati, San Francisco
79 (top) Walter Dräyer, Zurich
86 William E. Ward, Ohio
87 Michal Krejci, Prague
88 (top) Craig Kolb, Berkeley
(bottom) Frank J. Thomas, Los Angeles
89 (top) G. Paul Bishop, Berkeley
90 R. Shippy Moore
91 John Wesley
98 (bottom) David Arky, New York
99 Louise Allrich Gallery, San Francisco
100 (right) J. O. Bragstad, San Francisco
103 Pace Gallery, New York
109 Robert Hausser, Mannheim
111 Ray Jones, New Jersey
113 Frank J. Thomas, Los Angeles
116 Heidi Baumann, Kloten, Switzerland
117 Buro Sybolt Voeten, Holland
122 J. Ahrend
127 Walter Dräyer, Zurich
128 (bottom) Jerzy Sabara, Warsaw
130 (left) Marek Holzman, Warsaw
(right) Jan Nordahl, Södertälje, Sweden
131 (left) Marek Holzman, Warsaw
(right) Edgard Eriksson, Sweden
133 S. Koike, Japan
135 Walker Montgomery, Georgia
136 (top) Richard Davies, London
(bottom) Seitz/Krestofetz, Brookfield Craft Center, Connecticut
137 (top) Fred Van Ruen, Holland
141 (top) Robert Schlingemann, Amsterdam
145 David Arky, New York
150 (bottom) David Arky, New York

Page

154 (top left and right, bottom right) Richard Davies, London
155 David Arky, New York
157 (top left) David Arky, New York
159 Richard Davies, London
161 (top) Richard Davies, London
(bottom) Richard Davies, London
165 David Cordoni
173 (top) Roel Salomon, Amsterdam
174 Jeffrey Schiff, Boston
180 Wieslaw Maciejewski, Lodz
182 Jan en Fridtjof, Amsterdam
184 Jan en Fridtjof, Amsterdam
185 Linda Kooyman, Alkinaar, Holland
187 Bob Pettit, Brookfield Craft Center, Connecticut
190 Studio 68, Amsterdam
195 (bottom) Stedelijk Museum, Amsterdam
197 Louise Allrich Gallery, San Francisco
201 Jean-Pierre Beakdin, Quebec
203 The Dumbarton Oaks Research Library and Collections, Washington, D.C.
206 Karel Bauer, Berkeley
207 Walter Dräyer, Zurich
210 James F. Wilson, Texas
211 James F. Wilson, Texas
214 (bottom) Marija Brant, Zagreb
215 Nino lo Duca, Milan
219 Alexandre Georges, New York
220 John Allen, New York
222 Norman McGrath, New York
224 (top left and right) Courtesy of Lancaster/Miller Publishers, San Francisco
(bottom) William Hocker, San Francisco
227 Tom Haartsen, Amstel
228 Romek Pachucki, Australia
230 Jerzy Sabara, Warsaw
234 Jeanne-Claude, New York
239 Jerzy Sabara, Warsaw
242/243 Jerzy Sabara, Warsaw
244/245 Jerzy Sabara, Warsaw
248 (top) Colita fotografia, Valencia
(bottom) Colita fotografia, Valencia
250 Nino lo Duca, Milan
251 Nino lo Duca, Milan
252–253 C. Kaufman, Georgia

INDEX